Building Nature's Market

Building Nature's Market

The Business and Politics of Natural Foods

LAURA J. MILLER

THE UNIVERSITY OF CHICAGO PRESS   CHICAGO AND LONDON

The University of Chicago Press, Chicago 60637
The University of Chicago Press, Ltd., London
© 2017 by The University of Chicago
All rights reserved. No part of this book may be used or reproduced in any manner whatso-
ever without written permission, except in the case of brief quotations in critical articles and
reviews. For more information, contact the University of Chicago Press, 1427 E. 60th St.,
Chicago, IL 60637.
Published 2017
Printed in the United States of America

26 25 24 23 22 21 20 19 18 17   1 2 3 4 5

ISBN-13: 978-0-226-50123-9 (cloth)
ISBN-13: 978-0-226-50137-6 (paper)
ISBN-13: 978-0-226-50140-6 (e-book)
DOI: 10.7208/chicago/9780226501406.001.0001

Library of Congress Cataloging-in-Publication Data

Names: Miller, Laura J., author.
Title: Building nature's market : the business and politics of natural foods /
    Laura J. Miller.
Description: Chicago ; London : The University of Chicago Press, 2017. |
    Includes bibliographical references and index.
Identifiers: LCCN 2017005396 | ISBN 9780226501239 (cloth : alk. paper) |
    ISBN 9780226501376 (pbk. : alk. paper) | ISBN 9780226501406 (e-book)
Subjects: LCSH: Natural foods industry—United States—History. | Natural foods—
    Social aspects—United States. | Natural foods—Economic aspects—United States. |
    Counterculture—United States.
Classification: LCC HD9005 .M46 2017 | DDC 338.4/76413020973—dc23 LC record available
    at https://lccn.loc.gov/2017005396

♾ This paper meets the requirements of ANSI/NISO Z39.48-1992 (Permanence of Paper).

IN MEMORY OF MY FATHER, ARTHUR MILLER,
AN UNFORGETTABLE HEALTH FOOD SALESMAN

Contents

Preface and Acknowledgments

Over the years I have been working on this project, people have frequently asked me how I got interested in it. The answer is both personal and intellectual, and my explanation has always involved acknowledging my debts to the two people who launched me on this investigation. As a graduate student at UC–San Diego, I was lucky to take the last social movements seminar offered by the late Joseph Gusfield before he retired. At Joe's suggestion, I wrote my seminar paper on the natural foods movement, and his encouraging comments led me to pick up the project again many years later when I began to see similarities between the natural foods industry and the book industry, the subject of much of my previous research. These are both industries characterized by moral commitments to their work, and both have faced challenges in the contemporary era as they transition from a field of primarily small, independent firms to one of large, diversified corporations. More than just steering me to a topic where I could continue to explore these issues, Joe helped shape my way of thinking about them, and over the years, my respect for his approach to studying social movements has only deepened.

The other impetus for doing this project goes back even further, to well before I was born. My father, Art Miller, started in the health food business in the 1930s, when he was 15 years old, and he stayed with it for his entire working life. He was delighted, if perhaps a little baffled, when I began doing research on natural foods, and he supplied me with all kinds of leads as I started my hunt for data. When I contacted old-timers for interviews, his name provided instant entrée with people who remembered him with affection and respect—and who regaled me with stories of what a tough businessperson he could be. Because he died in 2009, he did not see this book come to fruition, and many questions I wish I had asked him must remain unanswered. But my academic research helped me better appreciate both who he was and the work that consumed so much of his life.

While it will become obvious that I have a great deal of sympathy for some of the ideals of the natural foods movement, I should make it clear that I am also skeptical of or indifferent to other claims from the movement's past and present, and by no means do I consider myself a natural foods activist. My family's background in the industry was, for most of my life, just that: the background to everyday life rather than something that was explicitly talked about. In the 1960s, ours was a household where it was considered equally mundane to stock the pantry with tiger's milk bars as canned corned beef hash; where boxed instant pudding was made with raw milk; where Wonder Bread was forbidden but TV dinners allowed for special occasions. The contradictions were many, but they were not experienced as philosophical conundrums; I assumed all parents had their arbitrary rules about food, and these just happened to be the ones favored by mine. Health foods were indeed a lifestyle choice that marked ours as different from most of my friends' families, though I did not realize when growing up just how marginal the health food world was. Aside from when business associates came to the house for dinner, or when we would attend health food conventions, where I liked to run around collecting free samples from all the friendly exhibitors, I did not pay much attention to this world. Unlike my older siblings, I never worked at my father's business, so what occurred there remained fairly mysterious to me. However, it was no accident that my first summer job was as a cashier at the local "organic market." I will always be grateful to Ron Smith for hiring me and for his kindness as I became accustomed to the highly idiosyncratic ways in which the market was run.

All in all, my childhood memories of the health food world are hazy; I am afraid I made a bad ethnographer as a youngster. Thus, I came to this project, if not as a full outsider, then still with considerable distance. Despite much that seemed familiar and that stirred vague recollections, I quickly discovered how little I actually knew about how the natural foods field operated, and how much there was to learn.

To that end, I am very grateful to all those people who allowed me to interview them. They interrupted their own busy lives, gave me tours of facilities, welcomed me into their homes, and graciously reached back in their memories to recall events and people long gone. I am also indebted to the many libraries I visited. I especially would like to acknowledge the assistance of Janice Little of the Heritage Reading Room in the Heritage Research Center at Loma Linda University, Sarah Hutcheon of Radcliffe's

Schlesinger Library, Jan Todd of the Stark Center for Physical Culture at the University of Texas–Austin, Cathy Lucas of Willard Public Library in Battle Creek, Michigan, and Garth "Duff" Stoltz of the Historic Adventist Village of Battle Creek.

Over the years, many people offered extremely helpful feedback, conversations, contacts, and encouragement. I apologize for not mentioning everyone here. A huge thank you to Nicole Newendorp for the years of our writing group; she patiently read my prose whether polished or rough, and her comments always helped me be clearer in my arguments. Thanks also to other former members of the writing group, including Kim DaCosta, Kathy Coll, and Melissa Brown. Thanks to Nicole, Kim, Kathy, and Cameron Macdonald for understanding what a difference a good library makes. I am grateful to Emilie Hardman with her deep interest in and knowledge of the politics of food; I benefited from her research assistance, our collaborations, and our numerous conversations. Many years ago, Chandra Mukerji taught me to care and think about consumer culture and historical sociology in ways I wasn't even aware of until I was working on this project. Thanks to Peter Conrad and Karen Hansen, who always made themselves available to talk about my research and offer advice; to Miranda Waggoner for research assistance; and to Cherie Potts and Pat Steffens for transcription services. Many thanks to the whole team at the University of Chicago Press, especially Doug Mitchell for his skill and enthusiasm in shepherding this project to publication, and Kyle Wagner for his gracious efficiency. Grants from the Theodore and Jane Norman Fund made possible much of my research.

I relied on the kindness of family, friends, and friends of friends to host me during research trips. In particular, thanks to Darshana and Jeff Kalikstein, Nancy Gerdt and Glenn Lyons, Jim and Michele Mosher, Liz-Ann Nelson and family, and Herbie and Mims Shepas. Thank you to my family for housing me, steering me to contacts, listening to my stories, staying interested, and helping me remember the people, products, and places that populated the health food world we personally experienced: Matt Miller, Vyvyan Tenorio, Roberto Johansson, Sylvia Miller, Noemi Johansson-Miller, Mahats Miller, Elias Johansson-Miller, Zach Tenorio-Miller, and my dear sister, Devra Miller, who died not long before I finished this project. It is impossible to enumerate all the ways Devra aided and influenced me over the years. But it is perhaps fitting to note that I derived my own eating and cooking style from hers. As anyone who studies food knows, that is one very important bond indeed.

CHAPTER ONE

Markets and Movements

Consider the following excerpts from a widely read book on natural foods:

> We know that certain food products of modern commercialism, such as white flour, refined sugar, corn syrup, candy, crackers, preserved meats and many other widely advertised foods, are lacking in the essential organic salts and vitamins. . . . And yet civilized man eats an ever increasing variety of factory-made products, which are devitalized in the process of manufacture and often contain harmful chemical preservatives.
>
> There is no doubt that the United States Government, through the Department of Agriculture, and the separate states through their agricultural colleges are largely to blame for these conditions. They have spent vast sums to propagate the idea of money-making by crop specialization; of industrial methods as applied to agriculture; of wrong soil fertilization; of farm life which is merely an imitation of decadent city culture. (Carqué 1925, 46–47, 93–94)

These words, with the possible exception of the reference to "organic salts," sound as if they could have been uttered by any number of twenty-first century advocates of sustainable, organic, small-scale farming practices, who promote a diet rich in unprocessed, fresh, nutritious food. But in fact, these passages were published in a 1925 book, titled *Natural Foods: The Safe Way to Health*, by Otto Carqué, an influential proponent of food reform. Along with writing numerous articles and books and lecturing on the subject of natural foods, Carqué produced his own line of dried fruit, nuts and nut butters, whole grains, honey, raw sugar, and olive oil that he sold through mail order, like-minded retailers, and his own storefront.

Carqué's ideas about how to achieve good health through diet, the ill effects on the food supply that come from a single-minded pursuit of material wealth, and the beneficial attributes of the natural world have been mirrored throughout the last two centuries by others working to reform dominant systems of food production and consumption. His pronouncements about the inefficiency of raising livestock compared to plants for human consumption, or the value of eschewing imported food for sustenance produced on native ground are echoed in the arguments of several generations' worth of natural foods advocates. But the continuity over time in the movement to promote natural foods goes beyond critiques of the prevailing agrifood system and beyond guidelines for sound eating practices. What Carqué also had in common with most leaders of the natural foods movement who came before and after him was involvement in commercial endeavors tied to natural foods. At the same time that Carqué forcefully condemned the commercialism that produced unhealthful food, a degraded environment, and the exploitation of both humans and nonhuman animals, he devoted his energies to businesses that turned the nature he revered into products sold to consumers. In this way, Carqué embodied one of the distinguishing traits of the American natural foods movement: commercial activities have been present since the 1830s and have been a significant part of the movement since the first systematic development of health food commodities began in the 1870s. Thus, for much of its history, the natural foods movement has to a large degree been constituted by a natural foods industry at the same time as it has retained a critique of the corrupting influence of commercialism on the social organization of diet and health.

Despite such continuities, the natural foods landscape of the twenty-first century United States does not, of course, look the same as it did in the 1870s or 1920s or even the 1970s. By the first decade of the twenty-first century, natural foods seemed to be everywhere. From hospitals to schools to workplace cafeterias, mainstream institutions were touting their healthy eating options. Public figures from film stars to the First Lady championed fresh-from-the-garden ingredients in everyday meals. Not only were broad segments of the population switching to organic milk and snacking on granola bars, but a broad variety of businesses, including major food corporations, sought to burnish their moral images and profit lines by selling goods labeled as *natural* or *organic*. By 2008, "all-natural," "organic," "whole grain," and "without additives or preservatives" comprised the most common set of claims made for new food and beverage products introduced that year, attached to 33 percent of new products released in the United States (" 'Natural' Tops Product Claims" 2009). This marketing strategy was inspired by the pace of sales, which continued to increase even during the recession that began in 2008. Whereas in 1970, retail sales of the category then called "health food" amounted to approximately $100 million (Wright 1972), they grew to $1.7 billion in 1979 (Research Department of Prevention 1981, iii). By 2011, retail sales of natural products totaled more than $73 billion.[1]

With natural foods now appearing to be simply another part of the mix of popular consumption options, it is easy to forget that not so long ago, this category was widely seen as embodying philosophical and political ideals, as well as culinary practices, far from the mainstream. Associated with nature cure believers, religious minorities, and other unconventional groups such as bodybuilders and hippies, natural foods were either ignored or mocked by most Americans. More organized opposition came from the medical establishment as well as agrifood interests and government agencies, which regarded users and producers alike as kooks and faddists, with more high-profile advocates branded as dangerous quacks. Segregated from the conventional food industry, production and sales were contained within a small, specialized sector that retained familial and other personal ties to its founders, many of whom were Seventh-day Adventist, Jewish, or immigrant. Although the constituency for natural foods steadily grew through the twentieth century, it was not until the 1980s that broad-based support for this approach to eating really took hold. One might wonder, then, how this shift in the fortunes of natural foods came about, and whether the mainstreaming process that has brought cultural legitimacy and market growth to this class of food represents a triumph of the philosophies of the movement that had promoted it since the nineteenth century.

The key to answering these questions takes us back to the situation whereby a movement confronting powerful interests in the realm of food production and policy has been sustained by individuals and organizations acting simultaneously as representatives of business and as self-conscious agents of social and cultural change. It may at first seem counterintuitive to consider an industry as leading efforts to shake up the status quo. After all, when social movements and private enterprise are considered in tandem, they are typically assumed to be adversaries. Along with a lengthy history of antagonism between labor movements and capital, citizen groups have mobilized over the last century to protest consumer exploitation, health hazards, environmental damage, and undue public influence on the part of for-profit companies (Hilton 2007; Pellow 2007; Seidman 2003; Soule 2009; A. Starr 2000). Indeed, some of the most visible protest actions of the late twentieth and early twenty-first centuries—such as those involving the antinuclear movement, or events taking place at meetings of the World Trade Organization, or the Occupy encampments—have targeted the corporate sector as, at the least, an equal partner with the state in perpetuating wrongs.

However, it is not always the case that private enterprise stands in opposition to movements for social change. Movements that seek to alter political, cultural, or social arrangements, and that fall on both the left and the right of the political spectrum, can include businesses and their representatives as active participants. Such overlaps between the private sector and social movements have been especially notable since the 1980s as people who considered themselves activists of various sorts in their youth become entrepreneurs who seek to "do well by doing good." Involving themselves in social change activity from environmentalism, to socially responsible investment, to campaigns to loosen marijuana laws, a variety of for-profit enterprises have made common cause with more classic social movement actors. These alliances are not without their skeptics, though, and are not always welcomed by others in business or activist circles. The ambiguous nature of this activity, which creates uncertainty about the extent to which the greater good and the corporate good can be simultaneously served, invites us to consider the consequences of merging citizen and entrepreneur identities and interests.

The prominent role played by industry in promoting a natural foods ethic and politics underlies the questions that are addressed in this book: What was the path that took natural foods from the marginal to the mainstream in the United States? What ideas and practices were altered along the way? In the course of providing answers to these questions, I consider a more general question: What possibilities open up and what limits emerge when private industry is involved in advocating for broad-based social and cultural changes? Before considering this latter question in more detail, it may be helpful to better identify just what the natural foods movement actually consists of.

Natural Foods as Material Good, Philosophy, and Social Movement

So far, I have been discussing the terms *natural foods* and *natural foods movement* as if what they refer to is self-evident. That is definitely not the case, and indeed, the contested nature of these terms is one theme that will come up repeatedly in this account. Nevertheless, a basic definition of *natural foods*, which would probably achieve consensus among advocates, is foods (and often other body-care products) that are subject to minimal processing or additives. Natural foods proponents have tended to promote diets centered on substances with direct origins in nature, especially fruits, vegetables, nuts, and whole grains. The common understanding among adherents that natural is equivalent to healthier gave rise to the term *health food*, originally coined in 1874 by Frank Fuller, a maker of bread products, and subsequently picked up and popularized by Seventh-day Adventist food companies.[2] As I will explain in chapter 2, *health food* refers more precisely to certain manufactured products targeted to those interested in a natural foods diet. Still, *health food* became the dominant way to refer to natural foods for about a century, notwithstanding those, such as Carqué, who were sharply critical of the slippage. It was not until the 1980s that the term *natural foods* regained ascendancy, for reasons I will explore in chapter 6. While I will employ the phrase *natural foods* when referring in a general sense to relevant food, philosophies, and the movement, following the custom of that era, I am more likely to use the term *health food* when discussing historical events and entities from the late nineteenth century up to the mid-1980s.

A natural foods *movement*, comprised of people acting collectively to promote such food, first took root in the United States in the early decades of the nineteenth century. The general goals of this movement have remained intact over time: advocates seek to integrate natural foods into their own and others' food-related practices and to further the conditions that make natural foods widely available and culturally acceptable. Drawing on the centrality of the nature–health connection, a key element of the movement has been a commitment to following and spreading food-related practices that bolster not only personal health but also the health of the natural environment. In this view, just as one should tamper as little as possible with the products of nature in order to receive their full benefit, one should respect the integrity of the natural world in order for its inherently good properties to be manifested. These abstract principles have spawned an array of more practical concerns, including opposition to the slaughter of animals and the greater resources needed to raise meat as opposed to vegetable food; the ecological effects of *monoculture*—that is, the intensive production of a single crop—as well as the application of synthetic fertilizers and pesticides; and the adverse effects of a food industry that is oriented to profit and controlled by large corporations. These various concerns, which arose between the nineteenth and early twentieth centuries, have furthered an interest in vegetarianism, organic and sustainable farming, food cooperatives, and other practices that seek to change how and which foods are produced and sold. They have also given rise to efforts to compel public policy and food-related institutions to make these practices economically feasible and socially legitimate.

It has never been the case that all natural foods proponents embraced all of these practices; one only has to compare "junk-food vegetarians" (H. Henderson 1987) with the enthusiasm among some natural foods advocates for eating organ meats (Davis 1947; Hewitt 1971; Albright 1982) to see how the particular commitments associated with the natural foods movement do not necessarily cohere. Indeed, following the typical path of ever-increasing specialization that characterizes the division of labor, the various strands of the natural foods movement now often pursue single-minded agendas as, for instance, one group campaigns for the legalization of raw milk while another concerns itself with keeping growth hormones out of the feed of dairy cows. Such diversity of purpose raises the question of whether one can even speak of a single natural foods movement or if what we have here is really an assortment of distinct, occasionally overlapping movements. Certainly, many scholars do choose to treat these strands separately. However, I believe it is useful to refer to the natural foods movement in the singular, not as a way to gloss over cleavages but to better recognize the intertwined interests and fates of those whose priorities might lie with vegetarianism, organic farming, combating genetically engineered life forms in the food supply, and so on. As I will argue in this book, what most unifies these various strands is a coordinated natural products industry that not only supplies so many of the goods these disparate advocates seek but also, through its communication organs, gatherings, and other opportunities for members to network with another, articulates the connections among these diverse goals.

Perhaps a more fundamental question, though, is whether efforts to promote the production and consumption of natural foods qualify as a social movement. After all, this is a field of people, practices, and beliefs that is directed at changing individual lifestyles, whose principal organizations are mostly unknown to natural foods consumers, and that is notable more for spawning new products than protests. Much social movement scholarship has preferred to study the organizational activity of those movements that target the state or state policies by engaging in coordinated collective action, especially outside of institutional channels.[3] However, by delimiting the range of movements studied in this way, we overlook significant social change agents who have consciously created ideologies and institutions that promote behavioral, cultural, and structural change.

Indeed, the scholarly literature contains a range of useful challenges to placing overly narrow strictures on the category of social movements. Together, these critiques suggest that not just movements with clearly defined political goals and organization, and not just protest activity by those disenfranchised from established social institutions, also deserve our attention. In particular, by broadening our focus, we can better study the cultural impact and aim of social movements.[4] For instance, the prevailing emphasis in American sociology has been on highly organized movements, with most analytical focus on formal social movement organizations, an outcome of the resource mobilization perspective, which explicitly directs attention to them (McCarthy and Zald 1977, 1216). Among others, though, Gusfield argues for a more fluid perspective on social movements that is "less confined to the boundaries of organizations and more alive to the larger contexts of change at the same time as it is open to awareness of how the movement has consequences and impacts among nonpartisans and nonmembers as well as participants and devotees" (1981, 323). As he says, by deliberately blurring the line between trend and movement, we can better assess how cultural meanings change over time and affect a part of the population larger than those who identify as activists.

Similarly, numerous scholars reject a narrow focus on the state (Calhoun 1993; Snow 2004; Van Dyke, Soule, and Taylor 2004). In the first place, nonstate institutional entities, such as medical or educational organizations, may be the target of movement action (Van Dyke, Soule, and Taylor 2004, 28; Levitsky and Banaszak-Holl 2010, 5). But along with challenging various institutionalized systems of authority, social movements can concern themselves with social, cultural, and economic matters that are embedded in everyday life and not just formal political institutions. Turner and Killian note that "broad movements for reform typically combine political with life-style objectives" (1987, 220). And according to Melucci (1989), cultural models that guide action and structure daily life, including exchange and consumption, can become the very ends of a movement. These "new social movements" tend to be centered on nonpolitical terrain, he claims. But they are still movements because their participants believe that personal needs are the path to changing the world. Going one step further, Offe suggests that the conflation of politics with the state is a false one and that what makes a movement political is that its actors intend to win recognition of their values as binding for the wider community (1985, 827). In this way, we may begin to understand how efforts oriented toward creating a mode of living, seemingly situated in the private sphere, can still be political by seeking to win public support for this lifestyle while discrediting rival lifestyles.

What we can call lifestyle movements are oriented to *spreading* cultural values represented in choices about everyday life.[5] Lifestyle is not synonymous with an entire way of life but rather refers to something more partial: patterned activities, tastes, and uses of material culture that express meaning about individual identity, preferences, and group affiliations. The sociological concept of lifestyle derives originally from Weber, who talked about status groups giving rise to styles of life that can be the basis of or requirement for social honor; that is, prestige. Significantly, what most clearly distinguishes one status group from another is its consumption of goods that are related to its style of life (Weber 1978, 937). As Bourdieu notes, the attention to style is about form over function, where the manner in which action is carried out is emphasized more than the ostensible purpose of action (1984, 5).

Most scholars addressing the politics of lifestyle emphasize either the way that lifestyle becomes a means of social differentiation, drawing boundaries between insiders and outsiders (Bourdieu 1984; Zablocki and Kanter 1976; Bellah et al. 1986; Holt 2000), or a means of expressing individual identity and achieving self-realization(Melucci 1989; Giddens 1991; Binkley 2007). Related to these emphases is the dimension of choice that comes to the fore in contemporary society: the right and obligation of the individual to determine his or her own lifestyle, even if the freedom involved in such choices is more perceived than real (Giddens 1991; Bauman 1990; Featherstone 2007; Slater 1997; Chaney 1996, 10). From this perspective, lifestyle politics are not so much about the quest for political power or the distribution of benefits by government but rather how public policy should or should not impinge on private life.

While these analyses help us comprehend the politics of everyday life and the way that consumption choices can, for instance, be used to mark others as morally inferior, analysts of lifestyle tend to understate how this kind of politics can develop into a movement, however diffuse, to extend a style of life. In such cases, the goal is not to maintain social differentiation but to break down categories of difference and bring as many people as possible within the favored lifestyle's orbit. Furthermore, while consumption choices are key to defining a lifestyle, a lifestyle movement is not just composed of consumers.[6] Since these movements usually require various goods to support a special style of life, they are often closely aligned with commercial interests. The producers who make that lifestyle possible are necessarily involved with the movement and have an interest in seeing the values and presuppositions underlying the lifestyle extended more broadly. Although that involvement may occur simply to take advantage of financial opportunities, in other cases, producers maintain similar commitments to consumers regarding the ideals of the lifestyle. Lifestyle movements, such as the natural foods movement, are thus particularly well-suited to highlight the phenomenon whereby philosophical ideals are joined to market interests.

Business as Movement Participant

The advantage of those perspectives that broaden a view of social movements beyond organizational activity directed at the state is that they allow us to consider culture, consumption, and lifestyle as central to the goals of a movement as well as what constitutes meaningful activity for movement participants. However, these perspectives still tend to abstract out the citizen-consumer as the sole agent of social change. When the private sector is considered, it is usually in terms of representing an elite against which that citizen-consumer makes claims. This analytical stance is likely an outgrowth of the empirical world where private enterprise is frequently (and justifiably) held responsible for so many social movement grievances. The result is that both social movement and business scholarship have shown increasing interest in the ways that private sector organizations try to circumvent, co-opt, or grant concessions to citizen demands for socially responsible action (Laufer 2003; Luders 2006; Clouder and Harrison 2005; King 2008; Soule 2009). What this perspective ignores, though, is how people in their roles as entrepreneurs and corporate actors can seek social change, not just as insiders with friends in high places but as social or cultural outsiders. It is important to recognize that members of the business world do not have a unified set of interests. Differences among firms or industries can pit an enterprise against other players in the market, and even position it to make the kinds of claims usually associated with an antielite citizenry, at the same time as it acts to safeguard its particular economic interests.

The phenomenon whereby business groups are concerned about the social good in similar ways to how individuals understand their roles as citizen advocates is perhaps most typically embodied in the concept of corporate social responsibility. The question of what obligations business-people have beyond their own immediate financial gain has long been a topic of discussion but, especially in the past, was generally conceived of in the more narrow terms of business ethics, such as honesty and fairness in pricing, product quality, competitive practices, and stance toward labor (H. Merrill 1948; McKie 1974; Brennan 1991). The 1960s, however, saw a rising concern with social responsibility in the sense of a company's role in contributing to the betterment of the world through corporate practices, philanthropy, and sometimes even more direct political action. Discussions about corporate social responsibility seemed to reach a zenith in the mid-1970s and then declined. But since the 1990s, there has been renewed attention to the issue of corporate social responsibility, both on the part of scholars, especially in business-related fields, and on the part of companies themselves (Vogel 2005; Quarter 2000; Piacentini, MacFadyen, and Eadie 2000).

As important as the corporate social responsibility approach is to understanding the moral dimension of private enterprise activities, it rarely considers corporations' direct connections to actions seeking to alter existing social institutions. Recent sociological scholarship, on the other hand, has recognized and examined the interaction between social movements and the private sector. This scholarship has included studies that show how a market or industry can emerge out of a movement, for instance, in renewable energy or recycling, and the extent to which movement values and cultural frames are retained within that industry (Lounsbury, Ventresca, and Hirsch 2003; Sine and Lee 2009; Vasi 2011; K. Weber, Heinze, and DeSoucey 2008). Other studies have examined how social movements can usher in new organizational forms, such as with craft brewing (Rao, Morrill, and Zald 2000; Rao 2009; Haveman and Rao 1997; Thompson and Coskuner-Balli 2007; Hiatt, Sine, and Tolbert 2009). Here, the focus is on innovation at the level of economic organizations or markets. This literature demonstrates that the fortunes of an industry may be strongly influenced by the character of a social movement. But that often leaves aside a consideration of what happens to the movement itself: how the movement is shaped and altered through its role in innovating economic forms and processes. I propose a somewhat different lens for understanding how both movement and industry are affected when the boundaries between them are blurred, one that observes that businesses can be not just allies but leaders of citizens engaged in social change efforts.

The case of natural foods lends itself to adopting this lens. It highlights the difficulty of judging activities as motivated solely by profit or by ideology, and it challenges overly rigid typologies that classify movements as either of the new type or the old, as left or right in their politics, or as radical or reformist in their aims.[7] While its environmentalist ethos and countercultural past make it easy to assume that natural foods advocacy fits with other movements on the left, it has on occasion been embraced by proponents of racial purity on the right and, more centrally, there is a strong libertarian streak running through it that defies typical left/right distinctions. Furthermore, the natural foods field combines cultural, economic, and political goals that are manifested in both everyday life and the public realm; it demonstrates the connections between private life and the private sector; and participants utilize both institutional and extrainstitutional channels to achieve their goals.

Although lifestyle issues are paramount, what distinguishes the natural foods phenomenon from an aggregation of private choices about how to lead one's life is that adherents desire to spread these ideals and practices to others. Efforts are made through the establishment of communication organs, advocacy groups, public speaking, and word of mouth to convince other individuals and organizations to engage in food-related consumption and production activities congruent with a natural foods philosophy. Moreover, the state is not irrelevant for the natural foods movement. There are four primary kinds of policy goals that are pursued. First is the goal of preventing prosecution or heavy-handed regulation of those selling or consuming natural foods, as in efforts to keep dietary supplements from being treated as equivalent to pharmaceuticals. Second, activity has been directed at achieving a more positive regulatory framework, such as the establishment of the National Organic Program, which sets standards for goods classified as organic. Third are actions that have been directed at equalizing government treatment, as in efforts to remove subsidies or other favorable treatment shown to producers of conventional food. Finally, efforts are aimed at creating direct government support of natural foods consumption, as in attempts to restrict genetically engineered crops or enact regulations banning certain additives.

Whether it be lobbying for favorable public policies, attracting new adherents, or elevating the public image of the movement, industry has long been at the forefront of leadership of this movement. From the late nineteenth century up through the present, a majority of the most publicly prominent individual advocates have had commercial interests in natural foods. Furthermore, corporate entities have been key players in efforts to achieve movement goals. Most natural foods followers are not members of an affiliated organization. Nevertheless, formal advocacy associations do exist and sometimes play an important role. What makes most of these groups look quite different from a typical social movement organization is the strong participation and leadership of for-profit representatives. This for-profit involvement applies not only to traditional trade associations but also to issue-oriented groups. The consequence is that such organizations are often shaped to promote their members' economic interests as well as to create public acceptance of a natural foods philosophy.

The industry that is now so central to natural foods advocacy did not create the original movement. As I will describe in chapter 2, the American natural foods movement arose in the early decades of the nineteenth century to promote an ascetic lifestyle centered on vegetarianism and a distrust of new techniques of food cultivation and production. There were a small number of commercial endeavors, primarily provision stores and eating establishments, which developed to serve followers after the movement took root. But a true industry of related businesses with the primary purpose of selling products geared to this lifestyle emerged only after John Harvey Kellogg established companies associated with the Battle Creek Sanitarium in Michigan starting in the last quarter of the nineteenth century. Originally motivated by a desire to further the teachings of the Seventh-day Adventist Church, Kellogg developed and marketed scores of new products to serve people interested in food reform. Despite the religious convictions that initially underlay Kellogg's efforts, his enterprises helped change an assumption that a natural foods lifestyle involves eating the simplest foods provided by God through nature to an assumption that such a lifestyle requires specialized foods manufactured by brand-name companies. Kellogg's attempts to straddle the line between entrepreneur and proselytizer also produced what would soon be a common theme in this field: conflict over whether movement goals were being subverted by profit considerations.

As health food businesses proliferated in the twentieth century, not all industry members were true believers in the merits of natural foods, and not all viewed themselves as participants in a cause greater than their own attempts to make a living. But as I will show in the following chapters, from Kellogg on through to the present, enough did that they were able to maintain the lead in defining the direction of this movement and give their commercial activities a missionary zeal. A central dilemma then became how to expand the industry and the public appeal of natural foods while at the same time preserving movement principles.

The Impact of Industry Involvement

Not surprisingly, as the natural foods field has grown, a number of scholars have examined the interaction and tension between alternative food movements and related commercial activities. For many of them, a central question is whether this relationship results in an institutionalization of the movement whereby movement activity gets directed into formal organizations and is vulnerable to co-optation by the state and conventional food sector. Among other works, Guthman's excellent account of organic agriculture argues that the growth of trade associations and certification agencies results in more radical goals being put aside (2004, 110–16). Similarly, Roth's older but still insightful account of health food (1977) discusses how the movement becomes more reformist than revolutionary after people make careers in the field. Although the significance of institutionalization is not her central concern, Maurer (2002) suggests that while an increased receptivity to vegetarianism on the part of mainstream food institutions offers new opportunities to the vegetarian movement, it does not fundamentally impact the movement. On the other hand, Thompson and Coskuner-Balli (2007) argue that in the face of corporate co-optation of the organic movement, it is possible to reclaim an original movement spirit in small niches, such as Community Supported Agriculture. Both Patricia Allen (2004) and Lockie and Halpin (2005) argue for more varied effects on alternative agrifood movements, with integration into, continued distance from, and reform of existing agrifood institutions all possible, along with the innovation of new forms.

While I agree with many of their claims about the effects of the institutionalization process, the separation between movement and industry has been overdrawn in most of these accounts. Instead, the overlap between industry and movement is so extensive and goes back so far that one cannot view industry efforts as simple colonization. Nor should we view the influence of economic organizations as in itself exerting a deradicalizing force on the movement. It is not institutionalization or participation in the market per se that acts as a conservative force, but rather the expansion of a receptive constituency that increases pressures on a movement to soften more radical expressions.

As I intend to demonstrate, the natural foods case shows that the participation of industry offers certain advantages to a movement, including the creation of stable institutions in the form of businesses and trade associations. These corporate structures provide the kind of long-term stability that can be elusive for citizen groups that have to depend on the goodwill of volunteers and often poorly paid staff. Moreover, trade groups can marshal the resources needed to hire lobbyists and law firms to defend their members' interests. While this has become a common strategy among wealthier nonprofit groups as well, most citizen groups find it difficult to raise the necessary funds. Additionally, through the consumer goods they provide, businesses can insinuate themselves into potential supporters' everyday lives rather than rely on those more compartmentalized (and generally rarer) moments when people are conscious of their obligations as citizens and are open to instruction from social movement activists.

These advantages have been significant in the natural foods field where, especially before the 1980s, there were few citizen-only advocacy groups independent of industry influence. Long-lasting trade associations, publications, and conventions tied members together in networks with regular interaction, information sharing, and coordinated action. Businesses, some in continuous operation for a half century or more, provided financial and logistical support, institutional memory, and continuity of personnel, as did those many individuals whose families worked in the field for multiple generations. The natural foods industry first established a formal lobbying, legal, and public relations arm in 1955 (Schiff 1957; Fred 1961) and has continued with such efforts ever since. Meanwhile, retailers acted as important centers of communication to natural foods followers, and some entrepreneurs gained a considerable public following through their lectures, books, radio shows, and television appearances.

On the other hand, citizen-only groups have on the whole not been as effective in attracting constituents and achieving their goals as have groups with some industry presence. Along with the difficulties of maintaining long-term commitments and adequate financial resources, problems related to infighting, cliquishness, autocratic leadership, and rigid expectations for purity of thought and action have limited the clout of many of the movement's citizen-based groups. Throughout most of natural foods' history, the marketplace actually provided a more hospitable environment that welcomed diverse followers compared with traditional social movement organizations, which demanded greater social and political homogeneity. This is not to say that the market is a truly democratic space. Obviously, there are economic barriers to entry (though they were surprisingly low until late in the twentieth century), and those who cannot compete will be cast aside. Moreover, throughout the natural foods industry's history, there were firms that were able to gain enough economic power to exert considerable control over other players in the field. Nonetheless, the social barriers to entering the industry, including education, gender, ethnicity (though only for those of European descent), and standards of propriety were relatively minimal, producing a haven for countercultural types and for entrepreneurs shut out of other economic sectors.

Natural Foods and Cultural Change

The space of marginality occupied by the natural foods field over much of its history is key to understanding its trajectory. The ways in which the field was dismissed and mocked spurred innovation, shaped relations with mainstream institutions, and ultimately gave entrepreneurs a means to expand the market. Marginality applied, in one sense, to the field's status in the commercial world. The segregation of natural foods from the conventional food sector was based less on consistently true differences in the properties of such food than it was on organizational divisions in production, distribution, and retailing that were rarely breached. Thus, for instance, items labeled *health food* were difficult to find outside of health food stores. But equally important was the field's cultural and political marginality. As chapter 5 will document, the field's social standing was so low that natural foods advocates periodically faced government crackdowns. Even when not subjected to state repression, those individuals who self-consciously identified with the movement tended to be viewed as irrational and extreme in their beliefs. Their intense faith in the moral authority of nature set them apart, not just from the average American but also from other food reformers.

The activities of American food reformers seeking social change through modifying dietary practices have been the subject of a large body of scholarship. Whereas an earlier generation of historians tended to draw a portrait of cultish movements dominated by eccentric personalities and outlandish faddism (G. Carson 1957; H. Green 1986; Schwartz 1986; Whorton 1982), many recent studies suggest that the moralism of past food reform efforts and the contemporary alternative food movement alike have acted to bolster the status of a white middle class by stigmatizing the eating practices of black Americans, immigrants, and others with few economic resources. More than just denigrating lifestyle choices, these scholars argue, middle-class reformers have used dietary choices as evidence of good citizenship and who rightfully belongs to the political community (DuPuis 2015; Veit 2013; Biltekoff 2013; Slocum 2007).

Although the connections that have existed between the natural foods movement and a social elite are important to understand, as I will discuss more fully in chapter 4, the earlier group of historians' fascination with food extremism is instructive. It helps us recognize that despite some common preoccupations among food reformers, they did not all share the same philosophies and were not all accorded the same social legitimacy. Indeed, reformers such as crusaders for the purity of the milk supply or Harvey Wiley and his allies, who spearheaded the Pure Food and Drug Act of 1906,[8] kept their distance from natural foods followers, whose perceived fanaticism discomfited groups claiming more respectability. This disdain shown toward reformers labeled extremists puts the moralism of natural foods advocates in a somewhat different light. A moralistic stance was not solely about drawing boundaries between the virtuous and the corrupt in the realm of food, but it also gave advocates the moral conviction to endure their marginal cultural status.

The considerable opposition that the natural foods lifestyle faced in the United States for most of its history suggests that it can represent some threat to the prevailing social order. First, and most obviously, the movement poses a challenge to economic interests tied to prevailing methods of food production and distribution. By claiming that conventional food is unhealthy and even poisonous, natural foods advocates potentially target much of the food processing industry and its supporting apparatus, such as the manufacturers of additives, as needing to be substantially transformed or eliminated altogether. And by arguing that most standard agricultural inputs do more harm than good, natural foods advocates threaten the makers of pesticides, herbicides, and fertilizers as well as the related trade in cultivars and their seeds designed to take advantage of those inputs.

The competition presented by natural foods to the conventional food industry has certainly resulted in pushback, from the millers and bakers of white flour in the early twentieth century to the giant chemical and bio-technology company Monsanto in more recent years. However, it is actually the ways in which the field has posed a challenge to state-sanctioned professional medical authority that has inspired the greatest antagonism toward natural foods over time. The natural foods field has directly defied jurisdictional claims of professional physicians, dieticians, and pharmaceutical companies by asserting an equivalent, if not superior, right to advise people on health issues and to develop health aids. Natural foods proponents have consciously turned their backs on decades of pronouncements from established scientific authorities about the safety of the conventional food supply and the ineffectiveness of much health food. This contempt for prevailing medical opinion is fueled by ambivalence about the kind of knowledge that requires scientific proof (an ambivalence seen in other debates, such as regarding evolution) and by a perspective that sees individual differences in how people respond to diet and other environmental factors as more important than statistical averages (a stance that can also help explain why some people demand access to drugs that have been banned by regulatory agencies). By denying that only certified experts are truly capable of understanding health, illness, and how to treat the body, the natural foods movement questions the very basis of professional authority.

These challenges to economic and professional interests were both originally related to a rejection of cultural ideas that equate progress with industrialization and technical innovation. The guiding concept of the natural in health care and food production represented a critique of the artificiality and fragmentation perceived as characterizing a modern existence. For advocates of natural foods, to live according to the laws of nature was a way to achieve harmony and balance in their lives. In this perspective, that which is artificial is not only dangerous to one's health but also enslaves one to materialism as it estranges one from an understanding of one's most basic needs and how these needs can be satisfied in a straightforward way. A respect for nature was also believed to translate into better relations with one's fellows. Otto Carqué was among the many who had no small hopes for making nature our guidepost: "The more closely and conscientiously we shall live in harmony with nature's laws, the more we shall hasten the coming of a higher order of society characterized by the reign of intellect, universal peace and welfare of all" (Carqué 1925, 10). For these critics of industrialism, it was obvious that a technically advanced society had not eliminated war, squalor, or superstition.

As I will describe in chapter 3, the early natural foods movement's refusal to uncritically embrace industrialization became associated with a range of countercultural styles, from unconventional forms of dress to unconventional business practices. These countercultural styles certainly contributed to natural foods' long-standing lack of legitimacy. But they also aided in natural foods' eventual popularization. Beginning in the mid-twentieth century, though not fully realized until the 1980s, the health food industry was able to transform its status by glamorizing the unconventional and showing how natural foods fit into fashionably bohemian lifestyles. Significantly, growing popular interest in natural foods preceded acceptance by cultural authorities, especially the medical establishment, and by political authority, especially government regulators. The conventional food sector, on the other hand, soon became eager to follow the money. As chapter 7 will discuss, attempts to redefine or break down the barriers that had previously existed between the concepts of natural and conventional food generated considerable debate and remain a source of conflict to this day.

My argument here in part parallels the valuable work of Belasco (1989), who similarly claims that a natural foods "countercuisine" challenged conventional science and the prevailing system of food distribution, though he downplays the countercultural and philosophical elements of the movement that existed prior to the late 1960s. He also exaggerates the role that consumers and others without a financial interest in natural foods activities played in leading the countercuisine, thus drawing a wider divide between citizen activists and opportunistic entrepreneurs than is actually warranted. Belasco's book was published in the late 1980s, a time when conventional food companies were aggressively moving to create their own connections to the natural foods concept and when complete co-optation of this movement seemed the likely outcome.[9] By considering a lengthier period of history, as well as the close overlap that long existed between movement and industry, I intend to show how the process of industry building in the natural foods field created dynamics that cannot be reduced to simple co-optation.

The case of natural foods suggests that the presence of industry in a movement produces a complex set of results. Indeed, the history of natural foods is filled with ironies. As I will show in the following chapters, a movement that began by emphasizing self-reliance and asceticism evolved into a lifestyle in which people depend on a vast array of consumer goods to meet its standards. Foods that were once chosen in part because they were more economical than conventional ways of feeding oneself and one's family were turned into high-priced "premium" alternatives to conventional fare. And a movement once derided as the outpost of the elderly, the sick, and the deluded became associated with the young, fit, and hip. Understanding how the natural foods field has both retained and repudiated the meanings that have shaped it for nearly two centuries helps us to better understand not just the current food landscape but also the interrelationship between economic and cultural processes.

Notes on Methods

My frequent use of the term *field* here, which encompasses both the industry and the movement, is meant to emphasize the indistinct boundaries between them. In thinking about the contours of the field, I borrow in part from social movement scholars who discuss a multiorganizational field (Curtis and Zurcher 1973; Klandermans 1992; Rao, Morrill, and Zald 2000), which includes diverse, nonequivalent organizations. However, to focus only on organizations as the essential core of the movement misses important individual actors who are loosely, if at all, connected to formal organizations. Writing from an organizational theory perspective, DiMaggio and Powell cast a much wider net, referring to the organizational field as the aggregate of organizations, regulatory agencies, consumers, and other actors that constitute an arena of institutional life (1991, 64–65).[10] While this definition makes sense in the context of studying how a firm reacts to the totality of its environment, I wish to indicate the identity of certain interests that sets some of these actors apart from others. Therefore, I include in the natural foods field private companies; trade associations; activist groups composed of any combination of industry members, citizens, and consumers; creators of communication media intended to promote natural foods; and other key individuals who view their enactment of a natural foods lifestyle as a means of proselytizing the philosophies that underlie it. Surrounding the field are other groups that occasionally interact with it in meaningful ways: uncommitted consumers, sometimes-allied environmentalists and others subscribing to "alternative" ways of living, conventional food manufacturers and grocers, conventional agriculture and allied industries, the medical profession, and government regulators. While my discussion will necessarily include many of these various actors, both inside and outside the field, my primary focus is on members of the natural foods industry as a way to better understand the role that they have played in shaping and furthering the adoption and legitimation of a natural foods lifestyle.

Researching this field as it existed over such an extensive period has involved utilizing a combination of methods. The interview portion of my research was intended to fill in aspects of natural foods' history that are not in the written record and to better understand the experiences and motivations of, and relationships between, those working in the natural foods field. I conducted fifty semistructured interviews with individuals who were part of the natural foods industry during its formative years or who were associated with key industry organizations and advocacy groups in more recent years. The interviews, most of which took place between 2003 and 2012, generally lasted between one and two hours and were conducted face-to-face except for three that were carried out via telephone. My informants included many industry "pioneers" who innovated new products, markets, or ways of carrying out business. All but about one-fifth started working in the field prior to 1980; a few of the oldest entered the health food business in the 1930s. Among them, they represented most of the major distributors, many of the major retailers and manufacturers, some of the best-known restaurants, and several authors of prominent cookbooks of twentieth-century natural foods; smaller and lesser-known firms were represented as well. Most of these individuals had worked at multiple organizations in a variety of capacities over the years and could speak knowledgeably about the industry as a whole.

While I was able without much trouble to locate old-timers in the industry who had worked in related jobs for most of their adult lives, it was much harder to find that kind of longevity and institutional memory for advocacy groups, at least in the sense of traditional social movement organizations. That speaks to both the small number of such citizen-only groups that lasted over time and also perhaps to the nature of activist work, which can easily lead to burnout or to the desire to make a more lucrative living as life circumstances change. However, as I have argued, confining a definition of advocacy work to citizen-only groups misses a great deal of relevant activity since much direct advocacy work takes place through trade associations or through nonprofit organizations that are not themselves involved in selling goods or services but whose mainstays are people who at one time or another worked in a natural foods business. Employing these broader criteria for identifying advocacy groups, eight of my fifty interviews were with people whose primary affiliations were with such organizations.

Our conversations covered my respondents' experiences in the field and their views on many of the issues confronting natural foods. I also solicited their ideas about who they considered influential individuals, organizations, and publications to better understand the networks of relationships in the field. In addition to the formal interviews, numerous informal conversations took place with many others I encountered at trade shows, public events, or in the course of locating and visiting my interview subjects. In most cases here, I do not identify my respondents by name, though I do frequently refer to the generation they came from or the type of position they held.

The other part of my research consisted of an analysis of a wide range of written sources, including industry trade publications, market research studies, natural foods cookbooks and guides, legal and financial documents, the popular press, and unpublished archival material. I consulted these sources to put together a reliable history of the field (because interview subjects' memories were incomplete and not always accurate) and to better understand the trajectory of the field's successes and challenges. The natural foods industry has not paid much attention to documenting its legacy, and unfortunately, much written material related to the trade appears to be lost. To locate available material, I visited twenty-one institutional and private repositories around the country as well as using online sources. I also collected additional unpublished and rare material through personal contacts and through purchases from private dealers, mostly via eBay.

Finally, I conducted observations and attended educational sessions at several natural foods trade shows and consumer festivals. And I collected and analyzed a variety of cultural material related to natural foods, including print, digital, audio, and visual items. This latter analysis helped me understand how the public image of natural foods has changed over time.

Starting with the first American advocates of vegetarianism and unprocessed foods in the nineteenth century, what I do in the following chapters is trace the history of the natural foods field as a way to show how natural foods went from the marginal to the mainstream, to show how industry has been a leader in this transformation, and to show the impact of industry on movement goals and outcomes. This narrative will encompass a diverse cast of characters, including religious groups and nudists, bodybuilders and Hollywood celebrities, naturopaths and crusaders against enemies of the medical profession. All helped, in one way or another, to shape the natural foods industry that exists today.

CHAPTER TWO

Escaping Asceticism

The Birth of the Health Food Industry

By the second decade of the twenty-first century, natural foods had a firm footing in urban, upscale, hip lifestyles, in scientific debates about such foods' effectiveness, and in left-leaning politics. One only needed to venture into any Whole Foods outlet and take note of the extraordinary array of raw, packaged, and prepared food choices, along with the retailer's popular nickname, Whole Paycheck, to find support for natural foods' reputation for healthy hedonism and consumers spending freely to simultaneously satisfy their gastronomic and socially conscious impulses. Meanwhile, doctors, research scientists, and government officials discussed in serious fashion evidence related to natural foods: What do the latest studies show regarding the body's need for vitamin D? Can the inclusion of more whole grains in one's diet reduce the risk of cancer? Are there nutritional differences between organic and conventionally grown produce? On the political front, campaigns against genetically modified organisms, junk food in schools, and agricultural chemicals linked to wildlife decline, among other causes, were easily embraced by Americans who identified themselves as progressive in their politics.

This contemporary image of natural foods as embedded in a secular discourse of self-indulgence, science, and social responsibility, and of being the food of choice of a cosmopolitan, affluent, white, fashion-conscious population, is only partially accurate. It leaves out lingering influences from a recent past that looked quite different, with users who skewed old and prioritized economizing and with scientific derision and dismissal of natural foods diets. But this contemporary image stands in particularly sharp contrast to the early natural foods movement, which started to take shape in the beginning of the nineteenth century. Until the turn of the twentieth century, the promotion of a natural foods lifestyle was in large part propelled by religious concerns and was intertwined with an ascetic lifestyle and disdain for the economic and social "progress" cheered by so many Americans at the time.

In this chapter, I describe the origins of natural foods advocacy and trace its transition from small clusters of people committed to asceticism, self-reliance, and a rejection of a commodified food system to a movement developing hand in hand with the industry serving and promoting it. The American natural foods movement of the nineteenth century did not emerge out of nowhere; it grew out of several other social and religious movements, some based in Europe, some homegrown in the United States, most far from the cultural mainstream. These movements included British vegetarianism and the Bible-Christian Church, American transcendentalism and the Seventh-day Adventist Church, and Anglo-American temperance. The American natural foods movement was also connected to alternative health movements such as hydropathy and, toward the end of the nineteenth century, nature cure practices coming out of central Europe. These various strands produced philosophical motivations that have defined the natural foods movement ever since: a reverence for nature, including a commitment to minimal impact on the environment and minimal harm to animals; opposition to the industrialization of food production, including a preference for locally grown and home-prepared items; and a belief in the health superiority of natural foods.

During the first half of the nineteenth century, advocates of a natural foods diet, the best known of whom were William Metcalfe, Sylvester Graham, and William A. Alcott, were committed to spreading the principles they believed were so important for personal well-being and the greater good. Through lectures, publications, and the formation of voluntary associations, they helped crystallize a movement of people based mostly in New York, New England, and Philadelphia. While the number of adherents remained small (historians have estimated it to be in the low thousands: H. Green 1986, 52–53; Nissenbaum 1980, 140; Whorton 1982, 119–20), their views became known to a much larger segment of the population, though familiarity did not generally breed respect.

For the many early proponents who made a connection to Christian ideals, a simple, natural, vegetarian diet brought one closer to grace, as it meant eating the unadulterated foods provided by God. Consequently, a natural foods orientation tended to promote limitations on consumption as the task was less to acquire specialized products than to obtain pure sources of the most basic food ingredients. Consistent with this perspective, the early leaders did not produce any commercial food products themselves; their entrepreneurial activities were limited to selling their publications and promoting their lectures. But their efforts paved the way for quasi-commercial endeavors as followers sought to put natural foods ideas into more consistent practice. Especially for people living in cities—and the early movement was mainly an urban one—gaining access to appropriately pure food could be a problem. Therefore, their ideals necessitated some kind of conscious engagement with the market. Adherents opened up boardinghouses and dining rooms that served vegetarian fare, and retail establishments catering to followers stocked vegetables, sugars, bread, and the whole-grain flour that was now named after Graham. By the middle of the nineteenth century, some natural foods believers had opened health centers, most notably water cure resorts, and continued to publish cookbooks, tracts, and newsletters. Still, it was only in the late nineteenth century, at a Seventh-day Adventist sanitarium in Battle Creek, Michigan, that the first truly systematic and successful effort to commercialize natural foods took place. Under the direction of John Harvey Kellogg, a number of meat substitutes, coffee substitutes, and cereal items were developed and widely marketed. The clashes over these efforts, which occurred between Kellogg and his brother and business partner, Will, and between Kellogg and other leaders of the Seventh-day Adventist Church, provided a model for the contradictions and tensions involved in marketing natural foods that have continued to mark the field ever since.

There have been numerous historical accounts written about nineteenth-century food reformers, and they have informed my own investigations. My intention is not to provide the same comprehensive stories of these reformers found elsewhere but to focus on the interactions between commerce and foundational principles of the natural foods movement, as well as on conflicts, both internal and external, that would provide considerable continuity in the preoccupations of those who identified with the movement. Externally, natural foods advocates encountered public sentiment that considered them eccentric at best and dangerous at worst, resulting in advocates occupying a culturally marginal position all the way until the late twentieth century. Internally, the movement faced the divisive question of whether broadening the base of support to include people who adopted some elements of a natural foods diet but did not embrace all associated philosophies was a worthwhile goal. These internal debates would also persist over the course of the movement's history.

Related to these conflicts, a decisive change realized during the nineteenth century was a shift in the leadership and center of the movement away from commercially disinterested groups and toward for-profit enterprises. This new generation of natural foods proponents inadvertently discovered the power of specialized consumer goods to attract new followers to its philosophical ideals. This shift came with a set of ironies: the new commercial enterprises sought to further the ideals of a natural foods lifestyle by mediating between nature and the humans who revered it, and they used industrial techniques to make available food that symbolized the rejection of the corrosive effects of an industrial order. When considering this contradictory relationship to industrialization, it is perhaps fitting that the movement begins near Manchester, England, one of the early centers of the Industrial Revolution.

Vegetarianism and Brown Bread

While beliefs related to a natural foods ideology, including vegetarianism and concerns over the adulteration of food, have been present for centuries in various parts of the world, a more coherent movement for natural foods, with its understanding that believers had a duty to spread their convictions to others, began to emerge in the early nineteenth century. The foundational philosophy was a variant of vegetarianism that made reference to biblical law and that saw the dichotomy between sickness and health as related to that between good and evil. Britain was a source of many of the ideas that underlay the American movement. Indeed, what appears to be the first United States–based group self-consciously promoting principles connected to a natural foods way of life was a religious sect called the Bible-Christian Church, which migrated from Britain to Philadelphia in 1817. The church was founded by William Cowherd in 1800 in Salford, England, on the outskirts of Manchester. Shortly after its founding, Cowherd developed the doctrine, which became core for Bible-Christians, of strict vegetarianism and abstention from intoxicating liquor. Cowherd, as did other vegetarians before and after him, cited the Bible as the basis for his teachings, scrutinizing passages related to vegetable and animal food and to the taking of life (Maintenance Company 1922).[1] In the church's interpretation, killing animals and eating their flesh was inhumane, an act of willful indifference to the suffering of living creatures and to the injunctions of God.

William Metcalfe, a minister in the Bible-Christian Church, led the group that settled in Philadelphia. Though the original intention of the migrating band of forty-one adults and children was to proselytize church doctrines, after they arrived in the United States, a majority abandoned their vegetarian and temperance ideals. With numbers greatly diminished, Metcalfe established his congregation and worked to spread Bible-Christian tenets beyond immediate members by publishing tracts and newspaper articles on temperance and vegetarianism (Metcalfe 1872, 18–19; see also Alcott 1859, 226–29). According to his son's published account of the church, Metcalfe viewed the public's resistance to vegetarianism as actually greater than that against temperance (Metcalfe 1872, 32).

By the 1830s, other voices advocating dietary reform were also being heard. For instance, the Philadelphia-based *Journal of Health*, edited by John Bell and David Francis Condie, did not directly call for complete abstinence from flesh foods, but it did argue that "it will be found that those who make use of a diet consisting chiefly of vegetable matter, have a manifest advantage in looks, strength and spirits, over those who partake largely of animal food: they are remarkable for the firm, healthy plumpness of their muscles, and the transparency of their skin." Using what was to become a key rationale for adopting a vegetarian diet, this piece not only touted the bodily benefits of such a diet but referred to the biblical description of the food consumed in the Garden of Eden, noting that "the fruits of the earth constituted originally the only food of man."[2] Like other vegetarians, Bell and Condie also advocated temperance, seeing alcohol, like gluttony, as a capitulation to excess that precludes both moral and physical health.

Far more strict in his commitment to vegetarianism, and more far-reaching in his organizational and literary activities, was William A. Alcott. As a young man, Alcott had taken an interest in the value of fresh air, exercise, and cleanliness for maintaining health. He also limited his meat intake and was completely vegetarian by the early 1830s.[3] In perhaps his earliest published essay on vegetarianism ([W. Alcott] 1835), Alcott laid out the various rationales for forgoing meat. They included the physiological case—the claim that humans' teeth and digestive system were designed for vegetable foods—and the "argument from experience" that throughout history, one could find societies that have subsisted wholly on vegetable diets. But three other reasons would become more central to a broader natural foods philosophy. The first one concerned the health effects of eating flesh: Alcott claimed that meat was frequently diseased and, even when not, had a similar detrimental stimulating effect as alcohol and other narcotic substances. Second, Alcott noted that far more people can be fed from an acre of land devoted to producing vegetable food than an acre used for raising animal feed. And third, Alcott discussed the cruelty of destroying "innocent" animal life and the Christian duty to feel compassion for beasts as well as humans.

Although he expressed frustration with a single-minded focus on diet that did not incorporate other elements of healthful living (Hoff and Fulton 1937, 711–12), Alcott was a key figure in establishing an American vegetarian movement, through his own writings, by disseminating others' endorsements of this mode of eating and by taking a leadership role in formal associations. Nevertheless, it was Sylvester Graham who became the best-known vegetarian advocate of the first half of the nineteenth century, and he remains so today, no doubt as much for his campaigns against masturbation as for his dietary advice.[4] Graham's views on the debilitating effects of food that he believed overstimulated the body were mirrored by his ideas about the dangers of sexual stimulation. But although Graham's views on sexuality are easy to mock, and his pompous manner has always invited skewering, his contributions to a natural foods movement are significant. His ideas attracted groups of people who developed a collective identity based on the way of life he promoted. And Graham went beyond vegetarianism to provide an analysis that spoke to the harmful application of modern techniques to food cultivation and preparation more generally. Along with vegetarianism, he advocated pure cold water and, most famously, brown breads baked in the home.

Graham moved from a short career as a Presbyterian minister to, in 1830, a lecturer with the Philadelphia Temperance Society. Although this position was also short-lived (Nissenbaum 1980, 81–82), he never abandoned his commitment to temperance but instead integrated it into a general philosophy of abstemiousness, which he promoted as an independent lecturer and writer. By his 1831 lectures on "The Science of the Human Life" and his 1832 lectures on the cholera epidemic, Graham was expounding on the benefits of a vegetable diet and properly prepared bread.[5] Influenced by writers such as Francois J. V. Broussais, who believed that illness resulted from overstimulation of the gastrointestinal tract (Nissenbaum 1980, 57–60; Whorton 1982, 41–43), Graham made connections between digestive health, the avoidance of stimulating agents, and moral sturdiness. "Whatever, in food or drink, or any other bodily indulgence or habit, impairs the sensorial power of the nervous system, commensurately impairs the moral sense," he claimed (Graham 1877, 243). Graham was a talented orator; crowds flocked to his lectures, the contents of which caused a sensation—not necessarily supportive—wherever he appeared. Soon after he began the lecture circuit, his teachings inspired groups of followers, dubbed Grahamites by dubious observers, who discussed his ideas and modified their diets according to his principles.

As part of his program of diet reform, Graham specifically campaigned against what was called *bolted flour*, which referred to a sifting process that removed the bran and at least some of the germ (as well as dirt and debris), leaving a whiter, lighter flour. Millers could produce several grades of flour through multiple rounds of sifting; the "superfine" whitest flour they hailed as the best. Not only did Americans develop a taste for white flour, but merchants also preferred it since it was less quick to spoil. After the steel roller mill was adopted in the United States in the 1870s, the process of grinding the wheat and separating out the germ and bran could be efficiently done at the same time. But even before then, the application of steam power to grinding and the development of various materials for bolting led to increased supplies of white flour.

In most of his written works, but especially in his *Treatise on Bread*, Graham made a case for using what has come to be called the *whole grain*. His reasoning was most obviously based in health concerns, but there was a moral dimension as well. On the one hand, Graham emphasized the healthful properties of coarsely ground flour made from wheat that was carefully cleaned by washing instead of bolting. He approvingly quoted Hippocrates, as well as the seventeenth-century British vegetarian Thomas Tryon, on the salutary effects of unbolted wheat bread on the bowels (Graham 1877, 627–28). (Constipation was to be a constant obsession among natural foods proponents for the next century.) Yet this was not simply an astute recognition of the value of roughage in one's diet. Graham's comments on the superiority of bread made from grain that has not had its components artificially sundered were in keeping with his broader message about the importance of a simple diet wherein varying foods are not combined in a single meal and the stimulants of spices and salt are excluded. In each of these cases, the original—that is, natural—composition of food is preserved in as pure a state as possible. It is partially for these reasons that Graham condemned commercially made bread since "public bakers, like other men, who serve the public more for the sake of securing their own emolument than for the public good, have always had recourse to various expedients in order to increase the lucrativeness of their business" (Graham 1837, 43) Those expedients included the use of adulterants such as "chemical agents" to make light and white bread out of poor flour (Graham 1837,

44). Already by 1832 and 1833, merchants in the Northeast were selling as "graham flour" the coarsely ground unbolted flour recommended by its namesake.[6]

As the previous quotation suggests, more than just the right ingredients were needed to make good bread. Along with disparaging overly refined foods, Graham warned that commercial preparations could not be good since the baker in business was primarily oriented toward profit. In contrast, he claimed, the wife and mother was first and foremost concerned with the well-being of her family: "Still, truth compels me to declare, that if we would have good and wholesome bread, it must be made within the precincts of our own domestic threshold; and by those whose skill and care are exercised more with a view to secure our health and happiness, than their own pecuniary interest" (Graham 1837, 49). Graham articulated a suspicion of the motives and methods of those who prepare food for commercial consumption, seeing an inherent conflict of interest between the profit-making mission of a business and the time and resources it will put into its products. Anticipating the place of bread baking in a do-it-yourself ethic that would be so prominent in the next century, Graham turned homemade bread into a symbol of freedom from the hazards of a commercialized food sector.

Leading the Ascetic Life

Stephen Nissenbaum, whose account remains the most thorough of Graham studies, has argued that the vegetarianism of Metcalfe differed sharply from that of Graham. Nissenbaum (1980, 39–40) notes that Metcalfe derived his views from a biblically based opposition to animal suffering, while Graham's rationale was primarily physiological. It is true that Graham had little to say about the plight of animals destined for the table. And the health and animal welfare lines of reasoning can appear dissimilar, especially if we are looking back from the vantage point of contemporary vegetarianism, where we easily find people who are motivated by one of these considerations with minimal regard for the other. However, Nissenbaum exaggerates the differences between Graham and Metcalfe. Both of them associated their ideas about diet with an understanding of what it means to lead a Christian life. Both of them saw virtue in embracing asceticism. And what tied together all these notions of health, morality, religion, and asceticism was a particular conception of the natural.

For nineteenth-century food reformers, the quintessential natural setting was not a wilderness untouched by humans but rather the Garden
of Eden. In this conception, *original* and *natural* are synonymous. Human misfortune is traced to the way that over time—especially because of
their own wickedness—people have become alienated from that simple
state of being where wants were few and easily satisfied. Therefore, recov-
ering humankind's original diet and the way of life that went with it is a
way to recover spiritual and physical health. When Graham claimed that
"fruits, nuts, farinaceous seeds, and roots, with perhaps some milk, and it
may be honey, in all rational probability, constituted the food of the first
family and the first generation of mankind" (1877, 317), he provided his
contemporaries with a powerful justification for building a diet formed
around these substances. An equation between the natural and a state of
grace can also be seen in the teachings of Metcalfe and Alcott. But of even
more importance for the developing natural foods movement, the elevation of the concept of the natural occurred with their followers.

For instance, Asenath Nicholson's 1835 volume *Nature's Own Book* was
the first vegetarian cookbook published in the United States; it became a
standard reference work for vegetarians before the American Civil War.
The section on recipes was actually something of an afterthought to Nicholson's more extensive commentary on the way of life that conformed to
Graham's philosophy and that was enforced in the Temperance Boarding
House that Nicholson ran in New York City. She wrote, "Let us go back to
first principles. and while bewailing the curse entailed upon us by our first
parents, see how far this curse *would have affected* us, had we obeyed the
original laws of nature" (Nicholson 1835, 6). In her view, redemption can
at least be partially found by going back to the foods originally eaten by
Adam and Eve. Indeed, Nicholson in her preface justifies the instructions
laid out in her book by attributing them to nature: "The writer makes no
pretension to originality, but has only followed out established rules, drawn
from Nature's own unerring laws" (1835, np).

Nicholson's book included the rules and regulations that Graham and
Nicholson established for her boardinghouse. The directives insisted on
plainness and simplicity in meals and warned against "unreasonable and
capricious demands for change and variety" (Nicholson 1835, 15). Although
animal flesh was not completely forbidden, it was discouraged, as was excessive consumption of sweets—though recipes contained what, from today's standpoint, would seem to be a heavy dose of sweeteners. The list of
boardinghouse rules described not only a strict dietary regimen but also a

complete code of conduct that promoted an ascetic existence. This code included cold sponge baths and the prohibition of a feather bed; mattresses were required to be made out of a hard substance such as hair (Nicholson 1835, 15).

As Nicholson's book exemplifies, a natural life was typically seen as an ascetic life, with nineteenth-century food reformers finding moral as well as health benefits in limiting the variety and quantity of their food intake. The developing natural foods diet, with its refusal of meat, spices, alcohol, coffee, refined flour, and elaborate food combinations, was strongly linked to the values of restraint and renunciation. As Gusfield has argued in relation to Graham, heightened appetite, both sexual and food-related, was seen as a product of civilization whereas what was viewed as a natural propensity for self-control allowed the individual to re-create an ideal moral order (Gusfield 1992, 84–87). This ascetic ideal valorized deprivation for its own sake, but it also grew out of a distrust of the consumer society that was then taking root in cities. Some reformers even posited a return to the land as the surest way to achieve self-reliance and independence from the commercial forces governing food provision. Such tendencies were perhaps best seen with those transcendentalists who were also followers of food reform.

Transcendentalism, the mid-nineteenth-century intellectual movement centered in New England, has been described as "a way of perceiving the world, centered on individual consciousness rather than on external fact" (Gura 2007, 8). In part, growing out of theological debates in the Unitarian Church, the movement saw self-consciousness as a path to connection with the divine. Although there was no unified doctrine of transcendentalism, some who identified with it were influenced by, adopted, and advocated food reform ideas. The most visible manifestation of this relationship were two communal endeavors of the 1840s: Brook Farm, founded by George Ripley in West Roxbury, Massachusetts, and Fruitlands, founded by A. Bronson Alcott and Charles Lane in Harvard, Massachusetts. In both outposts, residents (not very successfully) tried to create a simple and self-sufficient existence by producing for themselves all that they needed to eat, while also cultivating a rich spiritual existence (Francis 1997, 2010; Shi 1985; Gura 2007). Most Brook Farm residents were not vegetarian, though they did designate a Graham table for those who practiced Grahamism. Fruitlands, on the other hand, was fully committed to dietary reform and an ascetic existence (Swift 1973, 49; Shi 1985, 136).

Bronson Alcott was a cousin of William and the father of Louisa May

Alcott. He was primarily known for his educational innovations but was also committed to vegetarianism and an ascetic life in harmony with nature. Bronson Alcott's business partner, Charles Lane, an English reformer, provided the financial backing to purchase the land for Fruitlands, and they were joined there by about ten others, including the partners' children and Bronson Alcott's wife, Abigail. In Louisa May Alcott's satirical 1873 novel, *Transcendental Wild Oats*, based on the time her family lived at Fruitlands when she was ten years old, food—or the lack thereof—plays a prominent role. The story mocks the overly earnest commitment of residents to abstention from most foods. Meals consisted primarily of brown bread, vegetables, fruit, and water. On principle, Fruitlanders refused all animal products, forbidding dairy and eggs as well as meat. Condemning not just the slaughter of animals but their recruitment into servitude as well, Fruitlanders did without animal labor and, like Graham, opposed the use of manure as fertilizer, believing it to be foul like meat itself (A. Alcott 1843; L. Alcott 1975, 38, 89; Sears 1915, 38–39, 49). "Our present modes of agriculture exhaust our soil," Bronson Alcott declared (A. Alcott 1842, 426), voicing a concern about the health of the soil that would be elaborated on in the next century in ideas about organic agriculture. Anticipating another tenet of the twentieth-century natural foods movement, Lane noted, "It is calculated that if no animal food were consumed, one-fourth of the land now used would suffice for human sustenance" (1843, 119). Mirroring similar developments in England, the ideal of vegetarianism thus began to be tied to ideas about the conservation of the land.

In the quest for self-sufficiency, foreign-grown foods, such as rice and molasses, were also omitted from their diet. While today's natural foods discourse typically assumes that the valuation of deriving one's foodstuffs locally is a recent phenomenon, it has actually been integral to the natural foods movement since these nineteenth-century reformers articulated a connection between local sources of food and freedom from the complex system of exchange that underlay food imports. Lane and Bronson Alcott argued that food grown by one's own efforts allowed for a nutritious diet "without dependence on foreign climes, or the degradations of shipping and trade" (quoted in Sears 1915, 49–50). In their view, an ascetic existence offers freedom from the pecuniary interests and uncertainties of the market, from the guilt of taking the life of another creature, and from one's own physical appetites.

Unfortunately for the Fruitlanders' experiment, they were neither skilled nor disciplined farm laborers. Lane and Bronson Alcott preferred the intellectual component of their endeavor, so rather than experiencing a rural communal life full-time, the two traveled extensively to speak about its merits. The scanty attention to farm work, as well as strife over Lane's conception of family life and his promotion of celibacy (he later joined a Shaker community), led to the settlement being abandoned after only half a year. Brook Farm achieved more success but still struggled and finally folded after seven years. Short-lived as these two experiments in communal self-sufficiency were, they received a great deal of publicity and became a source of considerable commentary on the possibilities of collective living arrangements that were spiritually rich, materially poor, and in harmony with the natural world.

Indeed, public awareness of food reform more generally, especially Grahamism, was disproportionate to the relatively small number of followers. Notwithstanding the endorsement of some prominent citizens, public views were far from complimentary. Ridicule was the general rule, but opposition sometimes became more serious, as when Boston butchers and bakers threatened to attack Graham for his criticisms of them (Hoff and Fulton 1937, 694). In an 1837 letter to the *Graham Journal of Health and Longevity*, a secretary of an insurance company praised the Graham system but added, "I have known persons who are thorough Grahamites and yet are reluctant to confess it. They do not wish to be the subject of remark and ridicule" (Worthington 1837, 65). The mockery and incredulity of mainstream society helped constitute among natural foods reformers an identity as misunderstood nonconformists. While natural foods proponents often worked hard to counter stereotypes and their marginal status, a general unwillingness among the population to take them seriously actually helped this emerging movement to stay intact. After the initial wave of Grahamism died down, food merchants stopped worrying that their economic interests could be affected by the small group of people renouncing meat and white bread, and they simply chose to ignore the Grahamites. Perceived more as a curiosity than a threat, these food reformers thus continued their efforts mostly undisturbed, and with few concessions to mainstream sensibilities.

Taking Collective Action

Their numbers were small, and many Grahamites put the bulk of their advocacy efforts into temperance or other reform activities. But the movement for a natural foods way of life did find early institutionalization. As in contemporaneous social movements, food reformers formed publications

and associations to discuss and promote followers' views. Less typical were
the commercial endeavors they also sponsored.

Associational activity became formalized when an 1836 discussion group
in Boston, convened by John Benson, passed a number of resolutions expressing support for Graham's ideas and deploring the "popular prejudice" with which his doctrines were viewed. The group further resolved
"that the cause in which Mr. Graham is engaged *is not*, and ought not to
be considered, in any manner, as an individual or personal interest, but
as the common interest of humanity, which eminently deserves the confidence of every human being, and the decided support of every Christian
and philanthropist" (quoted in Hoff and Fulton 1937, 695).

This expression of the social character of Grahamism resulted in Benson, William Alcott, and others forming the American Physiological Society
a few months later, in February 1837 (Hoff and Fulton 1937, 696; Shprintzen
2013, 40–41). By May of that year, 127 "gentlemen" and 76 "ladies" had
joined the society (though interestingly, Graham was not among them[7]).
In keeping with the commitment to "use our best endeavors to effect the
formation of such societies in every place in which we have any influence,"
branches were established elsewhere in Massachusetts; New York; Oberlin,
Ohio; and Philadelphia where Bible-Christians made up much of the membership (Hoff and Fulton 1937, 700, 704; Maintenance Company 1922, 40).
Though it lasted only a few years, the American Physiological Society was
the most visible association promoting natural foods principles until the
American Vegetarian Society was founded in 1850.

In this latter organization, William Alcott and William Metcalfe again
took leadership roles, though it also included a new generation of advocates. The name of the association provoked at least some dispute; wrote
one supporter from Belchertown, Massachusetts: "I do not, however, quite
like the name which has been given to the Society; it does not cover ground
enough. A person may commit many and great outrages against the laws
of health, without travelling out of the vegetable kingdom. The narcotics
and spices are as bad, at least, as flesh. The forbidden fruit was a vegetable.
The Hindoos live upon vegetable food entirely, and yet they are among
the most degraded of the human species. 'Physiological Society,' or 'Graham Society,' would suit me better" (Filer 1850). Vegetarianism did remain
the focus of this organization, and as the ethnocentric comments of the
gentleman from Belchertown suggest, the American Vegetarian Society
remained rooted in a Christian frame of reference. Still, the group provided a means of connecting people with a wider range of interests related
to food reform until it folded in the late 1850s.

The many journals, tracts, and books that provided an outlet for the dissemination of ideas regarding vegetarianism, simplicity, and moderation in diet were another form of institutionalization. The interest in developing a literature on food reform was related to a desire to ground commitments in supporting evidence, which meant drawing on science and history as well as theology. To further their education, members of the American Physiological Society set up a circulating library of relevant works for their own use (Hoff and Fulton 1937, 707). Also important for spreading a set of principles connected to a natural foods way of life was the handful of vegetarian cookbooks published in this era. Especially before the 1870s, these cookbooks often devoted more space to explaining the rationale for vegetarianism than to actual recipes (L. Miller and Hardman 2015).

Two activities in particular were significant for involving the movement with commercial enterprises. In April 1837, the *Graham Journal of Health and Longevity* announced a plan by the American Physiological Society to establish a physiological market in Boston.[8] The next month, the *Journal* posted a request for farmers to supply samples, noting that preference would "be given to articles raised on physiological principles; they must be raised on a pure unadulterated soil, properly adapted to productions the most perfect in their kinds, without the aid of any unnatural or artificial process by which they may become the procuring cause of many of the diseases which afflict mankind" (Perry and Campbell 1837, 56). Under the direction of American Physiological Society treasurer, Nathaniel Perry, a provision store was opened on Fayette Court that September; it provided grains, vegetables, fruits, sweeteners, dairy products, and bread and crackers supplied by the Graham baker, Mr. Shipley.[9] With this store came a tacit recognition that few natural foods followers could abandon their urban way of life and move to the country to become truly self-sufficient; if existing markets were inadequate, followers would instead need to engage in alternative commercial activities to support the food-related practices to which they aspired.

Also serving those who wanted meals prepared according to Grahamite principles were several boardinghouses that sprang up in New York City, Rochester, and Boston in the 1830s.[10] Most did not survive for long, and commercial vegetarian cookery was hard to come by until much later in the nineteenth century. Indeed, vegetarian restaurants would continue to be hard to sustain until the twenty-first century, probably because of food that was more attuned to correct diet than to tastiness. The proprietress of a vegetarian water cure establishment wrote in 1854 of the difficulty of satisfying boarders with vegetarian fare, and she protested against William

Alcott's insinuation that she violated standards of purity by serving milk, eggs, sweets, and some variety in meals (M. Stewart 1854). Her remarks reveal the problems faced by eating establishments: a rigid interpretation of dietary strictures was likely to result in limited customers, while a more inclusive menu would invite criticism from purists. This dilemma was a foretaste of the types of conflicts that would become more common in a few decades when movement followers were increasingly transformed into consumers of movement-oriented products.

Testing the Market

In the second half of the nineteenth century, health reform became more diverse, with new influences both domestic and foreign, especially from central Europe. The Grahamite tradition was carried out most notably by advocates of water cure.[11] Water cure, or hydropathy, involved a regimen of baths and the ingestion of large quantities of water to treat ill health. Borrowing especially the ideas of Vincent Priessnitz of Silesia (now the Czech Republic), water cure took off in the United States in the 1840s, and by the mid-1850s, sixty-two water cure establishments operated around the country (H. Green 1986, 63). Once again, the Northeast, particularly New York state, was the center of movement leadership. The best-known American advocates—Joel Shew, Thomas Low and Mary Gove Nichols, Russell Thacher Trall, and James Caleb Jackson—were also followers of Grahamism, though they tended to refer to their mix of ideas about water, diet, exercise, and proper clothing as the *hygienic system*. They urged patrons of their establishments and readers of their disquisitions to take up vegetarianism and, in the case of Trall and Jackson, made available for purchase food items appropriate for a proper diet. By 1860, Graham flour and Trall's branded Graham crackers were being sold at 17 Laight Street in New York City, the site of Trall's Hygienic Institute, as well as via mail order.[12] Other grains were added to the supplies for sale,[13] but Trall appeared much more interested in selling the books he wrote and the journals he edited than in being a merchant of food.

A more significant move toward developing a market in natural foods was taken by James Caleb Jackson. What Jackson represented was a first step by a natural foods leader away from recommending simple foods derived directly from nature and toward the promotion of a complex, manufactured food item geared toward natural foods followers. Jackson ran a well-known water cure sanitarium, called Our Home on the Hillside, in Dansville, New York, where he counseled patients to give up meat, coffee, and tea. He developed Granula, described in an 1888 advertisement as "an incomparable, twice-cooked, food ready for immediate table use, prepared from the best Genesee Valley White Winter Wheat."[14] It was perhaps not as simple a substance as this advertisement made it out to be, as it required overnight soaking in milk to be thoroughly chewable.

Our Home Granula Co. claimed to have been producing Granula since 1863,[15] but this seems unlikely; I have found evidence of Granula's existence only from the 1870s. I believe instead that Jackson (or one of his sons) created Granula in the mid-1870s as a variation of granulated wheat. Granulated wheat was a substance similar to cracked wheat, the latter which was popular among Grahamites since it was not ground as fine as flour, preserving more of the whole grain. While a product called granulated wheat was available in Britain and Canada somewhat earlier,[16] it appeared in the United States in 1872, when Erastus Murray of Saint Paul, Minnesota, filed a patent for his process, which consisted of cracking the wheat, and then (contrary to Graham's teachings) bolting and scouring it to remove the bran and hull.[17] Shortly after Murray's product appeared, other similar items called "granulated wheat" were being sold, all marketed for their healthful qualities, and some advertised as a breakfast food.[18] Most such products, including Murray's, did not generate a substantial business.

One producer who did achieve some success was Frank Fuller. Fuller, a dentist who was governor of Utah during the American Civil War, established his Health Food Company in New York City in 1874.[19] His choice of words for the company's name was significant; while he resembled Grahamites in considering proper diet far better able than medicine to cure ill health, and he denounced stimulants and sweets, Fuller did not espouse vegetarianism. Moreover, he publicly excoriated Grahamism, though his chief complaint was, in the grand scheme of things, a relatively minor difference: Fuller charged that the coarse bran hulls left in Graham flour and cracked wheat damaged the stomach. Further distancing himself from Grahamites, Fuller downplayed the imagery of nature and instead kept his focus on the health-enhancing properties of his cereal wares.[20] Fuller did not claim affinity with the developing natural foods movement, and he was never fully embraced by hygienic food leaders, though users of his products included followers of health reform.[21] Fuller has likewise been left out of most published histories of natural foods. His status is noteworthy in that it marks the beginning of a pattern in natural foods sales whereby lines are drawn between insiders and outsiders, with the defining criterion being an acceptance of the broader moral framework through which the virtues of particular foods are understood.

Despite his absence from reformer circles, Fuller did have a lasting impact: he was the first to use the term *health food*, which would later be adopted by the industry serving the natural foods movement. Fuller applied this concept to his flours and grains. He also originated packaged, prepared products for people desiring wholesome food. Fuller made what he called "granulated wheat biscuit," and he manufactured a cereal coffee made from barley and wheat gluten.[22] Marketed as nutritious and especially good for those with "feeble digestion," these products were nevertheless not so different from substances homemakers produced in their own kitchens.

Without a more complete historical record, we cannot know whether Jackson or his associates were influenced by Fuller's goods. Regardless, the Dansville health reformers ended up manufacturing some similar items but took product development and marketing a couple steps further. In an era when distinctions in branding were beginning to matter,[23] Jackson called his food Granula, a name derived from granulated wheat (Canadian Patent Office 1895, 69). Granula was not to be used like any other grain or cracker but was already partially prepared and was meant to be consumed as a breakfast food. It was made by mixing Graham flour and water together, baking the dough in thin sheets, and then breaking it into small pieces and baking it again (thus, "twice-cooked"; G. Carson 1957, 67). First prepared for the benefit of Our Home on the Hillside guests, it proved popular enough to be sold to a broader clientele. By 1880, two tons of Granula were being sold each month, using mail order and sales agents based in Boston and Rochester. After a fire damaged the sanitarium in 1882, the Granula business was spun off into a separate company, and in 1883, production was moved to a separate facility in Dansville. In the 1890s, Our Home Granula Co. also started to sell a cereal-based coffee substitute called Somo. Ownership of the company changed hands a couple times, and after the Battle Creek businesses took off (as described subsequently), sales declined. Production of Granula stopped around 1921.[24]

Granula is sometimes touted as the first cold breakfast cereal. However, from my perspective, Jackson's primary significance is that by differentiating Granula from a biscuit or cracker or other familiar food items, he drew natural foods into the world of engineered food. That is to say, he invented a new product that appeared complex enough that, even if

derived from the pure elements of nature, it seemingly could not be repli-
cated by the home cook. Jackson himself was probably not much involved
in the actual business of selling Granula. Yet, this is not simply a case of
a leader taking more credit than is due for an activity that others carry
out in his name. Jackson's respected position in the health reform movement was critical for legitimating Granula as a hygienic food since, unlike
Fuller, he could not be dismissed as a mere merchant. This process of a
natural foods movement leader generating a natural foods business would
soon be repeated in a much more extensive fashion by John Harvey Kellogg in Battle Creek, Michigan.

The Morality of Health

Jackson's reach went much further than sales of Granula and Somo would
indicate, as his ideas about food and health also influenced leaders of the
Seventh-day Adventists, a religious group that originated in the 1840s as
a Millerite sect. William Miller was a Baptist preacher who predicted that
the Second Coming of Christ and the end of the world would occur in
1843, and then after that year passed without incident, in 1844. When the
Advent still did not happen (dubbed the Great Disappointment by historians), some of Miller's followers became completely disillusioned, while
others searched for an explanation without giving up on Miller's ideas entirely. One group, which believed that what occurred in 1844 should be in-
terpreted as a prelude to the Advent, was first called Sabbatarian and then
later Seventh-day Adventists due to their belief that saved Christians must
observe the Sabbath on the seventh day of the week (Numbers 1976; Bull
and Lockhart 2007).

   From early on, Seventh-day Adventist leaders took an interest in health
reform and vegetarianism (founder Joseph Bates became a follower of Grahamism in 1843; Numbers 1976, 128), but the notion of hygienic living was
made central to religious doctrine in 1863 when Ellen G. White, another
founder and the one who was considered a prophet by the denomination,
told of a vision she had that revealed the importance of healthy living to a
good Christian life. There is some dispute as to how much of White's ideas
were borrowed from Jackson, health reformer and vegetarian Larkin B.
Coles, or others; White and her husband, James, spent time at Our Home
on the Hillside in 1864, and prior to that she had been exposed to Jackson's writings.[25] But regardless of whether Adventists accepted White's

claim that all her revelations originated directly from God, her teachings came to hold special meaning for Adventists (and still do). In a series of pamphlets published in the two years following her initial health vision, White laid out a philosophy that emphasized the healing powers of nature and that denounced meat, alcohol, and the drugs prescribed by physicians.

For White, health practices and religious faith were inextricably linked. A healthy body went hand in hand with a devout spirit, and disease was seen as likely to be the outcome of disobeying God's laws. Furthermore, the spread of good health offered a means to proselytize religious ideals (Olsen 1972, 265–70). Corresponding to this philosophy, White reinforced the connections, which Grahamites before her had made, between God's will, the natural, an ascetic life, and health. She stated: "The Creator chose for our first parents the surroundings best adapted for their health and happiness. He did not place them in a palace or surround them with the artificial adornments and luxuries that so many today are struggling to obtain. He placed them in close touch with nature and in close communion with the holy ones of heaven" (E. White 1942, 261). For White, exposure to nature, simplicity in dress, the avoidance of stimulants, and a vegetarian diet "prepared in as simple and natural manner as possible" (E. White 1942, 296) made the drugs of physicians unnecessary.[26]

During her lifetime, White spoke and published extensively on matters of health and nutrition, and under her direction, the establishment of health institutes and restaurants became a central part of the Adventist mission. The first of these was the Western Health Reform Institute, modeled after Our Home on the Hillside, which opened in Battle Creek in 1866. Ten years later, the Adventists hired John Harvey Kellogg to run the institute, and in 1877, he changed its name to the Battle Creek Sanitarium. It was here that Kellogg directed the first truly systematic and successful effort to commercialize natural foods.

From the Garden of Eden to the Factories of Battle Creek

John Harvey Kellogg, raised as a Seventh-day Adventist himself, not only shared White's commitment to vegetarianism, whole grains, and a diet without alcohol, coffee, or tea but went beyond White in seeing such dietary practices as an inviolable commandment by God, even equivalent in importance to keeping the Sabbath. This stance eventually put him at odds with other church leaders, but for a quarter century he rose in influence within the Seventh-day Adventist Church. Kellogg's activities were numerous: he lectured extensively, published several newsletters and journals, and authored multiple books and pamphlets; he practiced medicine and invented various medical devices; and he set up educational facilities, foundations, and voluntary associations (Schwarz 1970).[27] He did not confine himself to dietary issues but advocated a variety of health practices; some of the more dubious ones—such as electric light therapy, enemas, and sexual abstinence—have made him a frequent target of derision and contributed to natural foods' reputation as the obsession of crackpots.[28] Leaving aside these multifaceted aspects of his life, I am primarily interested here in how Kellogg furthered ideas about how to achieve a natural foods way of life through the consumption of engineered food products.

Kellogg gradually introduced his dietary principles to the dining room at the sanitarium and developed special preparations to serve his patients there. One such food was Granola, a toasted granular cereal similar to Jackson's Granula but made from several types of grains and more convenient to prepare and eat. When questions were raised about the resemblance in form and name between Granula and Granola, Kellogg claimed that he was unfamiliar with Jackson's product when he created his own item and that it was his patients who saw a similarity to Granula. It was simply in order to distinguish the two, said Kellogg, that he called his substance Granola.[29] It is difficult to determine the accuracy of this story or just how much the various inventors of early cereal products knew about (or stole from) one another. Having little idea that their experiments would produce substances that would be valuable on the market, they did not initially bother with patents or trademarks. But Granola was just the first of several cases where Kellogg produced or named a product that shared similarities to another enterprise. In some situations, Kellogg appeared to be the originator, and at other times, he seemed to be the one doing the borrowing. But regardless of the originality of his creations, what set Kellogg apart from many of his competitors was his placement of his business activities in a broader philosophical and, at least in the early years, religious framework. For him, the food business was primarily a means to advance ideals of Christianity and the hygienic food movement. Kellogg was unstinting in his advocacy of food reform, which earned him respect among natural foods followers and helped to establish him as the preeminent entrepreneur of natural foods well into the twentieth century.

Initially, Kellogg's food efforts were directed at serving guests at the

Battle Creek Sanitarium and at educating them and the wider Adventist community about correct diet. In these efforts, he was aided by his wife, Ella E. Kellogg, who ran a test kitchen at the sanitarium, conducted cooking classes, and authored her own cookbooks as well as recipe columns for Kellogg's publications. Similar to other water cure establishments, the sanitarium made available Graham crackers for sale shortly after Kellogg assumed his position there.[30] From this beginning, a modest trade in biscuits, crackers, wafers, Granola, and other cereals was developed. By 1881, nineteen separate grain products were being produced by the Sanitarium Food Department.[31]

In the early 1880s, John Harvey's brother, William K. (Will) Kellogg became associated with the food department, and within a decade, Will was managing much of the business.[32] The venture went by several names over the years, mostly variations of Sanitarium, Sanitas, and Battle Creek Foods. The growth of the enterprise was recognized in 1888 with its formal organization as the Sanitarium Food Co. It was also in that year that John Harvey Kellogg first started referring to his products as "health foods." Prior to that, his goods were advertised as "invalid foods," but in April 1888, the switch was made. The new terminology highlighted the company's claim that its food preparations were directed "not only to persons belonging to the invalid class, but those who wish by 'good living' to avoid disease."[33] This change in terminology marked the transition to a new label for hygienic foods, one which came to be applied to any manufactured food associated with natural foods ideals. It also earned Kellogg a couple lawsuits from Frank Fuller, who took Kellogg to court for trademark infringement after Kellogg renamed his company the Sanitarium Health Food Company in 1893. Kellogg was forced to drop "Health" from the company name, but he won the right to refer to health foods as a generic category.[34] This semantic turn was significant for underscoring the health properties of this class of goods, while bringing into the natural foods movement a vocabulary for referring to hygienic *packaged* food.

The year 1893 was also the year that the Kellogg brothers decided to expand the food business. More grain products were added to the offerings and, later that decade, a number of meat substitutes made from nuts, wheat gluten, and yeast were being produced. John Harvey Kellogg claimed to have developed, over the years, between seventy-five and one hundred separate products.[35] However, product differentiation often merely meant a slight variation on an already existing substance. In 1899 alone, "new" nut products that were introduced included Nuttolene,

Nuttol, Nuttola, Nutta, Nut Soup Stock, Vegetable Egg, Manno, Granuts, and Coco-cream. Nuttola was initially the biggest hit of this group, while Vegetable Egg and Coco-cream were soon discontinued.[36] Will was no doubt responsible for many of the new products, as well as innovations in marketing, though John Harvey remained the more public figure. In 1896, food sales came to $150,000 (International Medical Missionary and Benevolent Association 1897, 138) and were used to fund many of John Harvey Kellogg's other activities; by 1900, sales had risen to $196,000.[37]

Today, the Kellogg brothers remain best known for having invented peanut butter and cornflakes. But it was the meat substitutes, the most popular called Protose, that exemplified the new kind of engineered health food. In the 1898 edition of her cookbook *Science in the Kitchen*, Ella Kellogg explained what made this product so desirable: "Protose, or vegetable meat, forms a most excellent substitute for the various flesh foods, resembling them in taste and appearance, and being composed of the same food elements. It comes in cans, all ready to slice and serve like canned meats, or may be recooked, and prepared into a great variety of palatable dishes" (E. Kellogg 1898, 398). Just as this cookbook included multiple Protose recipes, Kellogg publications regularly mentioned the benefits to be gained from the company's merchandise. In this way, the marketing of Battle Creek Sanitarium goods (see Figure 1) went hand in hand with John Harvey Kellogg's promotion of health reform ideals.

The reader might be forgiven for wondering how a canned meat substitute made from a somewhat ambiguous assortment of ingredients could have been integrated into a preexisting "natural" ideology that stressed simplicity and the unadulterated products of nature. Beginning with Granola, John Harvey Kellogg articulated a rationale for the manufacture of health food, one which presented his goods as not just healthful and natural but more suitable for human consumption than the basic foodstuffs obtained directly from nature. Kellogg argued that the human body will reject grain in its raw state and therefore cooking is necessary to make food more digestible. He claimed that what made Granola unique was not just that it was precooked but that it was done in such a way as to "dextrinize" the starch, meaning that the starch was broken down into sugars, a process Kellogg insisted made the food more easily digestible (J. Kellogg 1921, 257). Kellogg repeatedly referred to "dextrinization" when discussing his various food products. He asserted that dextrinization during the manufacturing process should be seen as analogous to the body's natural system of digestion; hence, the engineered food item need not be viewed

FIGURE 1. Sanitas Nut Food Co. advertisement, circa 1905. This advertisement, on the cover of a pamphlet about the Colorado Sanitarium, promoted some of John Harvey and Will Kellogg's most popular health foods. From the collection of Garth "Duff" Stoltz.

as something artificial. For instance, Bromose was one of Kellogg's earliest nut foods, made with the addition of starch and sold as small cakes (Schwarz 1970, 119). A promotional piece declared, "Bromose is not a mixture, but is a pure, simple, natural product. It is a thoroughly sterilized, predigested food, in which the starch has been converted into maltose and dextrin, the fat perfectly emulsified, and the albumin reduced to a state of the finest subdivision, so that it is quickly dissolved by the gastric juice."[38]

Descriptions of Battle Creek Sanitarium products typically emphasized both their natural qualities and the sophisticated manufacturing techniques that improved on nature in such a way as to conform to the body's requirements. Granose, the forerunner to cornflakes, was touted as "a preparation of wheat, in which all the elements of the grain are preserved, and by combined processes of digestion, cooking, roasting, and steaming, are brought into a state which renders assimilation possible with the smallest amount of labor on the part of the digestive organs" (E. Kellogg 1987, 141). Manufacturing is thus seen as a set of actions that preserve the nutritional integrity of the vegetable matter being processed rather than devitalize it.

Ironically, Kellogg's products, designed for a natural foods market, were some of the earliest engineered foods being sold in the United States. Bottling and canning technologies had been developed in the first part of the nineteenth century. But aside from relishes, condiments such as ketchup, and crackers and other baked goods, few combination (that is, multi-ingredient) products were available on the market. Even when canned foods gained momentum following the American Civil War, they were mostly preserved versions of single-ingredient foods such as meat, fish, milk, and vegetables (Root and de Rochemont 1976; Shephard 2000; A. Smith 1996). It was only late in the nineteenth century that canned, prepared, combination items such as pork and beans (manufactured by Van Camp), spaghetti (made by Franco-American), and soup (manufactured by Franco-American and Joseph Campbell) appeared (May 1937). Kellogg's products were among those inaugural heat-and-serve foods.

Although John Harvey Kellogg was fashioning brand-new food items, he minimized their strangeness by likening them to other familiar goods. For instance, patents for nut and gluten preparations emphasized their meaty flavor, consistency, and versatility of use. Actual meat may have been verboten, but plant matter was assumed to be more desirable if turned into faux meat. Additionally, far from deflecting attention from the fact that these were boxed or canned commodities, the Battle Creek Sanitarium companies stressed how much their products matched the convenience of other canned groceries. While condemning the output of the conventional meat, dairy, and grain sectors, Kellogg actually embraced industrial methods in his own enterprise. As well as inventing various foods, Kellogg worked out methods for industrial production, such as efficiently hulling beans and mass-producing biscuits.[39]

Through all these ways, Kellogg engaged in a process whereby prior meanings in a natural foods context were transformed in such a way as to make wholly natural substances appear more mysterious and alien, while new manufactured products became more familiar and comprehensible. The once straightforward and friendly items plucked directly from nature were now seen as foreign to the body, potentially undigestible and malevolent. In contrast, with Granola, Protose, and other products, Kellogg was offering a set of goods that would act in a predictable fashion, delivering the goodness of nature without any associated trouble. Thus, Kellogg advanced the assumption that natural foods are not just there for the taking from nature, but consumers need the interventions of a specialized manufacturer to mediate between them and the raw materials of the natural world.

It would be a mistake to dismiss John Harvey Kellogg's efforts as just a cynical maneuver to profit from gullible food reform followers. He was genuinely concerned about the nutritional needs of vegetarians and undoubtedly sincere about his belief in the physical and moral benefits of health food. But it is important to note that Kellogg could have taken an alternate path. Instead of encouraging the purchase of manufactured commodities, he could have disseminated information on how the home cook could prepare similar concoctions. Indeed, in *Science in the Kitchen*, Ella Kellogg included several simple recipes for making Caramel Coffee (one of Sanitas Food Company's best-selling products) and other coffee substitutes (E. Kellogg 1898, 360). Many of the other grain and nut products that Kellogg developed could also have been prepared in a modified fashion at home. Such dishes might be less convenient than opening a can, but they would have maintained the direct connection with nature and the self-reliance that still animated the belief system of Seventh-day Adventists and other natural foods proponents. This possibility was not lost on Kellogg's fellow food reform advocates. In a 1905 talk, by which time relations between John Harvey Kellogg and Ellen White were strained, White noted, "You need not be dependent upon the manufacture of health foods, in order to practice health-reform. . . . The health food business, in which a few have planned certain food combinations, has been allowed to take from the family cooks much of the work they should do. . . . Let us arouse ourselves and see what we can do individually, without leaning so heavily upon the food companies" (E. White 1905). Despite this warning, sales of goods produced by Sanitas steadily increased.

Broadening the Audience

The Battle Creek Sanitarium companies were industrious not only in inventing new food products but also in trying out new avenues for marketing and distribution. Early on, items were sold primarily via mail order, though advertisements encouraged consumers to ask their grocers to carry the products. By the first years of the twentieth century, less direct distribution methods were being used, with about 80 percent of products sold via grocers and general food wholesalers.[40] Sales agents were hired, and the sanitarium food companies sponsored displays and demonstrations around the world, at events ranging from world's fairs to medical association meetings. This turn in distribution and marketing coincided with a broadening of the customer base beyond the Seventh-day Adventist members and sanitarium patients who first comprised the clientele for Kellogg's health foods. Until 1906, about two-thirds of the Battle Creek Sanitarium food business came from Adventist individuals and institutions. At that point, the business gradually shifted to a more diverse audience.[41] This shift occurred in part because health food factories had been built under Adventist auspices elsewhere in the United States, including Boulder, Colorado; Saint Helena, California; and Portland, Oregon; as well as in Europe, Australia, New Zealand, and South Africa. No longer having a monopoly in the Adventist market, the Battle Creek group made a conscious effort to look elsewhere for customers.

It was recognized that only a very few of the Sanitarium line of products would attract interest among the general population. But sales possibilities were seen with the non-Adventist vegetarian market and with people suffering from ailments such as diabetes and digestive disorders.[42] Kellogg opposed the use of cane sugar, saying it is "hardly to be considered a natural food substance, for it is never found in nature in the condition in which it appears upon our tables." Instead, he preferred honey and especially fruits such as raisins, figs, and prunes for sweeteners (J. Kellogg 1903, 204–6). His companies developed a line of candy and other foods advertised as appropriate for diabetics and through this marketing effort brought many diabetics into the health food fold.

Significantly, after goods were systematically marketed to an expanded clientele, promotional material was stripped of the religious associations that were the original motivation for developing the food. Advertising copy almost never mentioned the Seventh-day Adventist Church and rarely mentioned religion at all. In an effort to cultivate various constituencies, the company reached out to not only those who might have been wary of church doctrine but also those who were suspicious of the array of health practices found at the Battle Creek Sanitarium. In 1907, an internal report recommended that the company "CHANGE THE CORPORATE NAME TO ELIMI-NATE THE WORD SANITARIUM. Entirely eliminate direct reference to the San-itarium except as an institution at which our foods are used, from our pack-ages, from our labels, literature, correspondence and advertising—place the business on such a basis that we can tell the people what we have and what it will accomplish without offending the sensitive feelings of the medical profession."[43] Instead, advertising focused on the scientific basis of a product's superiority. Thus, the meaning behind adopting a health food diet shifted from obeying the mysteries of God's commandments to rationally engaging with the comprehensibility provided by science.

Coinciding with the growth of the health food business in the 1890s, John Harvey Kellogg himself was moving away from Seventh-day Advent-ist leaders. As Schwarz (1972) has documented, Kellogg was disdainful of church officials who did not strictly adhere to a vegetarian diet, and he was resentful of efforts to control or restrain his various endeavors (see also Wilson 2014). Kellogg came to challenge Ellen White's authority and had doctrinal disagreements with other church leaders as well. Charges were even made against Kellogg that his book *The Living Temple* dem-onstrated an affinity with pantheism; evidently there were limits to how reverential one could be toward nature.[44]

But it was also the growth of the Battle Creek Sanitarium food enter-prises that produced increasing discord between Kellogg and his fellow Seventh-day Adventists, who saw a potential conflict between their re-ligious and health mission and the corrupting influence of profiteering. A church member summarizing complaints against Kellogg included this concern: "Commercial interests, instead of being considered secondary are permitted to come into the foreground, so that the income of money is often regarded as of greater importance than the gaining of a person's good will or winning to the Adventist truth."[45] White, still the most revered leader among the Adventists, took an increasingly critical tone toward Kellogg. In 1903, White communicated her concerns that an expansion of the health food business was diverting Adventists from the religious work that should be their priority: "I want to do all in my power to arouse our brethren to resist the temptation to erect many food factories and food stores for the manufacture and sale of health foods. There is danger that the minds of those engaged in the health food work will become absorbed in commercial interests" (E. White 1903). Rather than strive for continued growth by catering to consumers uninterested in the Adventist message, White preferred to focus on teaching the natural foods way of life to those who understood the spiritual importance of adopting the original diet of Eden (E. White 1942, 295–96).

For his part, Kellogg grew especially resentful over what he saw as "pirating" of Battle Creek Sanitarium recipes by other Adventists who then competed with Battle Creek by producing what Kellogg considered to be inferior goods that reflected poorly on the genuine articles.[46] Kellogg made sure that agreements with other Adventist sanitariums carefully spelled out which Battle Creek products could be produced and in what territories they could be sold. Kellogg additionally insisted that anyone working in his Sanitas Nut Food Co. sign a nondisclosure agreement, promising not to divulge anything about the business or put knowledge gained to any activity that could compete with Sanitas.[47] In refusing to divulge trade secrets, Kellogg claimed to be protecting the quality of health foods and the spirit of the health food mission. From the perspective of the church, on the other hand, his actions showed a misplaced interest in the bottom line and an un-Christian view of his fellow food reformers as competitors. Said White, "If through the wisdom donated by God for the benefit of His people, Dr. Kellogg has discovered something in regard to health foods, why should he feel that these productions are his own?" (E. White 1970, 47). White became increasingly insistent that Kellogg curb his ambitions and scale back his enterprises.

Tensions came to a head in 1907 when Kellogg was expelled from the Seventh-day Adventist Church. Kellogg retained control over the Battle Creek Sanitarium, which operated until his death in 1943, and most of its various offshoots. Though Kellogg was no longer officially active in Seventh-day Adventist affairs, Adventists around the country still purchased his products and read his health tracts.

This split was clearly the result of a power struggle between Kellogg, White, and other church ministers as they vied for influence among

Adventist members. But the tussle over control of the health food business also highlighted what would be an ongoing problem that emerged with the ability to commercialize health food: the possibility that the goals of natural foods advocacy were undermined by directing efforts (and profits) to expanding the business of natural foods. This is a type of dilemma not restricted to lifestyle movements; it is common to all social movements that must weigh the benefits of growth against the potential change in direction that can occur when new members with varying levels of commitment and diverse reasons for joining become part of a movement. In this case, while Kellogg was unquestionably successful in broadening the market for health food, Adventist leaders objected to the motivations of the new health food consumers. For the Adventists, consumer demand not accompanied by religious ideals was not a demand worth cultivating (E. White 1905).

Around the same time as his break from the church, Kellogg was also involved in disputes with other health food producers—including his brother, Will. The success of Sanitarium products motivated numerous entrepreneurs to enter the health food business. These copy-cat businesses, many of which planted themselves in Battle Creek, infuriated John Harvey, who called them "health food fakirs"[48] and constantly railed against them in speeches and writings.[49] Many such firms were short-lived and their founders were not always especially committed to natural foods ideals. Yet they did demonstrate the potential for an actual industry, with multiple manufacturers, to take hold and find a market.

A notable exception to the fly-by-night entrepreneurs was Charles W. Post, who first came to Battle Creek in 1891 as a patient at the sanitarium. Post went on to establish his own health center in Battle Creek and, in 1895, developed his own coffee substitute, Postum, followed by Grape-Nuts cereal in 1898. Post was a much better businessperson than was John Harvey Kellogg, being particularly skilled at advertising, and sales grew quickly. Although his original products directly competed with Kellogg's health food, Post's second cereal, Post Toasties (originally called Elijah's Manna), contained sugar and salt, and the company gradually moved away from the health food market (G. Carson 1957; H. Green 1986; Major 1963). This move toward the mainstream was also the path ultimately taken by Will Kellogg.

By late 1903, Toasted Corn Flakes was one of the Sanitas Food Company's biggest sellers.[50] Sales of Corn Flakes got a boost when Will, unbeknownst to John Harvey, added sugar as a flavoring to them. When he found out, John Harvey objected, but Will prevailed and the irresistible combination of sugar and breakfast cereal was normalized. A few years later, in 1906, with Corn Flakes serving a market that went well beyond natural foods followers, the brothers agreed that Will would lead the corn-flakes business as a separate company while still staying involved with Sanitas. However, relations between the brothers grew increasingly tense over financial and control issues, and Will withdrew from Sanitas management to focus entirely on Corn Flakes. The final break between the brothers came in 1908 when John Harvey renamed Sanitas as the Kellogg Food Company—one year after Will had rebranded his own product as Kellogg's Toasted Corn Flakes. There were multiple lawsuits between the brothers over several years, accompanied by numerous different iterations of their respective company names. But after the dust settled, Will was on his way toward building what would become one of the largest conventional food companies in the country—the Kellogg Company—while John Harvey pursued the much smaller and more specialized health food market with his Battle Creek Foods (H. Powell 1956; Schwarz 1970). Their personal split also helped to solidify the institutional division between health food and conventional food, with each sent along its own distinct production, distribution, and market tracks.

An Industry Takes the Lead

Among the legacies of the nineteenth-century natural foods movement are three in particular worth highlighting, one having to do with reformers' religious motivations, one with the way in which the movement became institutionalized, and one with the movement's orientation to an emerging consumer culture. First, while the movement expanded to include secular followers, an understanding of a natural foods diet as tied to religious beliefs remained an important strand in the first half of the twentieth century, especially among vegetarians. This way of seeing food choices as a means to restore a natural order and fulfill the way of life intended by God helped natural foods followers remain steadfast in the face of public ridicule and provided a strong moral dimension to their actions. Recognizing this continuity in motivation provides a corrective to those studies that equate natural foods advocacy (past and present) with religion simply in metaphorical terms, a discursive device often used to attribute irrationality and zealotry to natural foods adherents.[51] It is not that followers approached natural foods consumption *as if* it were a religion but that the philosophies underlying a commitment to natural foods grew out of concrete religious communities and beliefs.

Second is the issue of institutionalization. Throughout much of the nineteenth century, the natural foods movement existed at a low level of organizational activity, carried out by small but committed groups of people motivated by religious ideals, health concerns, and distrust of an industrializing and marketizing society. In the latter part of the nineteenth century, water cure establishments generated interest in natural foods, and occasionally, local discussion groups or clubs formed. But the only national association strictly dedicated to advancing natural foods ideals at this time was the Vegetarian Society of America, formed in 1886 by Bible-Christian Church minister Henry S. Clubb. The Seventh-day Adventists ended up filling the organizational void left by the paucity of advocacy groups. Through their sanitariums, restaurants, and publications, they spread the word about the importance of vegetarianism, whole grains, and plain unadulterated food. The health food factories started by Adventists, first at Battle Creek and then elsewhere, became increasingly important centers for developing and disseminating these messages. They set in motion an industry comprised of commercial organizations less likely than voluntary associations to collapse with the disappearance of any single leader. In this way, the natural foods movement and the new health food industry became merged.

Third and finally, it is worth considering the paradoxical role of consumption here. The natural foods movement that developed in the nineteenth century was influenced by a valorization of asceticism and a belief that eating the unadulterated products of nature was a means to achieve individual, spiritual, and social improvement. However, by the turn of the twentieth century, the efforts of people steeped in this worldview, especially John Harvey Kellogg, helped make the natural foods lifestyle as much about seeking out specialized consumer goods as about appreciating the direct fruits of nature. Similar to the process famously described by Max Weber (1976), in which the "inner-worldly" asceticism of the Puritans helped usher in the spirit of capitalism, the Christian asceticism of natural foods followers paved the way for a new industry based on providing specialized commodities that signified consumers' commitment to a natural foods way of life. This is not to say that the entire natural foods movement embraced the new health food; as I will discuss in subsequent chapters, there were vocal natural foods advocates who found health food a perversion of movement principles. But large numbers of natural foods followers did believe that Sanitarium and similar products added health benefits and variety to their diets, and regularly consumed them. With a national market established, other health food proponents gradually established shops, restaurants, and manufacturing facilities of their own.

For much of the nineteenth century, the politics of the natural foods movement included a denunciation of a developing consumer society that robbed citizens of the will to sustain themselves directly from nature. At the turn of the twentieth century, those people identifying with a natural foods way of life still saw themselves as engaged in a cause of serious social reform. But for those who were part of commercial enterprises, this commitment was accompanied by a stake in furthering the notion that a natural foods way of life was best reached through the regular consumption of health food commodities. The natural foods movement, increasingly being called the *health food movement*, was beginning to make the acquisition of consumer goods central to its purpose and identity, which necessarily shifted the terms of debate regarding the morality of market activities.

Ellen White and her allies cut off John Harvey Kellogg when he pushed the health food business to court a larger segment of the population. As a result, the Battle Creek Sanitarium companies were freed to develop along the lines of a regular business. Yet, the simple fact of being part of the capitalist enterprise did not lessen health food's marginal status. As I will describe in the following chapter, health food ran along a parallel track to the conventional food industry and helped nurture a counterculture.

CHAPTER THREE

Living and Working on the Margins

A Countercultural Industry Develops

In September 1904, the following poem was printed in *Sunset*, a widely read California-based magazine that helped popularize a Western lifestyle:

"To a Health-Food Girl," by Ruth Comfort Mitchell (1904)
Hail to thee, Granola Maid!
Kumyss cheek and silken braid,
Flower blooming in the shade
       Of the Protose tree;
Pious bearing, modest mien,
Hail, my Vegetarian Queen,
Hail, my healthy Nuttolene,
Zwieback fairy, thee!

Set my Glutose spirit free,
Lift thy Meltose eyes to me,
Say thou'lt be my Bean Puree,—
       All my cares beguile;
Sway me with thy grace imperial,
Say thou'lt be my Flaky Cereal,
Beam on me, while charms ethereal
Sterilize thy smile!

See, thy Granut tear-drop start!
Swear that we will never part,—

Give to me thy Whole Wheat heart,
    Let the skeptics scoff;
'Round thy waist my strong arm clinches,—
This is where my spirit flinches,
For that waist is forty inches—
    Let us call it off!

This piece, with its numerous references to Sanitas Food Company products, was in many ways typical of approaches to health food during that era. The specific image of the corpulent maiden was not especially common; it was more usual to depict health food eaters as on the brink of starvation. But what would have been familiar to *Sunset* readers was the humor that poked fun at the sincerity of health food proponents and that showed disastrous results from adopting such a diet.

Natural foods have increasingly become part of the mainstream since the 1980s, but for most of the last two centuries, followers were ridiculed and assumed to be the gullible victims of false prophets and promises. With these next three chapters, I depart from a strictly chronological account to discuss a number of themes concerning the relationship between the natural foods movement, the health food industry, and marginality during the first sixty years of the twentieth century. I begin in this chapter by describing how the health food business was transformed from a few scattered enterprises to a coordinated industry. This process was furthered by the industry's openness to unconventional people, beliefs, and styles as well as food. While the natural foods field's marginal status resulted in considerable public scorn, it also created a space where the field could develop largely free of interference from the conventional food sector. Chapter 4 will examine early paths to the mainstreaming of health food, with a particular focus on interest by Hollywood celebrities and figures involved in weight lifting and bodybuilding. And chapter 5 will discuss campaigns by the government and medical establishment to stigmatize health food and suppress the natural foods movement. Each of these chapters offers a distinct lens for viewing the growing field's ability to achieve social legitimacy and the nature of the challenge it posed to mainstream ideals and institutions.

During the first part of the twentieth century, the natural foods field was idiosyncratic in a number of ways. Most Americans did not believe the health claims of proponents, and they found a meatless diet and the new health food highly unappetizing. A refusal to take seriously the ideas of the natural foods field was reinforced by the fact that in the early twentieth

century, the small portion of the population who consumed this food
tended to be socially marginalized in other ways as well. The elderly and
the sick were disproportionately representative among health food consumers. The religious traditions of the nineteenth century continued to
have a strong presence, including sects with straitlaced expectations for
how to lead good Christian lives. Minority religious groups not only made
up a noticeable part of the clientele for health food but also were heavily
represented in the industry, running businesses from manufacturing to distribution to retail. On the other hand, the field was now heavily influenced
by central European immigrants who brought with them the philosophy
of naturopathy, which not only extolled a natural foods diet but also the
value of fresh air and sunshine, vigorous exercise, and a rejection of conventional medicine. The turn-of-the-century German *lebensreform* (life
reform) movement created affinities between natural foods and other unconventional practices associated with natural living, such as nudism, the
wearing of long hair and beards, and outdoor habitation. Although these
particular practices were limited to a small minority within the American
natural foods field, they were indicative of the field's general tolerance for
offbeat ideas and behavior.

Despite stylistic differences in expressing a natural foods way of life,
there was continuing ideological agreement among the various strands
about the moral and health properties of the natural. Thanks to the work
that John Harvey Kellogg and other entrepreneurs had done to develop a
health food market, a belief in the superiority of the natural could now be
channeled into the consumption of a growing array of specialized products.
The new industry itself was rather idiosyncratic. Businesses were founded
by people who saw their work as more profound than just earning a living;
entrepreneurs tended to have a moral commitment to the philosophies underlying the products they were selling. Small-scale enterprises dominated
the field, and opportunities were available to people lacking the financial
capital, educational credentials, and cultural backgrounds that could be required by more mainstream food or health ventures. One result was that
the industry was marked by ethnic and religious niches, most prominently
Germans, Jews, and Seventh-day Adventists.

By the 1940s, there could be found a small number of citizen-only advocacy groups, which existed to promote vegetarianism, organic farming,
and naturopathy and which consciously distanced themselves from the
health food industry. But these groups tended to be fragmented from one
another and troubled by infighting and heavy-handed leadership. As a
result, they were not especially effective in spreading their ideals beyond

a small core of the highly committed. In contrast, a desire to enlarge the market for health food and develop the fledgling industry shaped a business culture that was open to the participation and patronage of people with diverse styles, beliefs, and practices. Indeed, on the whole, the industry proved to be more welcoming than citizen groups, and the industry's ranks were more socially heterogeneous than were those of advocacy groups not joined to industry. This heterogeneity contributed to the industry's centrality in tying together the diffuse movement.

A willingness to work with a diverse group of sometimes unconventional characters facilitated the formation of trade associations that strategically worked to defend and promote a natural foods way of life. Annual trade shows brought together far-flung industry members year after year and helped create a network of people who, despite philosophical differences, discussed challenges and ways forward for the natural foods field. As I begin to show in this chapter, it was the participation of industry that led to both greater unity in the field and greater effectiveness in promoting a natural foods agenda. But that participation also helped shape movement goals in ways that were especially beneficial to the health food industry.

The Marginal and the Mainstream

So far, I have been referring to the marginal and the mainstream without much explanation as to what I mean by these concepts. Both notions connote a relationship to a symbolic location, one that is either near to or distant from a central place within society. Robert Dunne, who reviews the historical use of the term *marginality*, credits Edward Shils's juxtaposition of center and periphery with helping to capture the sense of marginality that is often employed today in sociology (Dunne 2005, 14). According to Shils, society's center "is a phenomenon of the realm of values and beliefs. . . . This central value system is the central zone of society. It is central because of its intimate connection with what the society holds to be sacred; it is central because it is espoused by the ruling authorities of the society. These two kinds of centrality are vitally related. Each defines and supports the other" (Shils 1975, 3–4). In contrast to the center, says Shils, sections of the population occupy the periphery, meaning that they are distant from both the central value system and those institutional positions that carry authority (1975, 12–13). While some scholars (R. Powell and Clarke 1976) have criticized this conceptualization for ignoring the ways in which marginalized people do interact with dominant institutions

and values, Shils's formulation helps us consider how a particular con-
figuration of values (or more broadly, culture) and limited institutional
authority can mark groups of people as socially suspect and subject to
censure. From ethnographies of urban immigrants to deviance studies to
examinations of subcultures to work on symbolic boundaries, scholars have
documented the experience of marginalization and how those affected have
suffered from, embraced, or resisted their marginal statuses.

The concepts of the marginal and the mainstream provide an especially useful vantage point for thinking about the nature of cultural politics. What is at stake here is the socially sanctioned ability to delineate
cultural categories that distinguish the legitimate from the transgressive,
what is normal from unconventional. In this sense, not just cultural values
but also cultural authorities who pass judgment on those values vie for
a place in the mainstream. Struggles to define what is mainstream and
what is marginal help us see that clout in the cultural realm can be at least
partially independent of other forms of power. Economic resources alone
do not translate into the right to define mainstream values, and cultural
authorities do not always overlap with economic and political elites.

Throughout the first decades of the twentieth century, there was little
question that health food and the people promoting it occupied the cultural margins. Studies of the natural foods movement before mainstreaming began in earnest in the 1980s note that followers would often hide their
consumption of health food to escape ridicule (New and Priest 1967, 17;
Roth 1977, 30, 104). Similarly, old-timers I interviewed all noted its marginal status in the early years. A characteristic remark from someone who
began working in the industry in the 1930s was, "In those days you were
looked upon as some kind of a freak if you're interested in health foods."[1]
This view of health food followers as "freaks" came from their rejection
of taken-for-granted categories of desirable food. The natural foods field
also discounted mainstream systems of health care and food production,
which were increasingly guided by scientific authorities who equated progress with technical interventions to manipulate human bodies and the substances they consumed. In contrast, the natural foods movement and the
health food industry continued to view nature as the ultimate authority.

Nature Is the Cure

Even following the establishment of the health food industry, the natural
foods field professed the moral and practical superiority of that which is

natural.[2] Nature was seen as superior because it is primary and original; for some natural foods proponents, nature was revered as the handiwork of God. Although nature was generally understood as pure and uncorrupted by human civilization, it was also respected because humans are themselves natural beings. As such, people would stand to benefit from being closely connected to nature, and their physical and spiritual health would improve if they were to take into their bodies the nourishment that the natural world means them to have.

During the first decades of the twentieth century, the ideas of numerous philosophers of the natural were in circulation among the American public and shaped the worldviews of natural foods advocates. The influence of such philosophers was material as well as ideological; the growing health food industry was indebted to these theorists of the natural who, through their books and lectures, primed the market for the industry's wares. Some of these writers were themselves engaged in related businesses, running sanitariums or shops, or developing their own branded products. There was no one preeminent sage of a natural foods philosophy. Indeed, the longevity of the natural foods movement has in part been due to the many thinkers who have been in conversation with one another, as opposed to more short-lived enthusiasms tied to the ideas of a single individual, as was the case with Horace Fletcher, whose directives to chew one's food with extreme thoroughness were embraced at the turn of the twentieth century and then faded away after Fletcher died in 1919 (H. Green 1986, 294). The multiple philosophers of a natural foods diet achieved highly loyal but nonexclusive followings. Those philosophers sometimes endorsed and cooperated with one another yet at other times condemned and competed with one another. While as a group they developed an ideology that elevated the natural over human inventions, they also showed that there was not a firm divide between theorizing and selling a natural foods lifestyle.

One influential expression of ideas about nature came from Adolf Just, a German proponent of a raw foods diet; his 1896 book, *Return to Nature*, was translated into English seven years later by the natural foods advocate Benedict Lust and widely circulated in the United States. Wrote Just (1903, 3):

> When we look at nature with an open, unprejudiced mind, and are not blinded by the teachings of science, we must arrive at the clear conclusion that man has become sick and miserable only because he no longer heeds the VOICES OF NATURE, and has thus everywhere transgressed the laws of nature, and lost his

way. Nature is forever unassailable in her justice; she punishes every transgression of her laws, but likewise rewards every return to obedience. *In all cases, and in all diseases*, therefore, man can recover and again become happy only by a *true return to nature*: man must today strenuously endeavor, in his mode of living, to heed again the voice of nature, and thus choose the food that nature has laid before him from the beginning, and to bring himself again into the relation with water, light and air, earth, etc., that nature originally designed for him.

Just was typical for this era in referring to natural "laws" that are violated at one's peril. Such inviolable directives mean that a natural foods diet is not a matter of personal preference but is the only way for all humans to fulfill their potential. This belief in a set of absolute rules that must be obeyed helps explain the frequent contempt expressed for half measures in adopting a natural foods diet and the grandiose claims commonly made for the effects of abiding by or ignoring a natural foods diet. For instance, William Howard Hay, a doctor who made natural foods the center of his "Hay system" of health care, claimed in 1934, "The fine art of cookery has had more to do with the degeneration of civilized nations than all other causes combined, simply because the usual cook violates every canon of digestive law" (Hay 1934, xv).

Discussions by natural foods proponents frequently used the imagery of life and death to describe food itself. The closer to nature, the more alive a food was, while foods turned dead when far removed from their natural state. Just as the producers of meat were equated with murderers, the makers of processed food could be likened to undertakers. Clarke Irvine, who founded one of the first health food magazines, *California Health News*, wrote in 1935, "No wonder man is sick" as he "preserves his food in cans with benzoate of soda and other embalming fluids" (Irvine 1935, 4). The term *processed food* was not yet common in the early decades of the twentieth century. Instead, natural foods followers spoke of "denatured" or "devitalized" food to refer to a process that removed that which is good, wholesome, living, and natural from food. These concerns seemed ever more urgent with the growth of giant companies that applied complex treatments, additives, and industrial methods to the production of meat, flour, sugar, crackers, dairy products, and canned fruits and vegetables.[3]

A variety of sometimes contradictory beliefs about what and how to eat came out of this belief in the inherent goodness of nature. Influenced by thinkers such as the Swiss doctor (and creator of Müsli) Max Bircher-Benner (Meyer-Renschhausen and Wirz 1999), one offshoot advocated

limiting what people eat to uncooked, or raw, foods. Another line of thinking concerned itself with food combinations and developed strictures speci-
fying which foods should not be taken together. Other natural foods proponents, such as Arnold Ehret, continued a theme from Sylvester Graham's
day by stressing limitations on food intake and advising frequent fasts as
a way to cleanse the body of impurities (Ehret 1924, 1926). Each of these
strands—raw food, correct food combinations, and fasting—meant to restore the body's natural balance by eliminating contaminants and empty
fillers. The flip side of this philosophy of omission, as I shall discuss shortly,
was the search for the best health foods—those additions to the diet that
would enhance health.

The belief in a natural foods diet often went hand in hand with a commitment to naturopathy. Naturopathy, sometimes called nature cure,
brought together various health remedies based in natural sources or natural living—hydrotherapy, air and sun baths, exercise, herbal medicine, as
well as diet; later on, the term also came to include homeopathy and chiropractic. The development of an elaborate theory of nature cure took place
in the nineteenth and early twentieth centuries, especially in central Europe through the practice and teachings of people such as Adolf Just, Sebastian Kneipp, and Louis Kuhne, who were all based in Germany. While
their specific regimens differed, each favored "drugless" healing, which entailed helping the body heal itself through natural processes. And for all
of them, a vegetarian, often raw-foods, diet that omitted processed food
was key.[4]

John Harvey Kellogg and other Americans traveled to Europe and
visited the nature doctors' health centers, and were clearly influenced by
them. But nature cure ideals were most fully integrated into the American
natural foods movement through immigrants who settled in the United
States, the most influential being Benedict Lust. Lust first came from Germany to the United States at the age of twenty in 1892. After becoming
seriously ill with tuberculosis, he returned to Europe and was successfully
treated by Sebastian Kneipp's system of diet and hydrotherapy. In 1896,
Lust immigrated to New York, this time with the intention of spreading
Kneipp's methods. Over time, Lust developed his own system of naturopathy, which found a following through the numerous outlets he and his
wife, Louisa, established: sanitariums, a naturopathic college, the American Naturopathic Association, and several influential books and periodicals (Kirchfeld and Boyle 1994). Lust also established what was probably
the first diversified health food store in New York City in 1896.[5]

Natural Living

Whereas the primary international influence on the nineteenth-century American natural foods movement came from England, the most important external source of ideas in the early twentieth century was Germany.[6] Lust and Ehret were both German immigrants, as were, among others, Henry Lindlahr, another prominent theorist of naturopathy, and Gayelord Hauser, probably the best known US advocate of health food in the first half of the twentieth century. Hauser's German roots were of great interest to mainstream health practitioners who sought to discredit him, such as the American Medical Association (AMA), which rarely lost an opportunity to mention his birth name (Eugene Helmuth Hauser) and birthplace (Tübingen, Germany) whenever discussing him.[7] Though it was quite typical for immigrants to Americanize their names (or for immigration officials to do it for them), the AMA's reports insinuated that health food proponents were attempting to deceive the public about the foreign origins of their philosophies. In actuality, what was likely most dismaying to mainstream medicine was the defiant attitude of these immigrants. Already by the late nineteenth century, nature cure enthusiasts in Germany were organized and active in defending their interests (Weindling 1989, 22–23). This tradition of fighting back against opponents (and doing so successfully) was brought to the United States along with their philosophies about health, diet, and lifestyle.

Their mix of ideas helped shift the American natural foods movement away from its prior emphasis on suppressing bodily (including sexual) appetites; the interest now was more about exhibiting rather than hiding expressions of physicality. Influential in this regard was the *lebensreform* (or life reform) movement of Germany that was in vogue from the late 1800s through the 1930s.[8] *Lebensreform* included a constellation of expressions of natural living: vegetarianism, nature cure, nudism, clothing reform (which entailed abandoning tight clothing such as corsets), and outdoor exercise, as well as other cultural and political expressions, including temperance and feminism. Participants in *lebensreform* rarely adopted all of these practices (vegetarianism and nature cure being the most common), and there were also significant political differences among people identifying with the movement; socialists, anarchists, and racial hygienists were all represented.[9] But what tied these various practices together was a critique of industrialization and urbanism, both of which were radically affecting

Germany at the turn of the century. The way to combat these forces, re-formers believed, was to adopt a lifestyle that symbolically and practically rejected the pernicious tendencies of modernity.

These cultural styles were integrated into the American natural foods field when German natural foods followers immigrated to the United States. These immigrants had an outsize influence on the American natu-ral foods field relative to their numbers, both because of their role as natu-ral foods philosophers and because many immigrants started health food businesses of their own. The wave of German immigrants also helped so-lidify California as a center of the natural foods field and to shift the stereo-typical image of a natural foods devotee from a humorless New Englander to a freewheeling Californian.

There was already a significant natural foods presence in California before German immigrants arrived at the turn of the century. Vegetar-ian societies existed in both Los Angeles and San Francisco.[10] Vegetar-ian colonies experimenting in communal living were also formed, such as Joyful News, established by Isaac Rumford in the 1880s near Bakersfield, and Societas Fraternia, established in the 1870s in Placentia by George Hinde and Louis Schlesinger. Both groups were motivated by religious ideals: Joyful News by devout Christianity and Societas Fraternia by a var-iant of spiritualism. Hinde's group in particular attracted notoriety; its members were dubbed "grass eaters" by the press, which reported rumors that they practiced free love and forced vegetarianism on hungry children at their Orange County colony. Their unconventional lifestyle attracted legal troubles as well, as when members were accused of starving a baby to death by substituting raw fruit for milk.[11]

Though attracting less publicity, food reform also found a home at some of the sanitariums and water cure establishments in the region; with its warm climate, Southern California was an especially popular spot for health resorts from the 1870s on (Baur 1959). Among them were Seventh-day Adventist sanitariums in Saint Helena (established in 1878), Paradise Valley (near San Diego) and Glendale (both established in 1904), and Loma Linda (established in 1905). Health food was produced at the Saint Helena and Loma Linda facilities.

In California's quirky mix of cultural experimentation, German natu-ral foods advocates made a home. German vegetarian groups were first recruited to the state by the Immigration Association of California in the 1880s.[12] But they came in much larger numbers in the early decades of the twentieth century, some directly from Germany, others after residing

elsewhere in the United States. Their ranks included the writer and lecturer Ehret, who also developed an herbal laxative that began to be sold
under the name Inner-Clean (later, Innerclean) by Fred S. Hirsch following Ehret's death in 1922;[13] Otto Carqué, another influential Los Angeles
writer, who also grew and marketed natural foods beginning about 1905;[14]
Emanuel Bronner, who first manufactured mineral seasonings in Los Angeles in the late 1940s and then developed the Dr. Bronner line of natural
soaps with Bronner's philosophies printed on the labels (Frost 1990); and
Herman Sexauer, who turned his Santa Barbara health food store into a
center for unconventional ideas in the 1930s and 1940s (Kennedy 1998, 159–
62). As these examples suggest, German immigrants helped make Southern
California into a place where teaching and marketing the natural foods life
were combined in varying ways.

Some of the immigrants also contributed to what would come to be seen
as an especially Californian countercultural style associated with natural
foods. Standard accounts of the American counterculture refer to it as a
phenomenon of the 1960s and 1970s, with perhaps an acknowledgment
of the 1950s Beats as predecessors. But many stylistic attributes of the
post–World War II counterculture actually have roots that go back much
farther in time. Natural foods followers were prominent among early experimenters with countercultural styles. One can look to the nineteenth-
century American transcendentalists who, along with their vegetarianism
and communal endeavors, were known for wearing long hair and flowing
clothes (Sears 1915, 19). While Massachusetts was the center of transcendentalism, California proved to be an especially hospitable environment
for people adopting certain traits of the German *naturmenschen* (natural
men), who maintained a raw foods diet, grew out their hair and beards,
and wore loose tunics and sandals (Kennedy 1998, 57–59); M. Green 1986,
57–62). In California, fresh fruits and vegetables were easily obtained, and
a temperate climate allowed for year-round outdoor habitation.

A group of men distinguished by their preference for raw foods, long
hair, loose clothing, occasional nudism, and living outdoors attracted attention in California in the 1920s. One of them, a German immigrant named
William Pester, was such a curiosity that tourists would come to his Palm
Springs outpost to gawk and take pictures (Wild 2008). Wrote Gypsy
Boots, the group member most involved in the health food industry, "We
attracted quite a bit of attention in those days [the 1940s], largely because
there were so many of us, and often we travelled together. . . . At times
there were as many as 15 of us living together in the hills, sleeping in
caves and trees." (Boots 1965, 7). Although their numbers were limited,

their cultural influence was not insignificant. With their distinctive look and dedication to natural living, they helped cement the popular association between natural foods and a countercultural eccentricity. This image received extra attention when the song "Nature Boy" became one of the top hits of 1948, boosting the career of the song's performer, Nat King Cole. Although the lyrics of "Nature Boy" do not directly reference natural foods, the song's unconventional composer, Eden Ahbez, caught the public's imagination, and reports frequently made reference to his long hair, preference for living outdoors, and raw foods diet.[15] The food Ahbez consumed was considered as much an oddity as his habit of going without shoes and his disdain for material possessions.

The term *Nature Boy* caught on as well, having a life beyond its musical origins, and was used not just as a label of derision but as one of admiration and self-description. A 1949 advertisement in *American Vegetarian* could read simply: "Nature Girls please write us: Nature-Boys Box 257, Tecate, Calif.," presumably with the expectation of attracting like-minded mates.[16] Gypsy Boots referred to himself and his gang as Nature Boys (Boots 1965). And in what is probably the most widely read book capturing a Beat sensibility, the 1957 novel *On the Road*, Jack Kerouac's protagonist, commenting on the colorful mix of people in Los Angeles, notes spotting "an occasional Nature Boy saint in beard and sandals" (Kerouac 1991, 86).

It would surely be a mistake to reduce the natural foods movement of California or elsewhere to the Nature Boy aesthetic. There were many other styles of life that characterized natural foods followers—and that were also countercultural—in the first part of the twentieth century. But the Nature Boy style is significant, and not only because it persisted with the counterculture that bloomed in the 1960s, as I will discuss in chapter 6. It also spoke to the willingness of the health food industry to cater to unconventional patrons and to make room for unconventional business partners. By the time Eden Ahbez's song became a hit, that tradition was already firmly in place.

Proselytizing through Food

In this small corner of American commerce, groups that were not always welcome in mainstream society could find an occupation. One of the notable features of the health food industry in the first half of the twentieth century is the heavy representation of particular religious and ethnic groups. Seventh-day Adventists remained a major presence, not simply through the Battle Creek Food Co. (as John Harvey Kellogg's company was called by 1921), but through church-owned Loma Linda Foods, church-affiliated Worthington Foods (originally called Specialty Foods, formed in Ohio in 1939), and individual church members who operated stores, restaurants, and manufacturing outlets.

Loma Linda Foods exemplified the combination of business and religious goals that characterized Adventist health food companies. It started in 1906 as a bakery attached to the new Southern California sanitarium. Like other Adventist sanitariums, Loma Linda produced, under the Sanitarium Food Company name, a range of health foods modeled on the Battle Creek line. But Loma Linda's ambitions outpaced those of most other Adventist outposts. The sanitarium grew into a multifaceted medical center, and its food manufacturing operations expanded considerably. The business adopted the Loma Linda Foods name in 1933, highlighting its regional identity and affiliation with the medical center.[17] In its 1935 articles of incorporation, Loma Linda Foods stated its purpose, which included sales, educational, and religious goals.[18] Over the years, religious motivations remained central to the enterprise and often reaffirmed, as in a 1942 sales report that assured its constituents that the company did all it could to operate "in harmony with the instructions given by the Lord."[19] Loma Linda saw its mission as a moral one and thus different from most for-profit endeavors.

Though they made a range of products, Battle Creek, Loma Linda, and Worthington Foods dominated the meat substitute (or, as it came to be called, meat analog) market (see figure 2). With the proliferation of mostly canned, complex nut, soy, and grain preparations,[20] the vegetarian aspect of their goods took precedence over avoidance of additives and extensive processing, a stance that resulted in condemnation from some parts of the natural foods field. There were occasional efforts by these companies to defend their claims to membership in the natural foods world, with Worthington Foods, for instance, explaining its use of monosodium glutamate by assuring customers that "MSG is a natural food element."[21] But with a firm base in Seventh-day Adventist consumers, these three companies were not hurt by disapproval of their production techniques, and sales stayed strong into the 1960s.

The Seventh-day Adventists had the most extensive industry involvement of any Christian denomination, but other sects also entered the field as part of a mission to lead the life they believed was ordained by God

FIGURE 2. Advertising brochure from the Battle Creek Food Company, 1930. It features the meat substitute Protose and a yeast-based flavoring powder called Savita. From the personal collection of the author.

and to spread their doctrines. Another group making forays into manufacturing was Shiloh, which was founded as a Christian communal colony in 1942 in Sherman, New York, by a Pentecostal minister named Eugene Crosby Monroe.[22] However, restaurants were the ventures undertaken most frequently by religious groups. They included a western Michigan sect, based near Adventist populations but following another Christian doctrine, named the Israelite House of David (later called Mary's City of David). Founded by Mary and Benjamin Purnell, the group established its first vegetarian restaurant in 1908 (Cawley 2000, 100). Another sect that linked vegetarianism to faith was the Unity School of Christianity, an offshoot of New Thought, which was founded by Charles and Myrtle Fillmore in Kansas City, Missouri (Donald Meyer 1988, 40–42). In 1906, Unity opened a vegetarian restaurant, which was quite popular for several decades and remained all vegetarian until the early 1960s (Ferruzza 2012). In one of its cookbooks, the group explained its purpose: "Unity Inn is not operated as a commercial venture, but as an educational movement to convince the public that a diet of fruits, nuts, and vegetables is really better suited to man's system than is a diet of meat" (Unity School of Christianity 1923, 3). For groups such as Unity, the provision of food in a commercial setting was primarily about utilizing a domain familiar to consumers in order to reach potential adherents. With that understanding, the group could view its business as about working for good rather than for profits.

All of these Christian sects were themselves culturally marginal, adhering to doctrines considered peculiar by larger denominations and often establishing utopian living experiments that set them apart from mainstream society. Whether living as a colony or not, in most cases they operated businesses that were physically attached to other church structures. This literal attachment served as a constant reminder that the business was an expression of a communal endeavor, and it presented consumers with a visible invitation to discover more about the spiritual ideals motivating the group.

An Ethnic Niche

In contrast, the context in which two of the major ethnic groups in the health food industry—Germans and Jews—operated was for the most part quite different. What they had in common with the Christian sects was that they were frequently regarded with suspicion or hostility by other Americans. Jews were regularly subject to negative stereotypes in the first half of the twentieth century, and the status of German-origin residents was highly precarious in the years around the two world wars. But what makes their activities not fully comparable to the Christian groups I have described is that both Jews' and Germans' health food businesses were not located in ethnic enclaves, nor were these businesses generally associated with other ethnically affiliated enterprises. They were not oriented toward serving their own communities, as was the case with many

Adventist companies, nor did they tend to build health food businesses as offshoots of an ethnic or religious identity, comparable to what Unity or Shiloh did. I have already discussed the presence of German immigrants and German Americans in the natural foods field and the direct connection to the German nature cure movement that helps explain their participation in similar endeavors in the United States. However, the reasons for the large representation of Jews in the health food industry are not as straightforward. It is worth considering this matter further, as it helps illuminate how the industry was able to attract people who worked to advance the natural foods field outside of typical social movement channels.

Reliable data are not available to help us understand the extent to which Jews made up the customer base for health food in the early part of the twentieth century. However, the number of Jews in the health food industry from the 1910s through the 1950s was certainly striking. Many of the individuals discussed in this and subsequent chapters were Jewish, such as Nature Boys Gypsy Boots and Eden Abez, and Jerome I. Rodale, who, more than anyone else, helped introduce organic farming to the United States. Jewish owners of prominent health food businesses included Emanuel Bronner of Dr. Bronner's; the Schulman family of Naturade; the Lessin family of Seelect; Eugene (Billy) Hamburg of Vegetrates; Eugene Schiff of Schiff Bio Food; and New York retailers Sam Brown of Brownies, Sam Rosenbloom of Health Food Distributors, and Solomon Kubie of Kubie's. This is not to say that a majority of health food manufacturers or retailers in the first part of the twentieth century were Jewish; there were scores of players who were not. But compared to the general population, it is clear that a disproportionate number of health food entrepreneurs, especially those whose companies were successful and long-lasting, were Jewish. Unsurprisingly, the largest concentration was in New York, but Jews were not confined to particular geographic locations; they could be found in health food businesses in most parts of the country.

Since they were not a majority, one might question any claim about just how significant the representation of Jews in health food manufacturing and retailing was. However, the situation was more clear-cut in wholesaling (or jobbing, as it used to be called) where a majority of the large wholesalers in the industry at this time were indeed Jewish. They included the owners of Balanced Foods and Sherman Foods, both of New York, of Health Food Jobbers of Chicago, and of the two companies that merged to become Kahan & Lessin of Los Angeles. Although the founder of Health Food Distributors of Detroit (unrelated to the New York retailer) was not Jewish, he sold the company not long after its founding to the Jewish family that maintained it into the twenty-first century. In fact, of the major wholesaling companies formed in the 1920s and 1930s (all of which continued to dominate health food distribution into the 1970s), only Landstrom of San Francisco and Akin of Tulsa were not formed by or passed on to Jews.

In an era when Jews were still seen as the Other, it was obvious to associates who was or was not Jewish. Their presence in the natural foods field occasionally generated some commentary. A 1922 *Vegetarian Magazine* column on "The Progress of the Movement," for instance, observed, "The best vegetarian restaurants are conducted by Jews and more largely patronized by them than Gentiles."[23] Yet, by and large, this was not a subject that appeared to be discussed much, at least, not openly. When I asked Jewish old-timers if there was an especially large number of Jews in the industry, they downplayed it. "I don't think especially, no, no. Just by coincidence," said one. "Not necessarily, but there were quite a few," equivocated another. It is quite possible that these men, with memories of a time when anti-Semitism was all too common, were habituated to not drawing attention to this feature of the industry. The next generation, of people born in the 1940s and 1950s, was more likely to acknowledge it and the sensitivities it could invoke. Most saw it as a curious phenomenon, but attached little importance to it. One respondent, however, suggested that the commonality between Jewish businesspeople made for a group of people who were comfortable with one another, resulting in a great deal of cooperation, even between competitors.

There has, of course, been a long historical association of Jews with commerce, which scholars often trace back to Jewish exclusion from other occupations (Muller 2010). In this way, health food may be like many other areas of commerce in which Jews engaged early in the twentieth century (Kobrin 2012). And their heavy representation in distribution in particular corresponds to the notion of "diasporic merchant minorities" that has been used to describe Jews' frequent entry into certain occupations (Muller 2010, 7). However, health food does not completely fit the classic model laid out by Edna Bonacich in describing the concept of "middlemen minorities." In analyzing why Jews, Armenians, Chinese, and other ethnic groups have so frequently acted in occupational capacities with a mediating function, such as between producers and consumers, or renters and landlords, Bonacich posits "highly organized communities that resist assimilation" (1973, 586) and that take on occupations where capital is liquid.[24] Yet, this description does not accurately fit in the case of Jews in the health food industry, as they mostly followed assimilationist paths.

What is especially noteworthy is that by and large, Jews in the health food industry were either secular or only mildly observant; unlike the Adventists, their attachment to natural foods did not emerge from religious convictions. On the contrary, Judaism, especially as it was practiced in Europe, has dietary practices traditionally quite meat-heavy, and in the United States, Orthodox Jews have generally dismissed vegetarianism (Jochnowitz 1997). Moreover, Jewish traditions of dietary purity did not give rise to nineteenth-century variants of a natural foods philosophy in the same way certain Christian teachings did. In sum, Jewish involvement in natural foods did not emanate from a communal impulse, nor from religious ideals. Neither is there evidence of a preexisting cultural fascination with the natural, especially among Jews of Eastern European origins.

It appears that for Jewish industry members, the initial attraction of the health food field was very much tied to this being an economic opportunity hovering outside of the mainstream. An industry that catered to people old and sick (in an era before social insurance programs alleviated their poverty) or people viewed as religious fanatics or who engaged in countercultural practices was wide open to anyone who wanted to try it out and who was willing to endure the mockery and low status that came with the territory. Health food retailing exemplified the lack of barriers that made it possible for socially marginalized groups to work in the field. Unlike typical neighborhood small businesses, the health food store was not an enterprise dependent on good relations with one's neighbors. Customers came via mail order or traveled from across the city to obtain products they could not find elsewhere. Being an upstanding member of one's local church or Elks Club—that is, of the kinds of institutions closed to Jews—was not likely to be key to expanding the business. Instead, a willingness to serve a diversity of people with out-of-the-ordinary philosophies and lifestyles was an asset.

But this was not simply an instrumental move into just any available occupational niche. Unlike so many other Americans, Jews were particularly open to working outside the conventional food and health care systems. Kosher laws meant that Jews were accustomed to recognizing and accommodating dietary restrictions, which extended to how food items are actually produced, even if they themselves did not observe such restrictions. Furthermore, Jews already had separate health care institutions. As Paul Starr notes, hospitals were an exception to Jewish assimilationist

patterns at this time. Jews built their own community hospitals to escape
the prejudice of existing facilities and to provide themselves with opportunities to practice medicine (P. Starr 1982, 173–76). These experiences
with nonnormative ways of meeting food and health needs may well have
made the health food industry appear to be a viable occupational option
to those Jewish individuals who were already consumers of these products.
Together with others in the field, Jewish entrepreneurs helped expand the
market for health food and, with it, spread the ideals of the natural foods
movement.

An Industry Expands

If one examines the list of products advertised in 1901 by Benedict Lust's
Kneipp Health Store on East Fifty-ninth Street in New York, a portrait
emerges of what the health food industry, outside of the Battle Creek
Sanitarium and its offshoots, then had to offer. (Lust did not appear to
carry any of Kellogg's goods—whether out of principle or competition is
hard to say.) The Kneipp store stocked a good variety of grains, cereals,
and breads, with an emphasis on whole wheat. There was an extensive selection of herbs and herbal remedies. There were also substitutes for coffee and dairy, nut butters, honey, soy sauce, several kinds of cocoa, and a
handful of other miscellaneous products listed under the category "health
foods." Aside from items house branded Kneipp or Lust, there were only
seventeen brands represented. Most of the store's foods were actually imported from Europe, as were most of the nonfood goods sold—toiletries
and linen clothes—though the books offered for sale were domestically
produced (see advertisements in Kneipp [1901]).

Thirty-six years later, Pleiner's Health Food Store and Whole Wheat
Bakery of San Francisco issued a catalog listing available products from
ninety-three companies (almost all domestic) in addition to house brands
and generic items. Of those company names, only one, Ralston, matched
a brand advertised by Lust in 1901. Many of the companies in the 1937
catalog, such as Alvita, Battle Creek, Hain, Carque, and Modern Health
Products, produced numerous distinct products; altogether, Pleiner's offered hundreds of choices of a range of goods. Still, much looked familiar
compared to the stock of the Kneipp Health Store of 1901. Whole grains
and grain products remained a primary focus. One could still find products such as vegetable oil, honey, and nut butters. But where Lust had

listed one or two types of each of these foods, Pleiner's stocked multiple varieties. And instead of carrying just cocoa for a treat, Pleiner's featured whole sections devoted to a range of "health candies" and sweets for diabetics. Moreover, entirely new categories now appeared, some clearly natural foods in the strict sense of the term, such as nuts and sun dried fruits, and others that were complex health foods, such as meat substitutes and vitamins. Other ingredients that are to this day still hard to find outside of natural foods stores—agar, seaweeds, carob—had also become part of the health food store's repertoire by the 1930s.[25]

As well stocked as it was, even Pleiner's was not comprehensive in carrying all types and brands of products that the health food industry now had to offer. Just up Market Street in San Francisco, Ruth's Health Food Store, and on the other side of the country, in New York City, Health Food Distributors and Brownies Natural Food Store carried many of the same products found at Pleiner's, but each also stocked brands not found at the others.[26] Taken together, their offerings and their ability to draw enough customers to sustain their businesses showed that a true health food industry, with numerous specialized, competing, and coordinated companies, had developed.

It had taken many years since Lust first opened his store to arrive at this point. Until the 1920s, when manufacturers and retailers of health food began to form in greater numbers, the commercial provision of natural foods was most firmly established with restaurants and cafeterias. Coming out of the boardinghouse tradition, as well as Seventh-day Adventist efforts to establish health food restaurants, vegetarian cafés were scattered here and there around the United States in the first decade of the twentieth century. It is impossible to say exactly how many existed; in his 1904 *Vegetarian Cook Book*, E. G. Fulton listed twenty-two of them, which surely undercounts the total. The restaurants could be found in cities large and small, from New York City to Fairmont, West Virginia (Fulton 1904, 251).

Restaurants played a significant role in the developing health food industry and natural foods movement. They served as meeting places and discussion spots for natural foods advocates. Vegetarian restaurants introduced diners to the possibilities of natural foods forms of cooking, and often to specific health food products, especially those coming out of the Battle Creek Sanitarium businesses. For instance, in 1906, the Vegetarian Pure Food Cafe of San Francisco, managed by Seventh-day Adventist church member Fulton, served many dishes based on Battle Creek foods, such as Nuttolene with Lemon, and Protose Sandwich, though a couple other brands—Horlick's Malted Milk and Grant's Hygienic Crackers—were also represented on the menu.[27] Restaurants not only served vegetarian fare, but many affiliated with the Seventh-day Adventists also sold Battle Creek Sanitarium products on the premises.[28] Over the next few decades, vegetarian restaurants would continue to be an outlet for customers purchasing food for their own meal preparations.

Restaurants provided ready-made vegetarian meals. The job of the natural foods home cook, on the other hand, was becoming both simpler and more complex as greater numbers of health food options came onto the market. Products offered the convenience of health solutions in a package but also necessitated the incorporation of specialized and hard-to-obtain commodities into one's dietary regime. In keeping with the Grahamite legacy of emphasizing whole grains, and the success enjoyed by Kellogg and other makers of breakfast cereals, many of the producers of health food in the first two decades of the twentieth century were suppliers of grain and cereal products. But by the 1920s, manufacturers had branched out to other kinds of items. Many such products were not actually food in any straightforward sense but goods meant to compensate for the consumer who could not properly observe an ideal natural foods diet.

The Battle Creek Sanitarium companies, as in so many other matters, led the way. Calax, which came on the market in 1907, was one of the first of many Battle Creek natural laxatives. Other brands of laxatives, such as the aforementioned Inner-Clean, not only proliferated in the 1920s but gave rise to companies that would become health food industry mainstays. One such company was Naturade of Long Beach, California, started by Nathan Schulman in 1926. Within a few years of its founding, the company's Ray-o-Lax, Kolen-Ade, and 3-in-1 Lax products were top health food sellers. Laxatives were certainly easy to come by outside of the health food market. But Naturade promised only natural plant sources for its products, with "no adulterants or chemicals" added, and agricultural growing contracts that prohibited insecticides or fertilizers other than those made from minerals.[29]

The 1930s saw the establishment of the most financially important new product line to enter the health food market: vitamin supplements. Vitamins—or, as they were originally called, vitamines—were identified by scientists in the second decade of the twentieth century but started to be sold as supplements by conventional retailers in the 1920s, primarily in the form of cod-liver oil (Apple 1996; Griggs 1986, 30–39). The sale of vitamin supplements got a major boost following the discovery of processes for synthesizing vitamins beginning in 1935. By the late 1930s, drugstores and department stores were selling synthetic vitamin pills, labeled simply as vitamin C, D, etc., alongside cod-liver oil and other substances marketed as being a good source of vitamins.

The natural foods field had taken an interest in vitamins soon after they were discovered. An appreciation for the vitamins found in foods was congruent with a philosophy venerating the natural since vitamins could be understood as the essential nutrients of vegetables, fruits, and whole grains. Indeed, scientific recognition of the importance of vitamins appeared to bolster the claims of natural foods proponents. The vitamin-rich quality of natural foods was seen by their proponents as further confirmation of such foods' superiority compared with devitalized (and devitaminized) meat, polished grains, and other processed food.

What became more contentious in the natural foods field was the promotion of vitamin supplements instead of simply vitamin-rich food. This debate is one that I will discuss more fully in chapter 7. Here, I am most interested in how the efforts to create vitamin supplements from natural sources, as opposed to synthetic varieties, created a whole new category of health food in the 1930s, one that over time became both extremely popular with the public and extremely profitable. In many ways, the manufacture of vitamins was a logical extension of the production of herbal, seaweed, and mineral remedies that health food suppliers were already producing. One early maker of vitamins for the health food industry was William T. Thompson, who began an herb importing company in Los Angeles in 1934. The following year, he created the Seelect brand of herbal teas. But he became increasingly interested in vitamins, and by the late 1930s, had sold his tea business to Joseph Lessin (who was related to the Schulman family of Naturade) to focus on manufacturing vitamin and mineral supplements from natural sources. The Thompson Co. remained a major vitamin producer in the health food industry into the twenty-first century.

Another of the first health food companies to develop vitamin supplements was Health Foundation of California, which produced its Vegetrate line of "nutritional adjuncts." Along with supplements for gastrointestinal disorders, diabetes, nerves, and weight control, there were ones for deficiency diseases, such as Vegetrate's Nutritional Blood Reinforcement, advertised as supplying vitamins A, B, C, and E. Fresh vegetables were best, the company acknowledged, but it suggested that compromises could be made without giving up a natural foods ideology. Since both children and adults "have their whims of eating," the product guide warned, it advised, "If your child, be he six or forty-six, 'won't eat this and won't eat that,' supplement his diet with VEGE-BROTH in order that he will receive the vital organic mineral elements as necessary to maintain health and life."[30] This solution to the problem of picky eaters was indicative of how the health food industry helped shape a more flexible approach to a natural foods lifestyle. Rather than insisting on purity in dietary choices, consumers could purchase a product to make up for an inability or unwillingness to adhere to strict standards.

Health Food Stores on the Front Lines of the Movement

The proliferation of branded health food at this time was not altogether unique; it paralleled the spread of conventional food brands. Yet, an important distinguishing feature of the health food business was that more than just commerce was at stake. Most early entrepreneurs tended to be as philosophically committed to the concept of health food as were those who sought out the products for their own use. Specific motivations for entering the health food business were not entirely uniform, but a few reasons were dominant. Some entrepreneurs, as I have discussed, were enmeshed in naturopathic or religious beliefs that were tied to natural foods. Personal health concerns were (and continue to be) another important motivating factor for entering the industry. One of my informants told me that his grandfather started a business in the mid-1920s while looking for health remedies for a chronically ill son. Similarly, another respondent reported that his grandparents opened a health food store in 1949 after his grandmother found that health foods helped her sickly children. In both of these cases, respondents reported being "born into" the industry, which was another common route into the field. In fact, of the fifty interviews I conducted, fifteen were with people from multigenerational health food industry families. They were not unrepresentative of industry composition during much of the twentieth century.

Demonstrating their commitment to advancing a natural foods way of life, businesses' promotional material frequently carried impassioned statements about the value of natural foods and, conversely, firm opposition to the conventional food and health sectors. For instance, the 1935–36 catalog of the New York retailer Health Food Distributors was a 135-page mix of product listings, advertisements, and advice on health, cooking, and reasons for adopting a natural foods diet. Topics included "The Legumes—Superior to Animal Protein," "Orthodox Medicine Discredited," "Natural Food Best Health Insurance," and "Vicious Methods of Commercial Agriculture." Health Food Distributors encouraged its patrons to feel that they were on the winning side of an expanding movement:

> The thin, scattered ranks of the erstwhile ridiculed and persecuted "faddists," "cranks," "nuts," "fanatics" and "extremists"—the ironically unfailing martyr-laurels of all pioneers of progress of all ages for their vision and courage of convictions—are growing by leaps and bounds, and their numbers are becoming legion. The hounded and prosecuted nonconformists and heretics of yesterday are becoming the revered and worshipped benefactors and patron-saints of the despairing and perplexed masses, seeking relief from their multiform ailments.[31]

For this retailer, the marginal status of natural foods could be turned into a badge of honor.

Considering the low profits to be had and the equally low public esteem for natural foods, health food retailing in particular appeared to be a line of business that only those who truly believed in the products would enter. With a few exceptions, dedicated health food shops were scarce in the first two decades of the twentieth century. Consumers wanting such food had to rely on mail order or perhaps had access to bakeries, restaurants, sanitariums, or special events where products were sold as a sideline. Battle Creek Sanitarium foods did have wider distribution, with about a dozen of its products carried by conventional grocers and jobbers in the first decade of the twentieth century.[32] As more goods labeled *health food* came on the market, they too could occasionally be found in conventional drugstores or department stores. The May Co. department store of Los Angeles even had its own health food department starting in the late 1920s. But a truly complete selection of such products could only be found in a dedicated health food store. Such outlets were starting to pop up in the 1920s.

As to be expected for this period of history, there was not a completely firm division of labor between production and distribution branches in the industry. Many enterprises served both functions before eventually specializing as the industry became more differentiated. Otto Carqué was the figure who perhaps best embodied the ways that natural foods advocacy and the production, distribution, and sale of natural foods could be bridged. Before his death in 1935, Carqué wrote books and newspaper columns, and he lectured extensively on the value of natural foods. Through these communication activities, he forcefully condemned the economic and political interests that underlay the conventional food sector. For Carqué, the production and sale of natural foods were truly meant to be an alternative to a corrupt food system. However, he rejected the term *health food*, saying, *"There are no so-called "health foods," any more than there are specific foods for the cure of specific diseases.* Health is primarily the result of living in harmony with nature's laws" (Carqué 1925, 96, emphasis in original). Carqué began his commercial endeavors in the natural foods field as a grower of fruits and nuts in California. He was especially interested in natural ways of preserving fruit, and he developed a process for storing and shipping grape juice without the addition of chemical or sugar preservatives.[33] He then went on to produce unsulfured dried fruit that became a health food store staple. Expanding his repertoire, he branched out to making nut butters, olive oil, honey, and flours as well. By 1912, his Carqué Pure Food Co. made products available to consumers by mail order, and then by the 1920s, he operated storefronts in Los Angeles.

In some cases, such as Berhalter's of Chicago or Nature Food Centres of Boston, health food shops grew out of existing bakeries. But by the 1930s, establishments were regularly being founded as dedicated health food stores. Still, such shops remained limited in number. When Brownies opened for business in 1936, it was one of only four full-service health food stores in Manhattan, the others being Lust's Health Food (the former Kneipp Health Store), Health Food Distributors, which opened around 1931, and Kubie's Health Shoppe, which opened around 1927. Southern California had the greatest concentration of health food stores at that time, which was fitting for what was becoming the center of health food production. *Health News* of 1938 listed forty-nine health food stores in the region stretching from San Diego to Santa Barbara.[34] Other cities and towns could maybe support a single shop, but with no industry-coordinated effort to generate new stores, their establishment depended on the initiative of individuals.

Stores tended to be small and run on a shoestring. They were not trying to serve the general food consumer and usually faced no local competition from other health food retailers, so they had little pressure to invest much in aesthetics; indeed, their shabby physical appearance became a sore spot for industry boosters. However, it also meant that entry costs were low. Said one informant about these early days, "To give you an example of how small a store was, there was a health food store on Vermont Avenue by the name of Stichler's Health Food Store. They used the front arcade of their house, a little tiny porch area in the front of their house, in which they had a few health food products, and [with that] they were in the so-called health food business." The dearth of health food outlets up until the 1960s resulted in health food proponents assuring would-be merchants that they need not be businesspeople—or have any relevant experience—to enter the field. Author and lecturer Gaylord Hauser (1950, 239) wrote, "If you like and understand just two subjects—food and people—a health food shop can be an exciting as well as a profitable adventure for the second half of your life. But do make it an attractive, good-health food shop, not one of those dreary little *ill*-health food places. Teachers, doctors' wives, ministers' wives, nurses, YWCA workers are especially well adapted to this sort of project." As Hauser's remarks suggest, retailing—unlike manufacturing—opened up possibilities for women to enter the health food industry.

In a disjointed field of natural foods philosophies and philosophers, with few voluntary associations making possible face-to-face interaction, health food stores, run by people committed to the concept of natural foods, became the principal point of contact for natural foods followers. Health food businesses were the primary means of distributing book and periodical literature that served as natural foods manifestos, and, as I will discuss more in chapter 4, retailers were frequent sponsors of health food lecturers. But beyond these traditional forms of communication, circulars, catalogs, and even product labels provided information and inspiration on adopting the natural foods life. Here on the store shelves, one could find the range of ideas in the field, articulated in literature or made material in food and ingestible health remedies. In a more personal vein, shop owners dispensed guidance and advice to people interested in a natural foods lifestyle. While this advice may well have included do-it-yourself suggestions, there was certainly an incentive to steer customers to the ready-made products that were becoming the hallmark of a commitment to the natural. The industry thus provided a visible face to the natural foods movement. It also provided an opportunity for people to earn a livelihood from their commitments to natural foods ideals.

Forms of Advocacy

The people running health food businesses spanned the gamut of ideologies connected to natural foods. But a recognition that they could advance both the natural foods cause and their entangled economic interests led, in the 1930s, to the formation of trade associations. Trade shows provided the setting that brought industry members together where they could discuss issues of common concern. One such event, the California Health Show and Trade Exposition, was held in Los Angeles in 1933, with speakers, demonstrations, and exhibitors.[35] Shortly thereafter, Ada Alberty, a health food producer, spearheaded a meeting, attended by fifty manufacturers and retailers, at which time the American Natural Food Products Association was formed.[36] Despite a spirited inauguration, the California-based organization seems to have soon petered out.

Four years later, a trade show attracting more people from the eastern half of the country provided the opportunity for another effort to band together.[37] Tony Berhalter, a health food store owner, organized a convention in Chicago in 1937 with the idea that it could be the occasion for merging industry personnel into the consumer organization, the American Health Food Association, that Berhalter had formed the previous year. Approximately 150 industry members attended the convention, probably the largest such gathering to have assembled up to that date. Discussions about the new organization resulted in a split, however, with the majority deciding to form a trade association that included all sectors of the industry but excluded consumers (Phillipps 1976). The resulting National Health Foods Association quickly became the principal organization representing the industry and one of the few truly national organizations promoting natural foods ideals. This organization and its subsequent incarnations sponsored health food lecturers, created communication organs, extended legal support to those accused of practicing unlicensed medicine, and lobbied local and federal governments for favorable legislation. Each year, the group held a convention, which solidified a network of individuals who got to know one another very well.

This organization, along with regional branches, helped create greater cohesion and cooperation within the still small health food industry, and it provided a forum in which the goals of the natural foods movement could be articulated. Yet, as a trade association, this group remained closed to individual citizens. An assumption was made about the congruence of health food industry and health food consumer interests and the ability of the industry to represent them. Even more fundamentally, ordinary citizens who embraced a natural foods lifestyle but did not identify as health food consumers had no real place in the organization's frame of reference.

With the formation of this association, the health food industry achieved formal leadership in the natural foods movement. Industry personnel continued to be represented in other organized efforts to advance the natural foods cause as well; in fact, in the first half of the twentieth century, there were very few organizations involved in promoting natural foods that were not in some way tied to commercial endeavors. This is not to say that everyone in the natural foods movement found the presence of businesspeople in their ranks benign. Some leaders of the movement did try to establish distance between themselves and the health food industry. The most prominent was Herbert Shelton and his American Natural Hygiene Association. Shelton frequently railed against the health food business, claiming, "Instead of selling patent medicines, it is selling patent foods."[38] He considered the move away from eating simple foods derived directly from nature as a betrayal of the natural foods philosophy: "Most of today's health food stores are parts of a gigantic nation-wide commercial scheme that sells almost everything except wholesome natural foods. Let us not kid ourselves; the whole natural life and nature cure movement, and not merely the health food phase of it, has fallen upon evil times and evil ways. Commercialism is the canker-worm that is gnawing at its vitals."[39] Yet, such protestations against commercialism were somewhat disingenuous. Although Shelton consistently rejected manufactured food products and did not market his own line of food items, his publications were filled with advertisements, not only for his books but also for his own health school. Similarly, many other leaders of the movement also combined advocacy of a natural foods philosophy with commercial activities, even if they did not necessarily manufacture or sell branded products. Most commonly, they authored publications, ran health spas, or provided consulting services. In this way, self-promotion became bound up with promotion of the cause, and heartfelt ideas about the natural foods life and the means for implementing them were literally for sale in a variety of forms. In this situation, where to draw the line between profit-minded and civic-minded activities was none too clear.

While social reform associations made up solely of disinterested citizens were rare in this field, there were naturopathic and vegetarian societies scattered around the country. Significantly, many voluntary associations, especially those focused on vegetarianism, continued to be infused with Christian morality and references, which could make them uncomfortable homes for Jews and other non-Christians. One person active in the New York Vegetarian Society was Symon Gould, who founded the American Vegetarian Party in 1948 and even ran for president on this party's ticket in 1960 (Iacobbo and Iacobbo 2004, 158–64). Partly because of his ambitions for the party, Gould was frequently in conflict with other vegetarian leaders, and on at least one occasion, tensions gave rise to public discussion of Gould's status as a Jew. After a letter containing an anti-Semitic tirade, but directed at no particular individuals, was published in the *American Vegetarian* (Kalus 1948), the newspaper's editor, E. L. Pratt, printed an apology, claiming that the letter had slipped through when he was away during press time (E. Pratt 1949b). But Pratt concluded his initial response with a footnote attacking Gould's honesty (E. Pratt 1949b, 8), and in a later editorial, Pratt accused Gould of attempting to use the letter "to excite readers of the Jewish faith to the extent of getting his fingers in their pockets" to finance a competing publication, along with other schemes Pratt said would undermine the vegetarian cause (E. Pratt 1949a, 1). The Pratt–Gould dustup served as a reminder that stereotypes of deceitful, avaricious Jews could crop up even among progressive reformers. It is also noteworthy for highlighting how embroiled in infighting citizen-based natural foods advocacy groups tended to be. What made industry a more tolerant place in which Jews and other religious and ethnic minorities could operate relatively freely was not that the business world was made up of more ethical or enlightened people; it surely was not. Rather, industry was not subject to the same demands for natural foods purity and loyalty that citizen advocacy groups made.

Indeed, until the 1950s, almost all of the field's nationally visible citizen advocacy organizations adhered strictly to the philosophies of their founders and did not welcome members who wanted to move the groups in new directions. Organizations such as the American Naturopathic Association (previously called the Naturopathic Society of America, which was founded by Benedict Lust) and the American Natural Hygiene Society (founded by Herbert Shelton in 1948) had little patience for those who questioned or violated their founders' rules of correct living. In contrast, industry entrepreneurs were generally quite willing to work with business associates who, in their personal lives, did not faithfully follow natural foods principles. This forgiving attitude makes sense when considering the market environment. In a capitalist context, a business is more likely to thrive when clients and associates are judged solely by their contributions to the economic health of the enterprise rather than by an entrepreneur's personal values. A good supplier or a good customer need not be the truest believer in or most steadfast practitioner of natural foods principles. Unlike more rigid advocacy groups, businesses welcomed even the most tepidly interested consumers and did not shun fellow industry members who ate meat, smoked cigarettes, consumed white sugar and flour, or engaged in other disparaged behaviors. As later chapters will explore, what was more controversial than the personal eating and health habits of industry personnel were compromises businesses made in the choice of ingredients used in manufacturing or the kinds of products stocked in a store. Whereas citizen groups scrutinized their members' private conduct for signs of a commitment to natural foods, businesses looked at an organization's or spokesperson's public face when evaluating whether they qualified as true natural foods supporters.

The ability to work with a heterogeneous group of associates allowed industry organizations to put aside differences over the finer points of a natural foods philosophy to further the field, including advocacy efforts. But the goals that were developed looked increasingly different from those that animated the nineteenth-century natural foods movement, with its emphasis on promoting ascetic and self-reliant lifestyles. What became central to the twentieth-century natural foods movement was protection of the right to freely manufacture, sell, purchase, and consume health food commodities without interference from the state or medical professionals.

The health food industry's small size, marginal status, and indifference to a mass market meant that it had little to lose by opening its ranks to nudists, religious devotees, antivaccination and antivivisection activists, and others viewed as eccentric or extremist. It could adopt unconventional standards of doing business and symbols of a counterculture without jeopardizing its core constituency. But as more companies were established, the industry had a growing interest in seeing the market for health food enlarged. That entailed altering, at least to some degree, the cultural images that led most Americans to dismiss natural foods. As I will discuss in the following chapter, the successes of the quirky health food industry created incentives to reach rapprochement with the mainstream.

CHAPTER FOUR

Feeding the Talent

The Path to Legitimacy

In contrast to most other consumer goods, the fact that "everybody eats" means that potentially anyone might endorse a food product. It is therefore not surprising that gaining celebrity approval of a natural foods item or diet is a favored promotional device of advocates today. Whether through a formal arrangement with a food company or informally through publicity about a person's eating habits, images of public figures who lend their names and faces to natural foods highlight out-of-the-ordinary individuals who decide to eat out-of-the-ordinary foods to achieve out-of-the-ordinary results.

First Lady Michelle Obama's organic vegetable garden at the White House, a public curiosity for years, became a central symbol of her health and fitness campaign, as well as her much admired physique and fashionable good looks. The picture of Paul Newman that has adorned every package of Newman's Own natural dressings, sauces, and other prepared foods is a constant reminder that a lack of preservatives in food can make for a well-preserved film icon. Former bodybuilder, actor, and California governor Arnold Schwarzenegger claimed to have favored natural foods as part of his fitness regimen and in 2013 launched his own line of nutritional supplements. In each of these cases, and many others like them, celebrities tacitly or explicitly showcase their health, good looks, strength, and glamour as testament to the qualities of the natural foods that they eat.

These associations between natural foods and political, entertainment, and sports celebrities are nothing new. Indeed, such associations were key to the long, slow mainstreaming process that commenced as soon as the health food industry was established. Beginning with John Harvey Kellogg's courting of high-society guests at his sanitarium, health food entrepreneurs understood that the dismal image of their field could be improved through publicizing their products' use by elite figures. The results of this process finally started to come to fruition in the 1950s and 1960s after the health food industry nurtured a group of spokespeople who attracted large numbers of followers, including elite entertainers and athletes. These years saw the first real successes in establishing natural foods as a culturally legitimate set of food practices.

A desire to achieve legitimacy for the natural foods way of life has been a perennial concern from the field's earliest years through the present. As soon as the movement arose in the nineteenth century, natural foods advocates resented the mockery and suspicion they were subject to, and they recognized that greater credibility would enable them to more successfully spread their ideals. With industrialization of the food supply intensifying in the twentieth century, it seemed ever more urgent to advocates that government and other socially central institutions be turned away from practices that were destructive of the land and of human physical health and spiritual well-being. But as the health food industry also grew during the twentieth century, more was at stake than simply validation of natural foods proponents' beliefs and identity. The industry additionally had a financial interest in expanding the customer base for health food, and that necessitated going beyond the fringe groups that made up most of health food's clientele through the 1930s.

There has never been just one single program used by the health food industry to reach a broad population. Mid-twentieth-century strategies ranged from generally fruitless attempts to gain medical doctors' approval of a natural foods diet to more concerted efforts to align health food with conventional values of professionalism, science, and even conventional food itself. As I will discuss in this chapter, such efforts to conventionalize health food had only limited success. The contradiction between simultaneously masking and accentuating a rejection of dominant beliefs and practices regarding nourishment and health care was simply too obvious. Furthermore, not all participants in the natural foods field were interested in mainstreaming; some believed it was more important to maintain the total dedication to a natural foods lifestyle that brooked no compromises to appease conventional sensibilities. The continued visibility of such proud nonconformists belied any claims by growth-minded industry members that health food was just another consumer choice of ordinary Americans.

Instead, what proved to be most effective in promoting health food was publicity involving Hollywood and physical fitness stars. Ironically, the industry needed the assistance of some of the most atypical people in society to induce regular Americans to try health food. It was the enthusiasm for health food among actors, bodybuilders, and weight lifters that helped set natural foods on the path to legitimacy.

The main focus of this chapter is on the 1930s through the 1960s, when the health food field generated star spokespeople, first in the form of lecturers, then as authors, and later, with more mixed results, as television personalities. These spokespeople became quite influential in physical culture and Hollywood circles. There were a number of direct business connections between the spokespeople and the health food industry, involving not just the sale of food products but also communication media promoting a natural foods lifestyle. Physical culture proponents, such as lecturer Paul C. Bragg, magazine publisher Bob Hoffman, and television host Jack La-Lanne, as well as a darling of the Hollywood movie crowd, author-lecturer Gayelord Hauser, all had their own lines of health food for sale. Each of these individuals helped spark greater interest in health food among entertainers and athletes, as well as among the general public.

Although bodybuilders and film stars occupied separate worlds, their mutual interest in vegetarianism and health food provided not just new customers for the industry but also visible supporters with little to lose by making public their unconventional dietary habits. These groups were themselves outside of the mainstream, and thus, they helped perpetuate health food's exotic image. But their status as performers lent glamour and, with it, some legitimacy to this food category. What further tied bodybuilders and Hollywood figures together was that they both embraced health food for purposes of enhancing personal appearance on top of good health, perhaps best captured in the title of Hauser's 1950 best seller, *Look Younger, Live Longer*. This emphasis introduced to the public an important new motivation for adopting such a diet. It also encouraged the industry to focus on the strength and beauty properties of health foods, while downplaying challenges to economic and environmental aspects of the dominant food system. By the middle of the twentieth century, the industry-led natural foods movement was having real success in attracting new enthusiasts. But with that success came a number of changes in how adherents defined a natural foods ethic.

Trying to Conventionalize the Unconventional

In their attempts to gain legitimacy for the natural foods way of life, proponents considered the obstacles posed by not just their food choices but also the people who ate these foods. In some cases, efforts were made to distance the field from its most marginal tendencies. Ray Van Cleef, a contributor to *Strength and Health* magazine, wrote in 1949 in regard to the upcoming American Vegetarian Convention:

> I do hope that the convention proves a huge success. To establish the organization on a firm and rational basis, it is vitally important that the "crack-pot" element be kept under control. Vegetarian movement must be promoted on a sane basis confined to the basic principals [*sic*] of the cause. Too many cults and other projects have allied themselves with the vegetarian movement in a way that definitely makes them far more of a liability than an asset. It is essential that the movement be devoid of the elements that have exposed it to ridicule and very distorted impressions. The objectives should not ignore reality and make fantastic claims. There is a need for a thorough house cleaning in the movement if any real progress is to be achieved.[1]

However, as others realized, such housecleaning would come at the expense of losing supporters. Members of the health food industry periodically expressed concerns about fraudulent practices within their ranks, but they rarely echoed Van Cleef's advice to purge people on the basis of holding peculiar beliefs or idiosyncratic ways of expressing them.

What was far more common in the industry than trying to shut out the more outlandish characters was to put forth a competing image of respectability and normality by associating health food with conventional styles and values, and sometimes even conventional food itself. This latter strategy was most apparent with the major Seventh-day Adventist health food companies. Throughout the twentieth century, the Battle Creek Food Co., Loma Linda Foods, and Worthington Foods worked hard to demystify their products and assure consumers that adopting a vegetarian lifestyle did not require that one exist outside the cultural mainstream.

The most obvious way in which this conventionalization approach was employed was by equating vegetarian products with meat. John Harvey Kellogg embarked on this strategy shortly after he started to sell nut foods. One of his first nut products, developed in the 1890s and called Nut Cheese, was not successful and was soon discontinued. Similarly, a product called Vegetable Egg appeared to be a flop as soon as it was introduced.[2] However, nut products that were meant to stand in for forbidden flesh foods fared better. An early advertisement for Protose buried the actual brand name under the headline "Vegetable Meat" and promised "a taste that can hardly be distinguished from best beef."[3] Kellogg's nut and gluten preparations were soon thereafter marketed as "meat substitutes," a label that prevailed in the industry until it was replaced in the 1970s with the more scientific sounding "meat analogs."

Consumers were assured that such products had the same taste as and other characteristics of meat. A Battle Creek Food promotional pamphlet noted, "One important reason why Battle Creek Vegetable Entrees have such universal appeal is that in color, texture and consistency they look like meats, meat spreads and sea foods."[4] Driving home the association, Battle Creek products sold in the 1940s included canned Vegetable Steaks, Vegetable Skallops, and Vegetable Burger. Recipes were offered that used these ingredients in similar ways as meat, such as Protose Hamburgers, Protose and Vegetable Balls, Soy Protose Goulash with Spaghetti, and Nut Meat Fillet.[5] The message was that vegetarians need not develop an entirely new approach to cooking. Giving up meat was as easy as switching from one brand of tinned food to another.

The dissonance of condemning meat while simultaneously trying to make alternative food as meatlike as possible was not lost on vegetarian advocates. One wrote a letter to the Worthington Foods publication *Chopletter* (named after its most popular product, Choplets), protesting a Thanksgiving suggestion to shape Choplets in the form of a turkey. The editors justified their feature by saying, "The shaping of the roast like a turkey was merely in keeping with the tradition of early Thanksgiving days."[6] Their intent was to bring vegetarians in from the sidelines by helping them take part in beloved, mainstream holiday traditions. Sometimes, the companies gave more extended defenses of their meat imitations. A Loma Linda Foods publication from 1958 told its readers:

> On the face of it, this may seem slightly ridiculous, but actually much thought has gone into the preparation of these foods. With more and more people every day discovering the wisdom of discarding their meat-eating habits, many feel a real need for foods that simulate meat in taste and texture. New converts to vegetarianism miss the familiar flavor of steaks, chops, or sausages they have been used to all their lives, and it poses an important problem as to how they may replace them. It is to meet the needs of so many of these people that Loma Linda and other food manufacturers have sought to perfect such palatable products.[7]

Other times, though, the companies seemed completely oblivious to the mixed messages they were sending, as with Worthington Foods' 1957 recipe contest, in which the first prize winner would receive a mink scarf.[8]

During the 1950s, a mink garment was a potent symbol of female luxury, and popular culture was full of references to women's desire for fur. Through its recipe contest, Worthington Foods suggested that vegetarian homemakers were really no different from other woman. Meat substitute marketing material frequently drew on this kind of conventional imagery, which seemed to declare that those who adopted health food could comfortably occupy the mainstream. From illustrations of well-dressed, light-skinned, happy families eating their health food in well-appointed surroundings to recommendations of party food and entertainment tips, the message was that health food consumers had the same aspirations and lifestyles as their meat-eating neighbors.

While the meat substitute companies waged the most explicit campaign to make health food into close copies of conventional food, there were other ways of linking health food to the normative, which were actually more widespread in the industry. These methods included a drive toward professionalization. The field's values could be made more legitimate and less threatening to outsiders by attaching them to some kind of professional expertise, which conventionalized these values by anchoring them in set standards and oversight by dedicated, experienced specialists. Support for professionalization could be seen in the field's trade associations and trade journals, which began forming in the 1930s and which embraced the task of disseminating information about best practices for aspiring entrepreneurs.

The attempt to project a more professional image also included the conscious use of symbols to make an impression on the public. In the 1930s and 1940s, the owner of the New York health food store Brownies had his employees wear white lab coats to create a professional look (Tardosky 1990). Health food manufacturers, such as Innerclean, achieved a similar result with product labels that were devoid of any images beyond the text, suggesting a no-nonsense approach to communicating the contents inside. Language was also used to this effect, as with one of the most successful health food manufacturers, Modern Health Products, whose very name broke with the natural foods movement's common critique of the pernicious effects of modernity.

Perhaps the most widely employed, though contradictory, method used to overcome natural foods' marginality was to appeal to science and rationality. Proponents typically aligned themselves with rationality, progress, and enlightenment, as summed up in the title of one of Otto Carqué's books, *Rational Diet* (1923), which suggested that the natural way is the most rational way. Natural foods advocates also frequently referred to their own and others' scientific studies to claim credibility. Worthington Foods reinforced many of the hallmarks of science and rationality—standardization, methodical action, cleanliness, and educational credentials—when it assured its customers:

> A modern laboratory is maintained at the plant where basic formulae for the products are worked out and control procedures are set up to insure a uniform product. Analytical, bacteriological analyses along with recovery studies are made in the laboratory, and experimental work for new products is being carried on constantly. Recipes for the foods are worked out and tested in the spotless white kitchen which forms a part of the laboratory. Mr. Warren Hartman, chemist at the plant since October 1946, holds an M.S. degree from the University of Michigan. He came to Worthington Foods after six years of experience as an employee in the Michigan State Department of Health laboratories.[9]

Yet, such attempts to create an alignment with science were a hazardous tactic. In his study of AIDS activists, Steven Epstein (1996, 335–36) describes conditions that allow for a social movement to gain credibility within a domain of science, such as already existing cleavages within science, or activists speaking the same language as science. These conditions were not present in the natural foods movement during the middle of the twentieth century. The scientific establishment was united in rejecting natural foods ideas. At the same time, natural foods advocates, in describing food as *vital* or *devitalized*, *acid* or *alkaline*, *natural* or *denatured*, used terms far from the language employed by scientists. Natural foods advocates could try to argue that science was on their side, but institutionalized science loudly begged to differ with them. On the whole, the strategy of claiming a conventional identity proved not to be especially effective in the search for new supporters. Instead, it was the encounter with charismatic personalities, rather than cold, rational science, that did the most to bring in new followers in the middle decades of the twentieth century.

The Lecture Circuit

In the present age, with mass communication synonymous with mediating technologies, it is easy to forget the power of the spoken word when in the physical presence of an orator. But well before mass media were used to galvanize large numbers of natural foods followers, health food lecturers inspired crowds large and small to try out a natural foods way of life. In the early twentieth century, it was once again John Harvey Kellogg who led the way. Kellogg was a prodigious communicator, publishing almost fifty books, numerous journals and newsletters to which he was the primary contributor, and countless articles and tracts. But he was perhaps best known for his public lectures, giving more than five thousand of them during his lifetime (Schwarz 1970, 82–87). Public lectures by proponents of natural foods soon became standard practice in the field. In cities with a significant movement presence, local advocates gave talks on a regular basis. For instance, in Los Angeles, a hotbed of such activity, Carqué was a frequent speaker, and a chiropractic doctor, Pietro Rotondi, offered weekly lectures in his home for years. Other homegrown teacher-philosophers included health food store and vegetarian restaurant proprietors, dentists, and naturopaths.

Whereas in the earlier years, such talks were mostly a local affair, the 1930s and 1940s became the heyday of traveling lecturers who toured the country to give their talks about natural foods and other natural health remedies. *California Health News* reported in 1933 that seven visiting health lecturers appeared within a two-month period in Los Angeles, with more soon on the way.[10] There were scores of such lecturers, but the most popular were probably Bragg, Hauser, Lelord Kordel, and Martin Pretorius. When they first started, they were hosted by health food stores or like-minded clubs and societies. As their fame spread, they sought out larger venues, typically renting an auditorium for their lectures. A 1932 *Los Angeles Times* advertisement announcing three evenings of lectures by Pretorius at the Trinity Auditorium promised "2,300 Free Seats!"[11] While even a star like Pretorius was unlikely to fill to capacity a hall that large, it was not uncommon for the handful of best-known health food lecturers to attract audiences of several hundred, and sometimes even over a thousand. Coming out of the nineteenth-century tradition of attending public lectures for purposes of self-improvement (Scott 1980), the draw of these events was nonetheless as much entertainment as edification, with crowds curious to see the personalities reputed to have such eccentric ideas and such stirring tales regarding the pathway to good health. After the free talk, the lecturers would sell their books and food products, mainly packaged under their own names. Before moving on, they frequently offered additional classes on nutrition and natural foods—for which they charged a fee.[12] Through their talks and classes, these lecturers stimulated demand for health food and often left behind newly committed devotees of the natural foods movement.

There was close cooperation between lecturers and the rest of the health food industry. Trade associations featured the best-known speakers at conventions and meetings to build morale and enthusiasm among members. And as they toured the country, most lecturers depended on industry personnel to arrange for venues and publicity for their talks. Health food stores were especially eager to help out. Brownies of New York City, for instance, had a lecture hall attached to the store, and owner Sam Brown invited speakers, local and visiting, to give free lectures once or twice a week. "People got something for nothing," he said. "And then they'd shop." In other cases, retailers or wholesalers helped book auditorium space knowing that some audience members were likely to turn into long-term customers.

The impact of the star spokespeople could be considerable. After Hauser directed consumers to health food stores to find the five "wonder foods" he recommended—blackstrap molasses, brewer's yeast, wheat germ, powdered skim milk, and yogurt (Hauser 1950, 25)—sales for these formerly obscure goods skyrocketed. Hauser was exemplary in promoting the health food industry; advertisements for his Modern Products brand regularly included the tag line, "at health food stores everywhere."[13] Even without such explicit support from lecturers, retailers relied on the lecturers' authority to draw customers, as seen in a 1957 circular announcing the opening of a new health food outlet in Chicago: "We carry all products endorsed by the leading HEALTH LECTURERS. Gayelord Hauser, Howard Inches, Walter Hodson, Paul Bragg, M. O. Garten, V. E. Irons, Martin Pretorius, Edward and Florence McCollum, Bernard Jensen."[14] Simply listing the names of these figures was a way to attract the public's attention.

Beyond the boost they gave to their associates' enterprises, many of the lecturers were directly involved in the industry, perhaps owning a health food store or, more likely, manufacturing a line of health food. Among the most successful such businesses were Modern Products (originally called Modern Health Products), founded by Hauser in 1925, and Bragg Live Products (a descendant of ventures Bragg started in the 1930s); both survive to this day. Hauser and Bragg themselves lasted on the lecture circuit for decades, continuing to attract curious onlookers and devoted followers who swore by their regimens. They also authored numerous books and, for a time, each ran health centers where they dispensed advice and shaped diet and exercise programs. Both men recounted the quintessential narrative of the natural foods lifestyle, each claiming that he was subject to debilitating cases of illness that no medicine could cure and then was not only healed but turned into a specimen of perfect health after adopting a natural foods diet. Furthermore, Hauser and Bragg are emblematic of the two worlds that provided significant constituencies for health food: physical fitness enthusiasts and film and television performers. Understanding the first group requires a brief return to the beginning of the twentieth century.

Supplementing Strength

Like some other health food advocates of the early twentieth century, both Hauser and Bragg were influenced by physical culture icon Bernarr Macfadden. The physical culture movement, which Macfadden helped define and promote, centered on bodily improvement: creating strength, a muscular physique, and good health through vigorous exercise and proper diet. While sharing a reverence for the natural, Macfadden differed from his contemporary, Kellogg, in that Macfadden celebrated bodily display and an active sex life; not coincidentally, although he claimed to be Christian, his religious convictions were rather tepid. To better disseminate his views, Macfadden started *Physical Culture* magazine in 1899. From there, he went on to create a magazine empire that included not just health and fitness periodicals but also, more profitably, pulp outlets such as *True Confessions* and *True Detective* and trade and consumer lifestyle publications such as *Modern Marriage* and *Model Airplane News*.[15]

Complementing Macfadden's focus on exercise was a belief in naturopathy and the health benefits of natural foods. Although not a strict vegetarian, Macfadden promoted the consumption of raw vegetables, advocated frequent fasts, and denounced white bread and other foods with highly processed ingredients. Macfadden's fitness magazines, along with many of the books he wrote, became vehicles for communicating his enthusiasm for natural foods; *Physical Culture* also was an outlet for others in the natural foods movement, who often contributed articles or advertisements. Macfadden never self-identified as a member of the health food industry, asserting in his book, "The only true health foods are those furnished by Nature, and if you adhere to them in all their natural simplicity, and refrain from eating beyond your power to digest, there will be no occasion for any one to search for other means of nourishment" (1901, 97). Still, he did market at least one food product, a breakfast cereal called Meline

(Ernst 1991, 117). He additionally operated a number of Physical Culture Restaurants that served inexpensive wholesome food; the first opened in New York City in 1902, and by 1911 the franchise had grown into a chain of twenty outlets in various cities (Ernst 1991, 28–29). In 1929, Macfadden purchased the former sanitarium of James Caleb Jackson in Dansville, New York, bringing new life to the now renamed Physical Culture Hotel (A. Merrill 1958). The resort provided naturopathic cures, vigorous exercise, and meals corresponding to natural foods principles. Much of the philosophy of the resort was summed up in a letter-writing contest it sponsored in 1959, a few years after Macfadden's death, the subject of which was: "How has vegetarianism, health foods, organiculture, natural living, physical culture and/or natural hygiene improved my health."[16]

Macfadden's significance for the natural foods field was, via his publishing empire, to strengthen the connection between natural foods and fitness. That link had been made elsewhere, as with the German *lebensreform* movement. But Macfadden spoke to Americans whose primary interest was in building and displaying strong bodies. For them, natural foods were not the center of a lifestyle that included a philosophical attachment to the natural world but rather a potentially useful tool to achieve a fit body for its own sake. In particular, bodybuilders and weight lifters took an interest in natural foods. In addition to Macfadden, several prominent musclemen, in both the United States and Germany, adopted vegetarianism, raw foods, or whole grain diets (Roach 2004; Wedemeyer 1994). As a result, even though natural foods advocates remained a minority in these circles, they often found a respectful hearing among their fellow physical culturalists. For instance, Muscle Beach, an area in Santa Monica, California, frequented by fitness practitioners, was welcoming of natural foods devotees, including the central Muscle Beach figures LaLanne and the female bodybuilder Relna Brown, who also worked at a Santa Monica health food store (Zinkin and Hearn 1999).

Among the most visible early health food entrepreneurs to introduce physical culture circles to the potential benefits of health food was the lecturer Bragg. The details of Bragg's life are somewhat murky. In a field where health promoters were known to embellish stories of miraculous cures, Bragg's accounts of his life and work were especially unreliable, a pattern reinforced after his death in 1976 by the heir to his business, his former daughter-in-law Patricia Bragg. The Braggs freely exaggerated Paul's accomplishments, claiming (wrongly) that, among other things, he founded the first health food store in the United States, he produced the first vitamins, he was the first to make herbal teas and honey available nationwide, and he was the first traveling health lecturer in the country.[17] Although his enterprises boasted of having a much older pedigree,[18] there actually is no independent evidence of Paul Bragg's involvement in the health food industry until the 1920s. After growing up in Washington, DC, he settled in Los Angeles by the early 1920s. There, in about 1924, Bragg joined forces with Fred Hirsch, the producer of Inner-Clean, to run a Los Angeles store called Health Food Products Co. In 1925, it was renamed the Health Center and expanded to include a lecture hall featuring nightly talks, a dining room, and a gymnasium.[19] Bragg appeared to have parted ways with Hirsch and branched out on his own with the Bragg Health Center in late 1928; he also began to travel extensively on lecture tours around then. For a time, Bragg seemed to be in direct competition with Hirsch; both health centers featured a Health Cafeteria, clinics offering treatments for intestinal problems, specialists to treat thinning hair, and, of course, lectures on diet and nature cure.[20]

Despite his self-aggrandizing tendencies, Bragg truly was an exceptionally popular health lecturer, and some of his company's products, especially his apple cider vinegar, remain a standard on health food shelves well into the twenty-first century. Bragg's philosophy of natural foods was quite similar to others of his day. He believed that health could be restored and "meals can be nutritious, appetizing, and satisfying to the palate, without including any of the processed, bleached, colored, sifted, bolted, denatured, degerminated, demineralized, polluted, chemically treated, and 'refined' foodstuffs that form the largest portion of an average diet, and that are responsible for the prevalence of sickness and disease among the American people" (Bragg 1935, 12–13). But what did set Bragg apart from many other natural foods lecturers was his emphasis on vigorous physical exercise. He was a follower of physical culture, and before his affiliation with the Health Center in Los Angeles, had acted as a physical education instructor for schools and YMCAs. Part of his lecture routine included showing off his muscles and sometimes performing feats of strength and endurance. In later years, his demonstrations included inviting people to jump on his stomach, a stunt originally practiced by Macfadden, and which Bragg even performed on the 1960s television program *The Steve Allen Show* (J. Kotulak 1963; Ernst 1991, 55). To dramatize his fitness even further, Bragg lied about his age, claiming to be more than ten years older than he actually was.

Bragg's message expressly countered the dominant image of natural foods believers as sickly or elderly people desperate for relief from their ailments. "Not for Sissies!" declared the headline of a 1940 advertisement for his food products and monthly newsletter (see figure 3).[21] Similarly, in a 1940 cookbook, a frontispiece family photo shows four Braggs, young and old, the three males bare-chested, and adults with rippling muscles. Posed sitting outdoors on a cinder block wall, there is no sign of food, or of nature for that matter, only the following statement: "Here are four generations of healthy Braggs. Each of them displays the highest type of physical perfection in normal weight, abundance of energy, vitality, and absolute freedom of [sic] sickness. They attribute their streamline functional perfection to the fact that they eat foods composed of all the minerals, vitamins, and vital factors for building a strong body" (Bragg 1941, 3). Through his continuous emphasis on how natural ingredients and branded health food play a part in building strength and a sculpted body, Bragg built bridges to a growing world of fitness devotees and paved the way for other health food entrepreneurs to come out of this world.

Those who followed included Vic Boff, a central figure in New York physical culture circles, who operated three successful health food stores beginning in the 1950s. Also coming from local physical culture milieus, but going on to achieve a measure of fame among the general public, was Jack LaLanne. LaLanne was first introduced to a natural foods philosophy as a teenager when he heard a talk by Paul Bragg. In the 1930s, LaLanne opened a gym and juice bar in Oakland, California, and proceeded to gain a local reputation as a muscleman. His reputation spread when he hosted *The Jack LaLanne Show*, an exercise television program that also pitched health food. First aired in 1951 in the San Francisco Bay Area, the syndicated show was broadcast to a national audience from 1959 to 1970 and then lived on through reruns. The show became something of a cultural touchstone, symbolizing a growing sector of the population who actively pursued good health without the assistance of medical or other professionals. LaLanne was circumspect in his on-air criticisms of the conventional food and health systems, but he enthusiastically promoted blended fruit and vegetable juices and other natural foods. He also marketed his own line of products off-air, including protein powder, supplements, and other typical health food (Delugach 1984; Goldstein 2011; Sandomit 2004; Stein 1988). Through the medium of television, LaLanne effectively showed off his physique, strength, and apparent good health to a large audience that had little previous familiarity with or interest in health food. He thus helped move health food closer to acceptance as a legitimate consumer option for enhancing personal well-being.

NOT FOR SISSIES!

Bragg Foods

are for people who
want to tingle with
the joy of living!

Bragg, his father, daughter and grandson Shocky,
always keep well and happy.

Alice Everett, perfect
example of vibrant
h e a l t h, has eaten
Bragg foods for years.

IF YOU ENJOY YOUR ACHES and PAINS
BETTER NOT DO AS THESE PEOPLE DO

No soft demineralized cereals for them!
> BRAGG MEAL is their breakfast. Made of four
> whole grains and wheat germ. Large box, **60c**

No caffeine drinks for them!
> It's always BRAGG'S **CALIFORNIA MINT TEA**
> **50c** a can

No CONSTIPATION for them!
> To relieve temporary constipation they use
> O. K. LAX — the family laxative. 50c a package

GOOD HEALTH FOOD STORES ARE PROUD TO SHOW YOU BRAGG FOODS!

Join our Health Family... FREE!

Every month Paul Bragg sends out his famous Health Bulletin
FREE to all who are interested in keeping well and young at any
age. Health Secrets galore. Write for your free copy today.

FIGURE 3. Advertisement for Bragg Foods appearing on the inside back cover of a 1940 magazine issued by Pavo's Natural Dietetic Foods of Minneapolis and St. Paul. Paul Bragg bridged
the health food and physical culture worlds. From the personal collection of the author.

While LaLanne's celebrity appeal drew ordinary Americans into the health food orbit, other entrepreneurs strengthened the connection between physical culture enthusiasts and health food. Most notably, these entrepreneurs helped make the category of nutritional supplements a key part of many fitness regimes, thus accelerating supplements' position as the most profitable segment of the health food industry. A 1950 survey of health food dealers found that vitamins and minerals already supplied 34 percent of store profits (Bernardini 1976). Yet, until the 1950s, nutritional supplements consisted primarily of vitamins and concoctions made of vegetables, minerals, or herbs, which were meant to relieve various ailments, especially constipation. Sometimes these products were marketed to help underweight individuals gain bulk, and they almost always promised increased energy and vigor. However, health food products promoted specifically for purposes of athletic enhancement took off only after people within physical culture circles began experimenting among themselves with nutritional formulas to improve performance. What became especially popular among weight lifters, bodybuilders, and other athletes were protein powders. Among the first was Kevo Co.'s 44, which appeared in 1950 and was sold in both health food stores and bodybuilding studios (Roach 2004, 30). Another protein powder released on the market not long after, Hi-Proteen, became one of the biggest-selling products to come out of the health food industry. It was produced by Bob Hoffman, an entrepreneur who adroitly straddled the health food and fitness worlds.

Hoffman was a weight lifter; his York Barbell Company, founded in 1938, sold training equipment, and he recruited and coached many weight lifting stars. Hoffman also published *Strength & Health* magazine, which he founded in 1932 and which became one of the nation's preeminent fitness periodicals (Fair 1999). Hoffman subscribed to natural foods principles, believing, like Macfadden and Bragg, that a natural foods diet benefited the fitness practitioner. "Eliminate foodless foods from your diet," he advised. "Eat natural food as much as possible" (Hoffman 1962, 9). *Strength & Health* became an outlet for Hoffman's ideas about nutrition, as well as a vehicle for promoting his products.

Historians Hall and Fair (2004) credit Bragg with first suggesting to Hoffman, in 1946, that he enter the health food business. Hoffman did so some years later, in 1951, when he began selling the York Vitamin-Mineral Food Supplement, and the following year, Bob Hoffman's High-Protein Food (soon renamed Hi-Proteen), which grew out of a similar product developed by bodybuilder Irvin Johnson (Hall and Fair 2004).

One health food manufacturer, who had been a weight lifter in the 1950s, recalled when Hoffman's protein powder first came out: "It tasted terrible!" Despite that fact, the regulars at the gym consumed it anyway, he added. As this informant noted, physical culture devotees would do almost anything to build muscle, and Hoffman's publications were filled with stories about the tremendous results to be gained from ingesting the right kind of protein.

Hoffman added more supplements to his line, but (after improving the taste) Hi-Proteen remained his biggest seller for decades, constituting half of all Hoffman sales in the 1960s (Fair 1999, 208). By then, several other companies were also marketing supplements geared toward athletes. Even in the early 1950s, Hoffman was not completely alone in this enterprise. Joe Weider was another fitness magazine publisher, maker of exercise equipment, and manufacturer of protein powder and other supplements; he was also Hoffman's main competitor. Indeed, the rivalry between these two figures continued long after their retirement and death, with associates insisting on one or the other's superior contributions or, conversely, nefarious practices. Although Weider also helped make health food supplements important to athletes, Hoffman was more involved in the health food industry and worked to advance it as well as his own business interests. Hoffman cultivated a high profile in the industry; by the 1966 National Dietary Foods Association convention (the primary convention of the health food industry at that time), only one other exhibitor took up as much floor space as Hoffman's Hi-Proteen Products and York Barbell companies.[22] Hoffman also held office in the National Dietary Foods Association as Youth Fitness Committee chair during the 1960s.

By promoting ideas about natural foods to fitness devotees, physical culturalists such as Hoffman expanded interest in a natural foods lifestyle. Moreover, the cultural image of health food was affected by physical culturalists' support. Certainly, bodybuilding remained an esoteric activity for most Americans; musclemen and musclewomen were generally seen more as curiosities than as role models. But they helped associate health food with athletic prowess and, as a result, brought average people looking for a performance boost into their local health food store. Vitamins, protein powders, and other food supplements—still found primarily in health food stores in the 1950s and 1960s—were increasingly taken by aspiring athletes who did not identify with the natural foods movement. Although they were uninterested in spreading a natural foods philosophy, these consumers did become important customers of health food stores and contributed to placing the industry on a sounder financial footing. They also demonstrated that health food could be consumed selectively and without attention to the ideological apparatus that gave rise to these products.

Health Food in Hollywood

Jack LaLanne and the men who became Mr. America were not the only celebrities who publicly embraced health food in the mid-twentieth century. Even more in the public eye were the denizens of film and television who became natural foods followers. Hollywood had been a symbol of physical culture since the 1920s (Addison 2003, 39). By the 1930s, it was also becoming one of the symbols of health food. The most obvious reason for this developing association was that screen actors were interested in managing all aspects of their appearance, and their admirers were interested in how they accomplished it. In an early nod to the film industry's willingness to try health food, a Battle Creek Food publication reported in 1927:

> Recently, Miss Nita Cavilier, one of the movie stars of Hollywood, gave a delightful tea and made it an occasion for serving health foods. A charming hostess, Miss Cavilier fascinated her Hollywood friends with the attractive dishes she brought out, intimately whispering to her guests that she was serving morsels of beauty and pep in the form of the well known Battle Creek Health Foods. And to use the parlance of Broadway, the party went over with a bang. When the movie stars take it up, you know it is the smart thing to do.[23]

The fact that Southern California had the country's largest concentration of natural foods followers and health food businesses made it easy for people in the film industry to find health food and strike up relationships with natural foods advocates. Some entrepreneurs cultivated these ties to burnish their reputations. Paul Bragg, for instance, made frequent mention of the stars seeking his counsel (e.g., Bragg 1946). Bragg did have celebrity clients, but the individual who did the most to associate the glamour of Hollywood with health food in the public's mind, adding to his already impressive talent for attracting new health food consumers, was Bengamin Gayelord Hauser.

Gayelord Hauser's background resembled that of many other natural foods followers, but he went on to become the most successful of his generation of health food lecturers, at least as measured by the size of the crowds he attracted and his ability to reach a mainstream audience. As a teenager, Hauser migrated from Germany to the United States where his brother, Otto, was living, but Gayelord soon went back to Europe after falling ill and finding no relief from American established medicine. In Switzerland, he underwent naturopathic treatments, recovered his health, and, after a period of study, returned to the United States. There, he received chiropractic training and, in 1923, opened a naturopathic clinic in Chicago, which included diet advice. In this capacity, he met Frey Brown, who became his companion and business partner, and Hauser started giving lectures at the clinic. In 1926, they left Chicago as Hauser began to lecture around the country. Around this time, the couple became partners in a Milwaukee health food company, originally called Milwaukee Whole Food Products and then Modern Health Products, in which other Hauser family members were also involved. Its major sellers at the time were a laxative called Swiss Kriss and a seasoning called Nu-Vege-Sal.[24] Within a couple decades, with Hauser's name as an endorsement and Brown's more direct involvement in running the business, Modern Products (as it was eventually called) was one of the most profitable companies in the health food industry.

The suave and good-looking Hauser's reputation as a speaker grew. Hauser and Brown settled in Southern California around 1930, though they frequently traveled on the lecture circuit. Hauser came to the notice of high society via Adele Astaire, who was the sister of tap-dancing movie star Fred Astaire and who became Lady Cavendish after marriage to an English aristocrat. Spending time in England and France in the 1930s, Hauser was embraced by European social elites interested in food reform (Hauser 1944; Lehman 1951). Back in the United States, he also circulated among the new American aristocracy: film stars. What especially elevated his public visibility was his friendship with and tutelage of actress Greta Garbo. By the time they met in 1939, Garbo was already a vegetarian (de Acosta 1960, 306), but Hauser made further changes in her diet, which appeared to improve her health. As she became good friends with Hauser and Brown, gossip columnists frequently reported on the "romance" between Garbo and Hauser, unfailingly noting his unconventional nutritional avocation. Said one such piece, "Why shouldn't the man Garbo would diet for be the man she'd follow to an altar?" (Haynes 1940). Much of the press was likely complicit in the knowledge that Hauser was gay and Garbo bisexual, and the public pairing of the two was more good publicity than good journalism. The romance facade was dropped after a few years, but Hauser continued his friendship with Garbo and advised other well-known entertainers as well, including Jean Harlow, Marlene Dietrich, Paulette Goddard, Gloria Swanson, Van Johnson, Zsa Zsa Gabor, and Bob Hope (F. Murray 1985).

Hauser made frequent references to his society connections, using them to bolster his appeal with the public. Underscoring his insider status with Elsie de Wolfe Mendl, he wrote in his 1950 book, *Look Younger, Live Longer*, "But we who know 'our Elsie' know that it is her immense vitality, her love of life which has made her not only an internationally famous hostess, but one of the most adored women in the world. Lady Mendl has long since adopted my Look Younger, Live Longer principles" (Hauser 1950, 212–13). Striking a chattier tone in his magazine, *Diet Digest*, Hauser confided in 1949, "When I have more time I must report what the Duchess of Windsor taught me about women's clothes. We had lunch together. The duke was also there, of course."[25] As self-serving as these sorts of remarks may have been, the interest by celebrities in health food was real. Columnist Art Buchwald (1959) quoted television writer Larry Gelbart (later of *M*A*S*H* TV fame) making fun of the "health nuts" who had taken over in Hollywood:

> It's very dangerous to be invited to someone's house for a meal. For one thing, you can't walk on their lawn because that may be your dinner. . . . Dinner? It consisted of boiled peanut water, wheat-germ pancakes, soybeans cooked in their own soy, carrot salad and cider vinegar. But that wasn't all. After we ate the food, the butler came in with a silver tray filled with jars of pills. "What are those for?" I asked foolishly. "They're the supplements," the hostess explained.

Some entertainers willingly lent their fame to the natural foods movement, such as Gloria Swanson, who advocated for vegetarianism, organic agriculture, and macrobiotics. The owner of a Los Angeles area health food shop recounted that when shooting the film *Sunset Boulevard*, Swanson, a regular at the store, agreed to meet with her customers, telling them, "better to eat the bug than the poison" in a pitch for organic produce. More typically, entertainers simply incorporated natural foods into their diets, neither announcing nor hiding their preferences. Expected by the public to be different from the average individual, and immersed in a social world where people's livelihoods required them to shape bodies for display, entertainers could afford to be nonchalant about adopting food habits that in other circumstances would invite loss of status.

EAT TO LIVE
Journal of Health

10 Cents

November

HELP YOURSELF TO SOY BEANS
•
DIET *for* HARDENED ARTERIES
•
UNSULPHERED SUNDRIED FRUITS
•
NATURE CURE MENUS *and* RECIPES

NATURAL FOODS INSTITUTE
807 ST. CLAIR AVENUE, N.E.   Telephone: CHerry 2349   CLEVELAND, OHIO

FIGURE 4. Front cover of *Eat to Live Journal of Health* with a picture of "Ilona Massey, United Artists Star." This November 1941 issue is an early example of consumer health food magazines placing film stars on their covers. From the personal collection of the author.

Hauser and Bragg were far from alone in drawing attention to Hollywood's interest in natural foods. From the 1930s through the 1960s, the health food industry frequently publicized this connection through advertisements and other promotional material. Nor was California the only base for establishing these relationships. Alvenia Fulton—who, in Chicago in 1958, opened what may have been the country's first black-owned health food store oriented to a black clientele—used the tag line "Diet Consultant to the Stars," as she advised figures such as Dick Gregory, Eartha Kitt, Ossie Davis, and Ruby Dee, among others.[26] The Hollywood theme was emphasized, not just by and for the benefit of individual entrepreneurs, but by representatives of the industry as a whole. Such references started to appear in the late 1930s[27] and became much more frequent during the next two decades (see figure 4). At its 1944 convention, the National Dietary Foods Association named film actress Barbara Hale as Miss Health Foods.[28] From the mid-1940s through the 1950s, *Let's Live*, one of the most widely read periodicals associated with the health food industry, featured performers on most of its covers[29] and during 1945 ran a monthly news column "about filmsters who take care of their health."[30] *Better Nutrition*, a monthly consumer magazine distributed through health food stores, also put film stars on its covers in the 1940s and 1950s[31] and by the late 1950s ran its own regular column titled "Report from Hollywood," which centered on a profile of a Hollywood health food fan. In one typical piece, actor Vincent Price informed readers, "I adore natural foods, especially fruits. In fact, I'm practically a fruit addict, and they have only the best at the Health Food Stores" (quoted in Braun 1964). Such remarks indicated support for health food businesses as well as for natural foods principles. In this way, key institutions of the health food field sought to transform the image of the natural foods lifestyle by associating it with personalities who were cultural role models for many Americans. With the help of celebrities, natural foods inched closer to the mainstream.

Speaking to the Mainstream

As a larger potential audience for natural foods ideas grew, lecturing started to become an adjunct to other ways of spreading the word. Of course, lecturers had long extended their reach through the use of multiple media platforms. They published books, wrote newspaper columns, and occasionally hosted radio shows. But for decades, the live speaker had been the main attraction. By the 1950s, lecturers were still important, but other media, capable of reaching a bigger and more diffuse audience, came into their own. Natural foods periodicals grew in number, though most had small readerships. One important exception was the series of magazines founded by Jerome I. Rodale, who was the most influential early American advocate of organic farming. Rodale's publications spurred an interest in organics, especially *Organic Gardening* magazine, founded in 1942, followed in 1948 by the *Organic Farmer* (the two merged in 1954). His *Prevention* magazine, started in 1950, had a broader natural health orientation and eventually became one of the country's biggest-selling periodicals, with circulation among the top twenty magazines by the mid-1980s.[32] Rodale's publications, as well as some other consumer periodicals, such as the aforementioned *Let's Live* and *Better Nutrition*, worked symbiotically with the health food industry. The communication outlets promoted health food through their editorial content, and health food advertisers became financial supports of the publications.

Not just periodicals but other natural foods printed material, including pamphlets and cookbooks, were key educational tools. The ability of books to reach a large, and more mainstream, audience became apparent by the 1950s. Hauser published his *Look Younger, Live Longer* in February 1950. It was the third biggest-selling nonfiction book that year, and the top-selling book (fiction and nonfiction) in 1951 (Hackett and Burke 1977, 152–56). *Look Younger, Live Longer* was a much-discussed phenomenon, with major news outlets marveling over how a health food proponent could become so popular; even as staid a publication as *Reader's Digest* excerpted the book. Booksellers' willingness to carry the book was what allowed it to become a best seller; prior to *Look Younger, Live Longer*, most bookstores shunned natural foods titles. Nevertheless, health food stores still moved large quantities of the book. In 1950, approximately two hundred thousand copies were sold through bookstores, and more than seventy-five thousand through health food stores (Hackett and Burke 1977, 163). Indeed, while Hauser's book removed the barrier to natural foods treatises being stocked in bookstores, health food distribution networks remained important sources of books. This strength was again demonstrated in 1965 when Brownies health food store set a record for the number of books of any kind sold at a New York City book-signing event, with eleven hundred copies of Carlton Fredericks's *Food Facts and Fallacies* selling in a single day.[33]

Hauser's various titles continued to do well over the years—by the 1980s, more than 50 million copies had sold (F. Murray 1985)—as did select other books. Another highly popular natural foods title was D. C. Jarvis's *Folk Medicine: A Vermont Doctor's Guide to Good Health*, first published in 1958. It became the second best-selling nonfiction book in the United States in 1959, and the top-selling nonfiction book in 1960, with a half million copies sold over those two years, and 4.5 million by 1975 (Hackett and Burke 1977, 177, 181, 12). Natural foods advocate Adelle Davis's biggest-selling books, *Let's Cook It Right* (1947), *Let's Eat Right to Keep Fit* (1954), and *Let's Get Well* (1965) were also major hits, selling a combined 10 million copies by 1975 (Hackett and Burke 1977, 15). The popularity of these books indicated not a readership that had adopted a complete natural foods lifestyle but consumers willing to be a little daring in their personal health and eating habits. They perhaps used apple cider vinegar as a remedy for colds or added some honey or wheat germ to the pantry, but they rarely gave up altogether on the "overprocessed and overrefined" (Davis 1954, 223) foods condemned by the best-selling authors.

An even broader sector of the population was exposed to natural foods ideas through the new medium of television. Health food advocate Lewis Arnold Pike developed what may have been the first television programming devoted to natural foods, *Diet Diary*, which aired in Los Angeles in 1952 (Millar 1972). As a local and short-lived program, it had a limited audience, though in the 1970s, Pike went on to host a syndicated celebrity-filled show, *Viewpoint on Nutrition*, which was sponsored by the primary health food trade association. The 1960s *Jack LaLanne Show* had much wider distribution; still, as a syndicated rather than network program, its reach was uneven. Instead of programming with an educational bent, it was comedic talk shows in the early 1960s that were the first truly mass broadcast outlets to offer the natural foods philosophy a platform, thanks mostly to host Steve Allen. Through such shows, television did increase public awareness of natural foods. But television favored the most spectacular displays of eccentricity by natural foods advocates and countered a Hauserian image of dignity and reasonableness with one of extremism and irrationality.

There was, for instance, Bragg's appearance on a 1963 *Steve Allen Show* episode that had Allen jumping up and down on Bragg's chest. And it is surely no accident that the only self-identified advocate who became a regular guest on television at this time was Gypsy Boots, the athletic and flamboyant "Nature Boy" (see chapter 3) who favored living outdoors and eating raw nuts and fruits. Boots first came to public attention as a contestant on Groucho Marx's *You Bet Your Life* in 1955. But he gained national recognition through his multiple appearances on the *Steve Allen Show*; he was a guest at least ten times between 1962 and 1964, playing the part of health food "kook" (S. Allen 1965, iii). Allen clearly respected Boots, but the show emphasized Boots's eccentricities, with much of the humor revolving around his eating habits. In one typical episode, Boots fed Allen nuts and raisins, with Allen remarking that he would do "anything to stop eating this strange stuff."[34] For Boots, these sorts of theatrics were the price of appearing on national television. As he recalled, "I did a lot of running around and yelling on Steve's show, but underneath it all was a serious effort to promote health" (Boots 1965, 62). Boots did bring wider recognition to the natural foods movement, but the entertainment bias of television accentuated the outlandish while giving short shrift to the serious. Such antics reinforced the skepticism of viewers already primed to dismiss natural foods. For average Americans to be willing to integrate natural foods into their diets, they needed reassurance that they could use particular substances without having to adopt the countercultural baggage that was still attached to a natural foods lifestyle.

Broadening the Market, Changing the Meaning

The way that star spokespeople such as Gayelord Hauser could captivate an audience, and the fascination that Americans had with celebrities who proclaimed the merits of natural and health foods, helped persuade a broadened range of Americans to experiment with these foods. But equally important in building a path to the mainstream were changes in the message itself. Less often was heard a religious rationale for trying natural foods. More muted was a reverence for nature and condemnation of industrial society. Assurances of good health and energy continued, consistent with statements of the past, but what was now at the forefront was an emphasis on beauty and appearance as an outcome of diet choices. The appeal of Hauser's books *Eat and Grow Beautiful* (1936), *Look Younger, Live Longer* (1950), and *Mirror, Mirror on the Wall: An Invitation to Beauty* (1961) was contained in the titles; by consuming vitamins, vegetable juices, and other health foods, he promised, the reader would achieve lasting good looks. The deepening emphasis on beauty was apparent in the rash of articles in natural foods magazines, starting in the 1940s and continuing through subsequent decades, with titles such as "Blackheads" ("Rub a little lemon juice on the inflamed spot"),[35] "Nutrition Builds Four Beauties" ("These four youngsters are models. . . . They ate whole grain cereals, plenty of fruits and raw vegetables just as soon as their baby teeth could cope with them"),[36] and "Beauty After Forty" ("The first rule of beauty is to have an internally clean, wholesome and healthy body"; Layna 1958). Throughout 1955, each issue of *American Vegetarian-Hygienist*, the monthly publication of the American Vegetarian Union, included a cover girl to illustrate how vegetarianism and natural living promotes beauty. As one typical caption said, "Our 'cover girl' this month is Miss Lenora Glick, a vegetarian lovely of Philadelphia, Pa. Lenora is an outdoor girl and a charming example of what Natural Living will do for beauty."[37]

The 1940s and 1950s were a turning point in the natural foods movement, as natural foods took on a wide array of competing meanings. The tension between simple foods obtained directly from nature and complex health food fabricated by commercial manufacturers had existed since Kellogg's early products. But now, the meaning of a natural lifestyle was stretched even further. For instance, Hauser's *Look Younger, Live Longer* did not end with diet advice. Hauser saw no contradiction in advocating plastic surgery, facial hair removal, and other techniques to improve on the natural-but-imperfect body. His message emphasizing individual well-being and personal transformation coexisted with pronouncements of other leaders who stressed the harm being done to the natural and social worlds by an industrial order. One such leader was Rodale, who not only advised eating organically grown produce for health reasons but also in the 1950s made the connection between a deteriorating food supply and those companies that profited from the spread of a "chemical ideology," stating, "We are involved in an economic, industrial system, a competitive cash culture, which is based on selling harmful things to each other. For every dollar we earn, directly or indirectly, we must take a certain quota of poison; otherwise the powers that control our destinies believe that our whole prosperity will collapse. What a mockery! And in this crazy system is involved the use of chemical fertilizers and poisonous insecticides" (J. Rodale and Adams 1954, 193). Hauser's upbeat invitation to explore new consumer opportunities and Rodale's forceful warnings against the false promises of consumer culture were in many respects contradictory. Yet both ideals were central to what the natural foods movement came to stand for as it moved forward.

Similarly, vegetarianism, which in the nineteenth century had been the original expression of the natural foods movement, was still a core value for some advocates but was increasingly pushed to the background by prominent spokespeople of the mid-twentieth century. Early in his career, Hauser advised consuming minimal amounts of meat, saying that even the most physically active persons should have a couple completely meatless days each week (1930, 21–23). By the mid-1940s, though, he reassured readers that he was not a vegetarian himself, and he warned against adopting strict vegetarianism without training in nutrition (Hauser 1944, 4, 16). Going even further, Adelle Davis insisted that meat is an essential source of nutrition. She was especially keen on brains, liver, kidneys, and other organs. Since their function in living animals is to carry on vital life processes, she reasoned, they help provide humans with some of the same when eaten (Davis 1947, 109). Her recipe for Brains in Casserole, made with wheat germ and American cheese (Davis 1947, 114), exemplified the mishmash of mainstream and unconventional styles that intrigued growing numbers of Americans.

Rodale was as much respected as Hauser and Davis within the health food industry. And the industry continued to have within its ranks staunch vegetarians. But the health food industry's financial interests were better served by spokespeople like Hauser who coaxed Americans into trying out a few additions to their diets than by those like Rodale who explicitly called on the public to reject an entire agroeconomic system. By showing that it was possible to eat health food in small doses and stay within the cultural mainstream, the moderate approach widened the market for health food, though it was accomplished by drawing in consumers with shallow commitments. The growing group of occasional health food consumers made possible the further expansion of the health food industry. But their presence also highlighted the ways in which primary goals of the natural foods movement—to broaden the base of support and to radically reform people's eating habits and the food production system—could be in conflict.

Despite the appeal of such star spokespeople as Hauser, the extent to which natural foods achieved legitimacy by this time should not be exaggerated. As the treatment of natural foods by television demonstrates, the link between the unconventional and glamour was still fragile. Even beyond the 1960s, as subsequent chapters will discuss, health food retained a reputation as unpalatable and marginal to the average diet, and enthusiasts who made natural foods a way of life were still viewed as eccentric and largely deluded in their beliefs. Moreover, despite the way that celebrities made natural foods less about morality and more about self-realization, the natural foods movement had not become depoliticized. As the next chapter describes, the field retained its defiance of conventional authorities, who in turn sought to quash it. This dynamic helped further solidify the identity of interests between the natural foods movement and the health food industry.

CHAPTER FIVE

Questioning Authority

The State and Medicine Strike Back

Despite gaining a foothold among new constituents in the mid-twentieth century, the natural foods movement remained small and with limited influence until the 1970s. Most Americans did not take its grand pronouncements seriously, and most of the country's central institutions—established systems of government, agriculture, industry, health care, and education—dismissed as nonsense the reforms advocated by its supporters. On the face of it, this movement appeared to pose little threat to dominant food and health practices. Yet, the movement and the health food industry that led it attracted fierce opposition from some quarters and, since the early part of the twentieth century, significant state-sanctioned repression.

In this chapter, I describe the conflict taking place between natural foods advocates and their opponents, hostilities that lasted for most of the twentieth century. While the natural foods movement had the potential to undermine economic interests in the food sector, its ability to realize that potential was minimal until the latter part of the twentieth century. Underscoring the movement's lack of clout in this area, conventional agriculture and food companies mostly ignored the natural foods field before the 1960s. Instead, what generated vehement condemnation soon after the health food industry came into existence was the movement's challenge to the authority of those who claimed expertise in the care of the human body. Underlying this challenge was a rejection of the ostensibly rational criteria those authorities employed—scientific consensus and calculable measures of efficacy—to determine what health practices were in the individual's best interests. In this way, seemingly private decisions about feeding the self became a proxy for social judgments on modern standards of rationality.

The health professions, including physicians, dentists, and dieticians, thus viewed activities by health food purveyors and related nature cure practitioners as not just economic competition, but also cultural competitors who called into question the very foundation of a medicoscientific worldview. Alarmed by the persistence of naturopathic philosophies, the health professions enlisted the state to help protect their privileges and status. Leading the fight was the American Medical Association (AMA), which conducted an active campaign to discredit the principles and promoters of natural foods. The AMA worked closely with government bodies, especially the US Food and Drug Administration (FDA), the Federal Trade Commission (FTC), and the US Postal Service, as well as nongovernmental entities such as the Better Business Bureau and conventional food trade groups, to suppress natural foods advocacy. As a result, from the 1930s through the 1960s, many of the most prominent proponents of natural foods were arrested, with some serving prison sentences, generally on charges related to fraudulent health claims.

The health food industry was a particular target of these efforts. Heavy involvement by commercial enterprises in the natural foods movement opened it up to charges of economic self-interest and exploitation of vulnerable consumers. The AMA and its allies cultivated sympathetic journalists and educators and utilized their own publications to steer the public away from health food products and businesses. Pressure was put on media outlets and lecture halls to deny spokespeople a platform for promoting health food. Especially in the second half of the twentieth century, legislation restricting industry activities was frequently proposed. And from the 1940s to 1960s, government raids of health food stores, in which books and other promotional literature were confiscated, put those businesses at the front lines of conflict between the natural foods movement and its opponents.

The targeting of health food businesses by institutionalized authorities helped define the terms of public debate and the direction that natural foods advocacy took in three key ways. First, adversaries reinforced the culturally marginal status of the health food industry by highlighting the industry's distance from the mainstream institutions that condemned it. Second, the campaigns against them deepened the sense by industry members that they were participating in a cause bigger than their own personal livelihoods. And third, such campaigns made the right to engage in commercial activities and to patronize commercial enterprises central goals of the natural foods movement.

The nature of the opposition to natural foods, and the corresponding importance placed on the right to consume the goods and services of the health food industry, introduced a strong libertarian strand into the movement. Natural foods advocates objected to regulatory agencies precluding individuals' decisions about how to care for their own bodies. With the government and organized medicine appearing dictatorial in their attempts to mandate drug-centered health practices, proponents of natural foods often joined forces with other naturopathic "health freedom" causes, including antivaccination and antifluoridation campaigns. Such alliances exacerbated the dim view of the natural foods field taken by government and health professionals. But these alliances also increased the ranks of supporters willing to be confrontational in their defense of the health food industry. By the 1950s, organized efforts to defend health food commerce came not just from trade associations but from citizen advocacy groups as well, the most effective of which was the National Health Federation. These efforts included rallying the public to oppose restrictive legislation, using the courts to challenge government actions, and on at least one occasion, marching on Washington.

Thus, by the middle of the twentieth century, and with lasting results into the present, the politics of natural foods were defined principally in terms of defying professional medicine's claims of exclusive jurisdiction over health matters and the related paternalistic policies of the state. In particular, the act of consuming unorthodox products with unproven worth held political meaning, as it represented a conscious rejection of the state's protections and the guidance of certified experts. The efforts of the health food industry's opponents had helped create a situation wherein manufactured consumer goods and the businesses that sold them became symbols of the superiority of nature.

Cultural Authority in Question

While the natural foods movement became more enmeshed with consumer capitalism as the twentieth century progressed, there were some natural foods followers who advocated renunciation of the entire industrial-capitalist system. Perhaps the best known in the first half of the twentieth century were Ralph Borsodi and Helen and Scott Nearing, who became models for the back-to-the-land movement. Beginning in the 1930s, the

Borsodi and Nearing families (separately) engaged in efforts to be completely self-sufficient and to live independent of market relations, growing food to satisfy their own needs, not to produce a surplus. Both families drew connections between an industrial economy made up of factories that enslaved workers desperate for a job and a factory system of food production that resulted in inferior nourishment (Borsodi 1933, 1947–48; Nearing and Nearing 1954). The Borsodi and Nearing endeavors represented an ethic that saw the antidote to capitalism in establishing small-scale, communal, subsistence farming endeavors as well as lifestyles with diets (in the Nearings' case, vegetarian) uncontaminated by synthetic additives or industrial processing.

The Nearings in particular would inspire later generations of do-it-yourself communards. However, most of their contemporaries in the natural foods movement did not bring with them an anticapitalist agenda. They were frequently critical of an alienating industrialization process in which large enterprises pushed out small-scale farmers and which put profits above quality and health in food. But at least before the 1960s, few natural foods proponents turned their backs on commerce altogether. Indeed, with so many involved in running small businesses—and a few gaining some wealth in the process—they tended to support the economic opportunities presented by a free market.

Even if expressions of radical economic reform were not the norm, the natural foods movement did seek to transform dominant systems of food production, distribution, and consumption, potentially threatening a vast array of private companies and associated networks of researchers and consultants. Still, during the first two-thirds of the twentieth century, most conventional food producers and distributors did not worry about an end to business as usual. Indeed, they rarely paid much attention at all to the natural foods movement. From a commercial point of view, there was no compelling reason to do otherwise; customers were not clamoring for health food in grocery stores, retailers were not asking their suppliers about natural foods lines, and farmers were not inquiring with the makers of synthetic fertilizers and other inputs about alternatives. Sales of health food or organic produce were simply too small to pique interest in capitalizing on them. For much of the conventional agrifood sector, then, natural foods were essentially irrelevant.

Similarly, the natural foods movement's ability to achieve other longstanding goals remained elusive. Natural foods advocates continued to challenge mainstream assumptions about the relationship between humans and nature, especially the view that nature is to be manipulated for

human purposes and that progress is equivalent to ever-increasing technical sophistication. And they disputed dominant beliefs about the symbolic
and practical merits of particular food substances and dietary customs,
questioning, for example, the superiority of meat. But these ideals had
limited popular appeal and, like the political economic critique of the conventional food system, would gain enough resonance to potentially effect
large-scale change only in the latter part of the twentieth century.

Thus, for decades on end, the economic, environmental, and culinary
challenges of the natural foods movement were easily shrugged off by opponents of its philosophies and goals. On the other hand, the challenge
that consistently provoked a stern backlash was the movement's defiance
of the state-supported domains of professional medicine, nutrition, and
science. The reaction of the health professions at first appears to be something of a puzzle since it was far out of proportion to any economic losses
they faced from natural foods followers deserting conventional medicine.
However, the active opposition of health professionals becomes more comprehensible when considering the challenge being made to their cultural
authority. These groups had not just economic interests at stake but also a
strong desire to preserve public deference in their areas of expertise. Their
outsize campaign against the natural foods movement demonstrates that a
cultural threat can be felt just as keenly as a threat to economic interests.

Paul Starr has described the rise of the medical profession in the nineteenth century and its eventual ability to command cultural authority, which
he defines as "the construction of reality through definitions of fact and
value" (1982, 13). After the professional authority of licensed physicians
gained legitimacy, Starr argues, they were able to achieve a near monopoly
over medical practice and exclude other kinds of practitioners, such as mid-
wives and chiropractors, through market control and government regulation. Among those to whom such exclusionary processes applied were naturopathic doctors and others employing natural foods as health remedies.
While the state was generally cooperative in erecting formal barriers to
block these rival practitioners, professional medicine's cultural authority
could be preserved only with continuous efforts to delegitimize its competitors in the eyes of the public. In this goal, professional medicine was not
entirely successful.

The primary way in which the natural foods movement undermines the
medical profession's claims to exclusive expertise in the care of the body is
not actually through putting forward a rival cadre of doctors but by suggesting that doctors of any kind are mostly superfluous. Joseph Gusfield notes

that natural foods movements are oriented toward a "popular medicine" that does not depend on professional physicians but instead sees ordinary people as capable of understanding and directing their own health (1992, 78–79). Although there is actually considerable variation in the extent to which individuals adopting natural foods bypass conventional medicine, a philosophy that views nature, rather than interventionist physicians, as the best healer of illness represents some degree of indifference to institutionalized sources of authority and knowledge as well as the incursion of alternative means for determining worth in realms that have been largely claimed by a rational-technical logic. Natural foods proponents were quite conscious of and explicit about the cultural competition they posed to the medical establishment. Stated a 1967 editorial in the *National Health Federation Bulletin*, "The holier-than-thou attitude of the AMA is unfortunate, particularly when every doctor knows, and will admit, if he is honest, that it is nature, not the doctor, which heals. True, each uses different tools, but the natural life force of the patient is the final determining factor. *So this healing power is not limited to the AMA*."[1]

The natural foods movement's philosophy of health clashes with the logic of professional medicine, not simply in its beliefs regarding nature but at a broader level, in three related respects. First, in contrast to professional medicine's emphasis on achieving consensus among experts who weigh replicable empirical evidence, movement followers favor personal experience as a valid determinant of truth. Second, the movement values religious, ethical, or political ideals as equivalent to calculable measures of efficacy and efficiency when developing food consumption strategies and assessing outcomes. And third, unlike the medical mainstream, which generally finds moderation in thought and deed both practically and morally superior, a natural foods philosophy may endorse a principled extremism. In sum, natural foods proponents rely on sources of knowledge and use standards for evaluating the merits of their behaviors that are not necessarily connected to the faithful application of the scientific method or to the cautious judgments of certified scientific experts.

When it comes to science, most of the claims of a natural foods philosophy cannot be definitively proven true, though most also cannot be definitively proven false. Certainly, scientific study shows that if left alone, nature does not always heal. Indeed, one need only look back on the respiratory scourges of the era before antibiotics to see how frequently sick people would worsen and die without the tools of contemporary conventional medicine. Furthermore, to this day, scientific research rarely determines that any single food substance cures or even protects against specific diseases. Nor does science show direct causal links between most government-approved additives, pesticides, herbicides, or bioengineered foods and specific illnesses;[2] nor is there proof that organically produced foods have more nutrients than conventionally produced food.

However, from a natural foods perspective, the narrow way in which medical science typically poses its questions, insists on consistent and replicable results, and demands a clear understanding of causal mechanisms represents a kind of tunnel vision that makes it unlikely to recognize natural foods' value. Medical science tends to deal with statistical probabilities and aggregates of people, and it selects treatments only when evidence shows that for a given population, such treatments perform better than placebos. For natural foods proponents, on the other hand, the existence of positive individual responses, as indicated by those individuals' subjective states of feeling, is proof enough that a natural foods diet has merit.[3] In this view, the absence of identical outcomes across a population is not a reason to discount natural foods; instead, it is important to acknowledge individual variation in how people respond to diet. Moreover, the reductive nature of science, which examines specific nutrients or indicators of specific physiological responses to nutrients, is at odds with the naturopathic philosophy of "holism," that is, considering how a health regime in its entirety—diet, exercise, relaxation, etc.—has effects on energy, vitality, and other imprecise but (from the individual's experiential perspective) essential measures of good health.

It is important to underscore that throughout the twentieth century, natural foods proponents did not reject the very concept of science. As I have previously discussed, they often tried to don the mantle of scientific authority by referring to scientific studies that supported their conclusions or that they themselves conducted. But what natural foods advocates did by and large reject were institutionalized gatekeepers with the ability to designate what is or is not good science and corresponding claims of consensus, by the mainstream scientific community, that a natural foods diet was ineffective and conventional food products were healthy.[4]

Furthermore, natural foods proponents did not accept the need to erect a fire wall between scientific approaches and other value-laden considerations when assessing the effects of their chosen diet. This standpoint confounded movement critics who often framed support for natural foods in psychological terms, seeing in followers' refusal to accept prevailing scientific evidence an irrational emotional response. Asserted one medical researcher who equated interest in health food with faddism, "Food faddism persists, I believe, despite incontrovertible scientific evidence denying its special validity, because an effective appeal is made by faddists to the emotional drives of people and not to their intellects" (Olson 1955, 777; see also, among others, Olson 1958; R. Smith 1960, 145; Gittelson 1972). In some cases, observers assumed that natural foods followers must simply be psychologically disturbed. Suspicion that natural foods enthusiasts have personality disorders resulted in a number of studies in the 1960s and 1970s examining, or simply commenting on, their mental health or thought processes (New and Priest 1967; Bruch 1970; West 1972; Calvert and Calvert 1975).

However, natural foods followers' indifference to the kind of knowledge that depends solely on scientific proof was not about psychological deficiency. Rather, it was about allowing religious, political, or ethical ideas to tip the balance in nutritional debates, which were, and continue to be, marked by considerable scientific uncertainty. Especially when scientists do not know enough to say with confidence which foods in what quantities are best for human consumption and when their pronouncements regularly change, then other, seemingly more eternal values can hold authority. In this way, the natural foods movement defined the field of nutrition as moral terrain. And it was clear to advocates that the medical professions were most decidedly not on the side of morality.

The Scourge of Faddism

Although today it may seem common sense that a healthy diet is one rich in fresh fruits and vegetables and whole grains, this view has only very recently become an accepted piece of wisdom among large parts of the American public and nutritional experts alike. In contrast, for most of the twentieth century, scientists, government officials, and the medical establishment endorsed processed foods and meat-heavy diets, and they scoffed at vegetarianism, health food, organic agriculture, and other aspects of a natural foods philosophy. While the general public tended to simply laugh off natural foods practices, many health professionals and their associations—including dieticians, nutritionists, dentists, and physicians—devoted resources to actively combating the natural foods movement, with the health food industry a particular target.

Health professionals largely insisted on the pointlessness of organic and health food while praising the modern industrialized system that produced a plenitude of inexpensive food.[5] The favored label critics used to describe natural foods followers was "faddists," meaning people with foolish and fleeting enthusiasms, who were easily swayed by spokespeople out for self-promotion and profit. The real problem with faddism, health profession-als believed, was that faddists could see alternative healing practices, or even their own intuition about health care, as equivalent to the expertise of trained physicians, dieticians, and the accumulated body of knowledge that drives conventional medicine. As a result, individuals might cavalierly ignore their physicians' instructions and assessments of the worth—or worthlessness—of particular food substances or diets, and they might even decline to consult with regular doctors altogether. This concern was stated explicitly by a Circuit Court of Appeals judge in a 1947 case charging health food manufacturer and promoter Lelord Kordel with making misleading claims about his products: "The danger in this system lies not in any positive unwholesomeness of the articles themselves. As to them as such there is no charge and it may be that they are quite harmless in and of themselves. The danger however, lies in the fact that ignorant and gullible persons are likely to rely upon them instead of seeking professional advice for conditions they are presented to relieve or prevent."[6] Three decades later, the issue was be-ing discussed in the nutritional literature in almost identical terms. As one pair of researchers put it succinctly, "The most serious problem, as men-tioned above in other aspects of food faddism, is the advocation that the reader be his own diagnostician and doctor" (McBean and Speckermann 1974, 1076).

Nutritionists, dieticians, and home economists had long been eager to bolster their own professional credibility by defining health food as a fad and a social problem, and they continued to be key players in denouncing a natural foods philosophy for most of the twentieth century.[7] Likewise, they were also frequently supporters of, and supported by, the conven-tional food industry. Perhaps the most prolific and vociferous individual critic of natural foods in the middle decades of the twentieth century was the nutritionist Frederick J. Stare, head of Harvard University's Depart-ment of Nutrition and the most visible spokesperson for the Nutrition Foundation, an organization of food and chemical producers founded in 1941 and involved in funding and publicizing food-related research. For a quarter century, Stare acted as editor of *Nutrition Reviews*, published by the Nutrition Foundation, and he reached a more general audience through a nationally syndicated newspaper column he wrote for more than thirty-five years. Stare used these organs to condemn the range of tendencies found in the natural foods movement and the health food industry and to defend food additives, white flour, and the use of pesticides in agriculture.[8] Stare's characterization of the natural foods field drew a sharp contrast between victimized followers and profit-driven promoters who preyed on the public's fears to sell them unneeded goods. Combining his defense of conventional food and his criticism of natural foods, he testified before a US Senate committee in 1964: "There is not one single case in the medical literature where there is a single individual whose health has ever been impaired by eating any kind of a food product that had pesticides or insecticide residues left on the food product. . . . So, to scare people saying that you have to buy organically grown food on which no insecticides have been used is only done by those people who have such foods to sell."[9]

Stare had a close relationship with government regulators; he was frequently brought in as a witness for FDA and FTC cases against alternative health practitioners. He cooperated with other food and health organizations, including the AMA. And he cultivated relations with popular media outlets, which readily gave him a platform to air his views. Stare's attacks on natural foods grew more forceful as natural foods grew in popularity, receiving such a wide hearing that on two occasions, members of the health food industry sued him for defamation. In one case Stare was acquitted, and the other suit was dismissed in federal court.[10] The outcomes of these two cases were not surprising since the standard for what is considered libel is quite high in the United States. Indeed, it is doubtful whether the plaintiffs truly thought they would win. Instead, their decision to devote scarce resources to such legal fights was more likely an effort to preoccupy Stare and divert him from his attacks on the health food industry (see F. Murray 1984, 180). At those moments when the natural foods field was attracting greater popular support, Stare's crusade not only hurt health food's public image but also threatened to attract restrictive legislation by government regulators.

The AMA's Crusade

Stare remained a thorn in the side of the health food industry for many years. But even the activity of Stare and his Nutrition Foundation could not compare to the actions of the American Medical Association, whose campaign against the natural foods movement was more long-lived, extensive, and organized than that of any other group. Much of what made the AMA's campaign so effective in marginalizing natural foods is that it went well beyond the commitment of any single individual, being core to the very mission of the medical profession and its organizational bodies. Since its formation in 1847, the AMA had resolved to stamp out a large variety of health practices it deemed quackery. Its efforts included the 1913 formation of a Propaganda Department, under the direction of Dr. Arthur J. Cramp, which investigated and publicized reports of fraudulent claims for the efficacy of health substances, devices, and treatments. The department's name was changed to the Bureau of Investigation in 1925, and then, the Department of Investigation in 1958. For more than sixty years, until the department was finally shut down in 1975, it amassed files on those suspected of illegitimate activities and used multiple means to discredit them (Halling 1947; Field 1982; Hafner, Carson, and Zwicky 1992, viii–ix; Young 1967, 129–37).[11] Included in the department's purview were a wide range of nostrums, patent medicines, and people without medical credentials calling themselves doctors.

Food was one area that got considerable attention by the investigation department and other offices of the AMA. "Of all the people of all the world, Americans are most cursed with faddists; of all the faddists that occupy our attention the food faddists are most eccentric and most comical," wrote Morris Fishbein, the editor of the *Journal of the American Medical Association*, in a volume on quackery (1932, 252). In 1929, the AMA formed its Council on Foods, later called the Council on Food and Nutrition, which issued reports on nutrition and monitored food advertising. The council was committed to discouraging what it considered to be food faddism; it regularly published columns in the *Journal of the American Medical Association* and occasionally produced special educational materials to that end.[12]

From the 1930s through the 1970s, the character of the AMA's criticism of natural foods did not change much. The AMA denounced most variants of a natural foods philosophy but directed its real outrage at health food promoters and the very concept of health food. Concern by physicians about this rival form of health care was exacerbated by the fact that the health food industry was made up of for-profit enterprises, which cast doubt on the purity of health food purveyors' motives. The statements of AMA officials showed what little store they put in the sincerity of people selling a natural foods way of life, and instead they assumed that health food dealers were solely out to make a buck by conning a gullible public with smooth promises of better health.

Of course, there is no disputing that health food promoters often engaged in considerable exaggeration of what health food substances could accomplish, and the pursuit of sales shaped the nature of the arguments health food promoters made. A 1930s promotional catalog for Vegetrate, for example, promised that its various formulas could cure digestive disorders, headaches, hay fever, asthma, high blood pressure, poor complexion, menstrual cramps, and overall "mental and physical bankruptcy."[13] Over the course of the twentieth century, companies grew less bold in their claims, but advertisements in the health food press still frequently made unlikely assertions about product merits. They ranged from the specific, such as a 1959 advertisement for Superb, a product that purportedly would "restore color to grey or faded hair in 30 days after 30 years grey,"[14] to the highly vague, such as an advertisement the same year for Faulkner's Super All-Natural B-Concentrate: "If you've lost some of your energy and zest for living, you've been feeling depressed, irritable or can't concentrate as well as you can, add *Vitamin B Complex* to your daily diet. You will be delighted with the results!"[15] Obviously, such claims were hyperbolic or even outlandish. Yet, while not condoning these pronouncements, it is worth remembering that the AMA did not turn the same skeptical eye to nutritional claims for products from the major food companies. But then, conventional food companies did not encroach on medicine's turf by calling their products *health* food.

What the AMA and similar critics could not acknowledge was that two sets of motives—a genuine belief in the virtues of health food and a desire to cash in on it—could be joined together in such a way that proponents saw their actions as advancing a social good as well as personal interests. Unlike members of the health food industry itself, the AMA did not try to distinguish between true cynics and true believers; in the eyes of medical officials, sales of health food were an inherently cynical enterprise. Because health food businesses had an obvious financial stake in advocating natural foods, the industry was left wide open to charges of hucksterism and consumer exploitation. Although physicians also had a financial interest in treating patients, their recognized status as professionals, rather than entrepreneurs, allowed them to profess to be disinterested. The AMA utilized the medical profession's prestige as well as considerable material resources to quash health food entrepreneurs whether they were driven by moral commitments or not.

The AMA collected its information on natural foods advocacy from a number of sources. Concerned physicians, conventional food companies, and citizens sent in examples of natural foods literature, announcements of lectures and other events, and even samples of health food products or their labels. The AMA clipped news articles and sometimes used commercial information services.[16] Perhaps most aggressively, the AMA occasionally sent out its own undercover investigators. A "special agent" report on a 1932 lecture series by Paul Bragg on "Sex Secrets of the Polynesians" deplored the talk as "without any question, the filthiest, most ungrammatical harangue in the English language that we have ever listened to" and noted with satisfaction that a citation was issued by the San Francisco District Attorney's Office.[17] AMA agents were still attending Bragg lectures in the 1960s, taking particular note of derogatory comments Bragg made about professional medicine.[18] Another major target of the AMA was the National Health Federation; at least two AMA agents became members of the organization between 1966 and 1970, receiving the group's literature and attending some of its meetings.[19]

Yet, perhaps because of the vast number of people and tendencies that caught the AMA's attention, its files remained patchy; they included minutiae on minor players in the natural foods field while having nothing on some of the larger companies, trade organizations, and publications. There was also a midwestern bias to the information collected, reflecting the AMA's headquarters in Chicago. Despite its prodigious efforts to be a clearinghouse of information about what it saw as fraudulent health practices, the AMA produced—and acted on—a highly partial and often inaccurate picture of the natural foods movement.

The AMA encouraged health professionals, educators, journalists, civic leaders, government officials, and citizens to consult the organization to check on the legitimacy of health practitioners and communicators. The organization's eagerness to provide such information could be seen, for instance, in the nine-page response it gave to a 1937 request from a Massachusetts Agricultural Experiment Station professor for information on health lecturers to be used in a bulletin on food fads.[20] In the 1950s and 1960s, the AMA made available to medical societies, schools, clubs, and community groups a kit on food faddism with printed material and an exhibit for display featuring a recording of a door-to-door salesperson's pitch for food supplements. The organization also produced a film called *The Medicine Man*, which spotlighted the perceived problem of lecturers who spread food faddism. The AMA proudly reported in 1964 that the film had been shown more than fourteen thousand times, including more than one thousand television broadcasts.[21] With an eye on the next generation, some efforts were specifically directed to youth and their teachers. Science and civics textbooks suggested that readers write to the AMA for information on quacks and similar topics (Halling 1947, 1036). And in the 1960s, the AMA provided materials focusing on health food and chiropractic for use in teacher training courses on quackery. One distressed health food proprietor in Tacoma reported that children exposed to such a program would come by her store calling out, "quack, quack" and spitting on the store's windows (Carpenter and Moffett 1967, 4–7).

As well as making its own position known, the AMA sought to minimize the ability of the health food industry to reach a wider public. Oliver F. Field, a former FDA inspector and the director of the AMA's investigation department from 1948 to 1973, was especially proactive about contacting groups that gave health food proponents space for disseminating their views. For example, in 1966, he wrote the executive director of the Los Angeles County Medical Association expressing his surprise and displeasure that lecturer Bernard Jensen had been invited to speak at a photography club event being held at Cedars of Lebanon Hospital. The executive director wrote back the following week to assure Field that the matter had been resolved and Cedars would no longer be hosting the talk.[22] Similarly, Field sometimes contacted newspapers about their relations with health food figures. In one case in 1963, he both telephoned and wrote to a *Chicago Daily News* advertising service manager expressing disapproval about an advertisement for a Paul Bragg lecture the newspaper ran. Earlier that month, a set of feature articles on Bragg and advertisements for his lectures carried by the *Chicago Tribune* earned a letter from Field detailing government actions taken against Bragg over the years; for good measure, Field included a twenty-seven-year-old article on charges against Bragg of tax fraud and seduction of a minor. "In the circumstances, it appears that the *Tribune* is doing its readers a disservice in publicizing Mr. Bragg. We thought it was doing a much greater service when [reporter] Miss Browning was exposing Chicago quacks," Field wrote.[23]

Journalists varied widely in how much they consulted with professional medicine for information on the natural foods movement. In some cases, the AMA had success in enlisting journalists to write disparagingly about the movement. Numerous articles closely mirroring the AMA's description of health food appeared in the early 1970s in publications such as the *New York Times*, *Vogue*, and *Life*.[24] A 1972 *Good Housekeeping* article on "The Facts about Those So-Called Health Foods" rehearsed the standard arguments by critics: health foods were an unnecessary expense;

plants do not differentiate between chemical fertilizers and organic fertilizers (the latter almost always defined by natural foods critics as animal manure rather than the compost actually favored by organic proponents); starvation and malnutrition from poor crop yields could be the result of giving up chemical pesticides and fertilizers; enriched foods present an improvement over nature; and a belief in health food can lead people to delay seeking out necessary treatment from doctors. "In addition, the Good Housekeeping Institute says there is no such thing as a 'health food' because no single food supplies, in the proportions required, all the nutrients needed by human beings," the article concluded, using a definition of *health food* that no health food proponent would actually endorse.[25]

Sometimes media coverage was far more focused on the salacious than the scientific. Gayelord Hauser's popularity among celebrities and the public made him a frequent subject of scrutiny, and his sexuality was one means by which journalists could discredit him. The press almost never blatantly stated he was gay, but critical articles used innuendo, for instance, making a point of discussing the residences Hauser shared with Frey Brown, who was frequently depicted as mainly interested in the money Hauser could bring in (Lehman 1951; Busch 1951). One gossip magazine was less subtle. With the headline, "Gay Gaylord [*sic*] attracts rich women like a dog attracts fleas. Here's the INSIDE STORY on this suave, handsome huckster who can switch from saffron juice to sex without batting an eyelash," the 1956 article noted, "Brown and Hauser are not only business associates. They have lived together ever since they started out on their 'health crusade.' Even at the height of Hauser's affair with Garbo, the two men were inseparable, which has led some cynics to call *this* Hauser regime a rather 'queer design for living'" (Mabrie 1956). Yet, the same outlets that provided a platform for health food critics would also report on the growing interest in health food, belying its reputation as a short-lived fad. In this way, the media were unreliable allies in the campaign against health food. Other social institutions, especially federal government agencies, proved to be more faithful opponents, consistently collaborating with the medical profession to curtail health food activity.

Medical, Business, and State Alliances

The health professions led the fight against the natural foods field, but they were not alone in viewing the field as a menace. Other sectors in society could also be mobilized to oppose the activities of natural foods advocates. Until the 1970s, few people working in the conventional food industry took health food seriously, but there were sometimes exceptions to this complacency, and health professionals looked to make common cause with organized business interests whenever they could. In the nineteenth and first half of the twentieth centuries, manufacturers in flour milling and baking were the most prone in the conventional food industry to express worry and irritation about natural foods, noting advocates' condemnation of white flour and synthetic food ingredients.[26] A 1933 letter to the AMA Bureau of Investigation from a representative of a baking soda manufacturer asked about the Chicago Health Food Company, which had been distributing pamphlets on the dangers of baking soda. The correspondent offered a reminder of his company's role as an advertiser in the *Journal of the American Medical Association* and asked "how best to combat the nefarious attack on baking soda." The AMA's Arthur Cramp replied with the reassurance that the pamphlet material "is such rank nonsense that it seems hard to believe it will do very much damage."[27] The AMA continued to defend the safety of commercial leavening agents and, after vitamin and mineral enrichment of white flour began in the 1940s, joined the baking industry in embracing white bread (Council on Foods of the American Medical Association 1939, 377; Wilder 1956).

The primary form of business cooperation with AMA efforts against the natural foods field came not from the food industry but via Better Business Bureau affiliates around the country.[28] The Better Business Bureau frequently turned to the AMA for the latter's views on the legitimacy of a local business, and the Better Business Bureau in turn transmitted such information to its constituents. For instance, in 1947, the Better Business Bureau of Spokane contacted the AMA for guidance when a local newspaper wanted Better Business Bureau approval before carrying an advertisement for a Carlton Fredericks book. After hearing from the AMA, no such approval was forthcoming.[29] By the mid-1960s, the national Better Business Bureau reported progress in convincing media outlets to not accept health food advertising.[30] It also encouraged its member businesses to deny health lecturers space for their events. In these ways, the Better Business Bureau, as the voice of established and trustworthy business, helped define health food firms as illegitimate and worthy of public suspicion.

Such actions reinforced health food's marginal status and were experienced by natural foods advocates as unjustified harassment. Still, an even more effective means of disrupting and discrediting the health food industry was to marshal the power of the state. The AMA engaged in frequent interchange with federal, state, and local government agencies; information was shared between offices to better coordinate the monitoring and prosecution of people and organizations involved in health food. The actions of government were to some degree based on constituent concerns about misrepresentation and adulteration of food, especially in the first few decades of the twentieth century. However, the government's crackdowns on the health food industry were far more forceful than the occasional citizen complaint would warrant. Yet, government's willingness to collaborate with the AMA should not simply be attributed to trying to accommodate an especially vocal interest group. As Michel Foucault has argued (1990, 2153), modern forms of power show their strength less by taking away life (as with executions) and more by managing life, a key component of which is the regulation of biological processes. By allying with professional medicine and demarcating the boundaries of acceptable behavior in eating and health practices, the state could more effectively regulate the maintenance of life and exert control over people's choices regarding seemingly private matters.

A key debate concerning health food in the United States, especially nutritional supplements, is whether this category should be legally defined as a food or a drug. That decision has important implications for how it is regulated, since food items do not face the same restrictions as drugs regarding proof of beneficial effects before they can be sold or incur limits placed on quantities purchased or sources of distribution. Until 1976, when federal legislation put it firmly in the food camp, the status of health food was ambiguous, with variation existing between state laws and inconsistencies in court opinions.[31] At the federal level, both before and after the 1976 legislation, health food fell under the jurisdiction of the Food and Drug Administration; the FDA has the authority to safeguard the safety of both food and drugs, to ensure that descriptions of substances are accurate, and to monitor whether health claims being made cross the line into statements that can only be made about drugs. The FDA has frequently used its authority to brand health food a public menace. But until the 1980s, it was rarely done because of concerns about the intrinsic safety of an item. Instead, the FDA's focus was almost always on misbranding—that is, false or misleading claims made about a good—and on the legitimacy of those people making claims about health food.

In this capacity, the FDA's dealings with the AMA were multifaceted. The AMA often brought to the attention of the FDA persons, firms, or voluntary associations that medical officials believed were engaging in bad behavior. The AMA also encouraged citizens to contact the FDA with similar complaints about health food purveyors. As part of their public outreach efforts, the AMA and FDA worked closely together to produce educational material discouraging the public from using health food. One initiative that highlighted their collaboration resulted in four National Congresses on Medical Quackery, held from 1961 to 1968. These events were full of workshops, talks by government and medical officials, and exhibits on a range of practices considered quackery, with health food often getting center stage. As one skeptical report in the *New Republic* related, "You left this two-day convention with the feeling you had been at a training camp for finks who on their return home could make a collect telephone call any time to the Food and Drug Administration to rat on any doctor not a member of the American Medical Association, the one credential agreed by all to be as authentic as an FBI badge" (Rideway 1963). The FDA went through periods of increased attention to the health food industry, often corresponding to periods of heightened AMA activity. During times of enhanced vigilance, FDA efforts to patrol the health food arena included sending out undercover investigators to enroll in lecturers' classes or apply for jobs as sales canvassers, done with the prospect of overhearing proponents overstep the legal line of what constituted a false claim about a product. Prosecution would then follow (Crawford 1951).

Other federal and state agencies also took action against the health food industry, including the Federal Trade Commission, which has authority to regulate claims made in advertising, and the US Post Office, which could become involved in punitive measures when items intended for unauthorized purposes, or their promotional material, were distributed through the mail. Government action often took the form of warnings, fines, and suspended prison sentences, but it sometimes meant shutting down a firm's operations or jail time for people making or selling health food. Among the earliest federal government actions against health food entrepreneurs was the 1910 prosecution of Frank Fuller, head of the Health Food Company (see chapter 2), who was charged with misbranding his bread product, Health Food Manana Gluten Breakfast Food. The US Department of Agriculture contended that the statement contained on the product label—"It has accomplished a great work with the sick"—was false and misleading because it implied that the product had medicinal value. Fuller pleaded guilty and received a suspended sentence (United

States Department of Agriculture 1910). Another early industry figure, and one who was a frequent target of law enforcement, was the naturopathic doctor and health food store owner Benedict Lust. Beginning in 1899, Lust was arrested sixteen times by New York state officials and three times by federal government authorities, usually on charges of practicing medicine without a license (Kirchfeld and Boyle 1994).[32]

Accusations of practicing medicine without a license or falsely claiming a medical credential were one type of problem that health food promoters, especially lecturers, encountered. Bragg, who ran afoul of the law on numerous occasions, incurred a hundred-dollar fine in 1936 after a lecture series in Washington, DC, that authorities viewed as akin to diagnosing disease and prescribing Bragg's own products.[33] More typically, though, health food promoters were brought up on charges of product misbranding or fraudulent product claims. During the late 1950s and early 1960s, the FDA successfully carried out more than two hundred misbranding actions (Herbert and Barrett 1981, 92–93). Such actions ensnared prominent and respected health food industry figures and fly-by-night entrepreneurs alike.

Were these individuals guilty of the practices with which they were charged? Undoubtedly, they sometimes were, though in other cases, one could take issue with the rather broad definition of something such as "practicing medicine without a license," which posited a lecture to a crowd as equivalent to a medical examination. The point to be made, however, is not that health food entrepreneurs were virtuous in their business dealings, as many most assuredly were not. Instead, it is important to recognize that health food promoters were singled out for behaviors, such as grossly exaggerating the benefits of products and services, which are commonly accepted as standard marketing practices in commerce. It was the selective enforcement of the letter of the law, which was applied to health food businesses in far greater proportion than to conventional businesses, which created among natural foods advocates a sense of solidarity and commitment in the face of what they saw as spiteful harassment.

Dangerous Books

Perhaps the most startling move by the federal government to quash the health food industry and the associated natural foods movement came with attempts to shut down key channels of communication. One agency that was not as cooperative as health food critics would have liked was the Federal Communications Commission (FCC). In 1961, the AMA and Harvard University nutritionist Frederick Stare urged the FCC to take action against radio broadcasts by "unqualified" nutritionists; the suggestion was made to perhaps revoke the licenses of sixty radio stations that allowed such broadcasts. Stare and the AMA were in particular targeting health food lecturer and author Carlton Fredericks, who had a daily radio program heard around the country. In this instance, the FCC declined to be the arbiter of correct nutritional advice but retained the authority to intervene if it determined that fraud did occur.[34] A few years later, Stare was again complaining that the FCC was lax in cracking down on "charlatanism" since it permitted Fredericks and television exercise host Jack LaLanne to remain on the air.[35]

In contrast, government agencies were more aggressive in going after printed material. As discussed in chapter 4, books played an important role in spreading a natural foods philosophy in the mid-twentieth century. Books served the cause even better than television did at this time since advocates who appeared on television were so frequently cast as buffoons, while book authors and sympathetic publishers could exercise greater control over the messages that audiences received. A tradition of strong First Amendment protection and relatively weak libel laws in the United States has meant that in general, authors can present their views in print with limited outside interference, especially those writers who avoid sexual content.[36] There were some, such as Frederick Stare, who nevertheless suggested that Congress consider how to legislate against health food books.[37] Although lawmakers did not agree to venture into the legal minefield of prior restraint, the federal government did try to regulate natural foods books, largely by redefining them as extensions of actual health foods. In the 1950s and 1960s, the FDA and the FTC targeted natural foods treatises, their publishers, and the health food stores and distributors that sold them by claiming that such materials' mention of various health food substances constituted labeling of or advertising for specific health food products.

The opening gambit in this campaign came with the Kordel case. Lelord Kordel was one of the more prominent mid-twentieth-century lecturers and authors. Like other health food promoters, he sold a line of his own branded products. In 1945, the federal government charged Kordel with misbranding drugs and fined him $4,000. The basis for the charge was that along with shipping his vitamin, mineral, and herbal supplements to dealers across state lines, Kordel also shipped pamphlets and circulars about arthritis and other health topics, which discussed these supplements. The pieces of literature had their own prices stamped on them, and some dealers sold the pamphlets separately, while others included the literature gratis with the sale of supplements. The heart of the ensuing legal case hinged on whether the literature, which was sometimes shipped to dealers in the same container as the supplements, but usually not, "accompanied" the Kordel supplements. In the 1948 US Supreme Court decision upholding the government's position, Justice William O. Douglas wrote, "In this case the drugs and the literature had a common origin and a common destination. The literature was used in the sale of the drugs. It explained their uses. Nowhere else was the purchaser advised how to use them. It constituted an essential supplement to the label attached to the package.... Every labeling is in a sense an advertisement. The advertising which we have here performs the same function as it would if it were on the article or on the containers or wrappers."[38] The decision in this case set a precedent that government agencies and the courts subsequently used in upholding the legality of linking natural foods literature with specific health food articles.

Following the disposition of the Kordel case, the FDA and FTC pursued several other high-profile health food authors and moved from associating labeling with booklets to an association between labeling and formally published books. In 1951, the FDA seized 120 jars of Plantation Blackstrap Molasses, 25 copies of Gayelord Hauser's best seller, *Look Younger, Live Longer*, and 26 copies of a booklet by Cyril Scott called *Crude Blackstrap Molasses* from a Rochester, New York, health food store. The manufacturer of Plantation Molasses, the Allied Molasses Co., had an agreement with Hauser to use a picture of him on the label along with the words, "Recommended and Endorsed by Gayelord Hauser." With the Rochester Nature Food Centres store displaying jars of molasses and the book together, the government said that the books served as labels for the molasses. And since statements in Hauser's book extolled the benefits of blackstrap molasses in general (though never mentioning any specific brand), the FDA charged misbranding.[39] Later that year, Farrar, Straus, & Young, the publisher of *Look Younger, Live Longer*, advised health food stores to not refer to the book in any way when selling any food mentioned in *Look Younger, Live Longer*.[40]

During the 1950s and 1960s, health food retailers reported FDA inspectors entering their stores to examine literature and product labels.[41]

Among the actions taken by the FDA involving health food books as labeling were the 1961 seizure of supplements, along with Carlton Fredericks's book *Eat Live and Be Merry*, from a Varna, Illinois, health food store, and the 1962 seizure of 58,000 safflower oil tablets along with 1,600 copies of Herman Taller's best seller *Calories Don't Count*.[42] Kordel was the subject of two other FDA actions in 1961: first, when the agency seized 198 jars of honey along with booklets and leaflets about honey from his Detroit retail establishment,[43] and second, when Kordel was indicted following a lecture series where he sold his books and food products. For this latter incident, Kordel was fined $10,000 and served a year in prison.[44]

While the FDA focused on books as equivalent to labeling, the FTC pursued books as forms of advertising. This was actually a dual strategy, with the FTC primarily scrutinizing the content of marketing material promoting books to determine whether it additionally acted as advertising for health food items and secondarily looking at whether actual book content constituted advertising for health food. Although it generally did not have the authority to prohibit the expression of ideas in a book, the FTC asserted that promotional material for a book did not have the same protections as the book itself. The FTC issued complaints of false claims in advertising for natural foods books at least as early as 1957.[45] However, most such actions occurred in the early 1960s. For instance, in 1963, the FTC brought charges against the same book, *Calories Don't Count*, that the FDA had targeted a year earlier. The FTC said that the book, published by Simon & Schuster, was used as advertising for safflower oil capsules and that promotional material for the book made false medical claims.[46] That same month, the FTC filed a complaint against publisher Farrar, Straus and its advertising agency for making false, misleading, and deceptive health claims in its advertising for Hauser's book *Mirror, Mirror on the Wall*. The complaint identified both self-contained advertisements and the copy on the book jacket.[47] Similarly, the FTC filed a cease and desist order in 1964 against an advertising brochure for J. I. Rodale's book *The Health Finder*, stating that the brochure made unfounded health claims (Kilpatrick 1965, 1967). After these cases against some of the biggest-selling natural foods books of the era, publishers were more careful about what was said in their advertising, though they did not stop publishing natural foods books altogether.

All these actions by the FDA and FTC caused considerable consternation in the natural foods movement but received relatively little public attention, probably because even though mainstream publishers were behind many of the targeted books, it was the not-fully-respectable health food stores, rather than regular booksellers, which faced government raids. Through their actions, government agencies demonstrated not only their opposition to the health food industry but also that they took for granted that philosophical ideas about health food could not be separated from the ingestible commodities that put those ideas in material form. The linking of literature with food products was then a way both to impede the sale of health food and to halt the ability of advocates to publicize natural foods ideals.

The issue of confiscating literature finally came to a head with another court case, which was decided at the end of 1964. In this case, copies of two popular D. C. Jarvis titles, *Folk Medicine* and *Arthritis and Folk Medicine*, along with a cider vinegar–honey product whose manufacturer was mentioned in the two books, were seized from the New York health food wholesaler Balanced Foods. Balanced Foods fought the initial judgment against it, and a US Circuit Court of Appeals ruled in favor of the wholesaler. In the majority opinion, Judge J. Edward Lumbard said that there was no evidence that the books and the food product were jointly promoted. Moreover, while never mentioning First Amendment protections, the judge did draw a line regarding the FDA's ability to police the written word. "It is not disputed that [Jarvis's] claims were misleading, but the Federal Food, Drug and Cosmetic Act was not intended to deal generally with misleading claims," he wrote. "In our view, the Food and Drug Act was intended to deal with such claims only when made in immediate connection with the sale of the product."[48] Following this case, the FDA pulled back from its campaign against natural foods books. Literature was still sometimes seized from stores, but only if placed immediately adjacent to a food item. As a practical matter, health food stores tended to simply create separate sections for books. In this way, the health food retailer could straddle the line between dispenser of food and dispenser of philosophy.

The Movement Gets Organized

While the right to sell natural foods books was more secure by the late 1960s, government continued to erect other barriers to conducting business. In the 1960s and 1970s, local officials used sanitation laws, zoning restrictions, and building codes to harass health food stores, some of which were stymied when trying to sell fresh or bulk food (Roth 1977, 60). But a bigger threat came with proposed policies to curb the sale of supplements, which were a financial mainstay of the health food industry. These policies included a set of FDA proposals in 1966 that would have, among other things, set minimum and maximum potencies that were vastly different from what was typical among supplements and required that supplements carry a notice on their labels stating that there is no scientific basis for routinely using them.[49] These and other proposed regulations were tied up in congressional hearings and the courts for years. Perhaps the most controversial was a 1973 proposal by the FDA to require a doctor's prescription for high-dosage forms of vitamins A and D. *High dosage*, in this case, was defined as more than 150 percent of the FDA's Recommended Daily Allowance and would have covered a large proportion of the A and D vitamins sold in health food stores (Schmeck 1973; Bentsen1973). By this time, however, the health food industry and its allies had mobilized large numbers of citizens to oppose the restrictive measures.

During the first half of the twentieth century, although individual natural foods proponents defied authorities, organized collective efforts to oppose government action were uncommon. Achieving legitimacy was very much on the minds of health food industry leaders, and confrontation with the government, especially in the absence of much public support, would likely only underscore health food's marginal status. The desire to avoid trouble helps explain why some in the industry adopted the rather ambiguous term *dietary food* rather than *health food* to describe their businesses, and likewise, why the primary trade association, the National Health Food Association, changed its name to the National Dietary Foods Association (NDFA) in 1943 (see figure 5). But by the 1950s, with growing public interest in health food, the NDFA and regional associations were more assertive in fighting back. Under the NDFA's auspices, the industry formed the Public Relations, Education, Legal, Legislation, & Lobbying program in 1955. Initially, it was mostly focused on public relations, but in 1959, a more combative phase was signaled when attorney Milton Bass was retained as legal counsel (Bernardini 1976; F. Murray 1984, 201–6). For decades, Bass was the principal lawyer for most cases involving industry fights with the government. Subsequent trade association name changes also registered the industry's growing self-confidence. The National Dietary Foods Association became the National Nutritional Foods Association in 1970 and then the Natural Products Association in 2009.

The health food industry trade associations, along with an allied citizen advocacy group, the National Health Federation, were leaders in the

FIGURE 5. Banquet at the 1956 National Dietary Foods Association convention in Pasadena, California. Photograph by Weaver Photo of Los Angeles. From the personal collection of the author.

campaign against supplement restrictions in the 1960s and 1970s. Their efforts included testifying before Congress, lobbying, and filing lawsuits, all typical activities practiced by private interest groups. But they also engaged in activities that spoke to the movement's outsider status. Simultaneous with the 1963 AMA–FDA National Congress on Medical Quackery, the National Health Federation held a National Congress on Health Monopoly just a couple miles away from the quackery event.[50] And showing that street protest was not off-limits for businesspeople, a group of health food retailers, manufacturers, and wholesalers even held a march on the capitol building in Washington, DC, in 1975 (F. Murray 1984, 126–27). But most decisively for affecting public policy, health food advocates became highly successful in mobilizing citizen opposition to restrictive regulations.

Retailers encouraged their customers to write letters to government officials, and the National Health Federation distributed postcards for supporters to send in. Reaching beyond the most committed health food users, the national trade association arranged for spokespeople to appear on radio and television calling on consumers to make their wishes known to their legislators (F. Murray 1984, 133). Throughout these campaigns, advocates emphasized the issue of freedom of choice in health and dietary matters. In 1966, following the FDA's announcement of rules limiting the maximum potency of vitamins, the National Dietary Foods Association took out a telling advertisement in the *Washington Post* depicting a fictional dialogue between a health food store's owners and customers outraged at the rules. In it, one customer says, "If this is consumer protection, I can get along without it!" When the store proprietor remarks, "The FDA claims there is no scientific basis for the routine use of vitamins. They say you don't need them," another customer in the vignette replies, "Must I provide my government with scientific proof that I need something? Can't I just *want* it?"[51] This piece gets to the heart of the politics of natural foods as they had developed in the twentieth century. At stake were the conditions of natural food—particularly health food—sales and consumption. Advocates asserted that the state and scientific elites do not have the right to impose on individuals their standards of health care efficacy or to intervene in a mutually desired relationship between producer and consumer.

These campaigns were highly effective in riling up consumer opposition to government interference in their dietary choices. The FDA repeatedly reported being flooded with letters and petitions protesting attempts to tighten regulations over access to supplements.[52] Congressional representatives were similarly inundated; following the 1973 proposal to classify high-dosage vitamins as drugs subject to a physician's prescription, an estimated one million letters were received by members of Congress about the issue (Lyons 1973; F. Murray 1984, 134). All these efforts against regulation finally proved successful. In 1976, the Health Research and Health Services Amendments of 1976 were signed into law; they included a Vitamins and Minerals provision that gave broad freedom to the sale of supplements and confirmed their legal status as a food.[53]

The industry's ability to enlist consumer support in its quest to maintain control over the sale of supplements demonstrates that businesses are able to mobilize constituents to affect public policy. But this is not to say that private enterprise acts in identical ways to citizen advocacy groups. Defined by their dedication to a cause, citizen advocacy groups are frequently explicit in stating goals, dismissing doubters, and condemning adversaries. Bold gestures and passionate rhetoric can inspire supporters and force opponents to take notice. In contrast, businesses, which need to maintain relationships with customers, suppliers, and regulatory offices, tend to be more cautious when it comes to expressions of dissent that could alienate those partners. While this may limit the radicalism of business participants in a social movement, these same tendencies can also make industry's participation in advocacy efforts more stable over time compared to citizen groups. The role played by the health food industry's main citizen group ally of this era, the National Health Federation, highlights some of these differences between private enterprise and voluntary associations in social movement activity.

The National Health Federation was founded in 1955 by Fred J. Hart, whose activities manufacturing electrical healing devices previously got him into trouble with the FDA. The National Health Federation was formed as a "health freedom" organization with the goal of preserving citizens' rights to choose their own forms of health care. The organization was blunt in its criticisms of the AMA, accusing the professional association of exercising "dictatorial influence" over government agencies and stifling debate about conventional medicine's guiding principles (C. Pratt 1966). The National Health Federation was not the first American organization of its kind; in the second decade of the twentieth century, the American Medical Liberty League and the National League for Medical Freedom were formed to oppose government intervention in health matters and to support health philosophies outside of conventional medicine (Petrina 2008). However, those earlier health freedom organizations were short-lived and did not gain the same kind of public support that the National Health Federation did. By the end of 1971, the National Health Federation had approximately forty-nine thousand members and a staff of thirteen (Crecelius 1972).

The National Health Federation had a number of issues on its agenda, including opposition to the addition of fluoride to public water systems, opposition to mandatory vaccinations, and support for unorthodox cancer remedies—positions that put it at a considerable distance from prevailing scientific wisdom. Adding to its reputation as a culturally fringe group, defense of the health food industry was a central goal from the organization's beginning. Indeed, there were close connections between the National Health Federation and the health food industry. Several of its officers had their own health food businesses, such as Kurt Donsbach, who ran a Southern California health food store, and Royal Lee, a vitamin manufacturer and author of numerous natural foods pamphlets that were widely distributed. Among its long-term members and financial supporters were many prominent individuals and businesses in the industry, including manufacturers, wholesalers, retailers, and magazine publishers.[54]

Eventually, though, the National Health Federation's close cooperation with the health food industry dissipated, along with the group's national visibility. For approximately twenty years, from its founding until the mid-1970s, the National Health Federation was highly effective in helping to secure legislative victories and in showing the clout of the natural foods movement. But the organization became considerably weakened when a split developed in 1980 among organization leaders over accusations of mishandling of funds.[55] As in other natural foods citizen advocacy groups that preceded the National Health Federation, leaders with strong personalities became flash points for disagreement, and periods of infighting left the organization highly insular. Although, as subsequent chapters will discuss, industry trade associations also had periods of conflict, the necessity of industry members putting aside ideological and personal differences in order to conduct business helped to keep relationships intact and to maintain the health food industry as a force in the natural foods movement.

A Libertarian Politics

The National Health Federation is significant not just for its moment of political clout. Additionally, this organization and the assortment of issues it championed highlight somewhat curious tendencies in the politics of the natural foods movement. Despite contemporary assumptions that natural foods supporters occupy the left side of the political spectrum, the natural foods movement actually confounds any simple attempts to characterize it as left or right in its politics. Instead, the most widely shared political strand running through the movement has been libertarian, with both left and right variants represented. In the face of so much repression from established authorities, the natural foods movement developed a deep commitment to the right of individuals to determine their own health practices without being subject to the views of reigning medical opinion or the paternalism of the state. This libertarian philosophy makes it possible to understand how a group such as the National Health Federation could both support the countercultural natural foods movement and show sympathy for positions such as equating water fluoridation with communism.[56]

Indeed, people who might normally be at political odds found themselves strange bedfellows in the natural foods movement. The movement had a tradition of left-wing attacks on the power of conventional agrifood interests, such as the previously discussed figures Borsodi, the Nearings, and Rodale. But there were also those on the right who feared socialist encroachment on free enterprise, such as natural foods advocate Howard Inches, who warned of communist infiltrators trying to get a foothold in the food reform movement, and the John Birch Society, whose publication, *American Opinion*, published a lengthy denunciation of the FDA's "Big Brother" efforts to restrict vitamins (see figure 6).[57] The resonance of the natural foods movement for the political right is perhaps best exemplified by the fact that for decades, the strongest supporter of the health food industry in Congress was Republican Senator Orrin Hatch of Utah, a state with a large presence of health food businesses.

What the various branches of the natural foods movement continue to have in common is antipathy toward a paternalistic state and health sector seeking to determine how people treat their own bodies and evaluate their own well-being. In the mid-twentieth century, both left and right came together to reject heavy-handed regulation and to ensure the continuing availability of health food by supporting those entrepreneurs who supply alternative health remedies. Thus, the natural foods movement's primary demand vis-à-vis the state was to be left alone, with much less effort put into trying to achieve public policies that would mandate natural foods goals, such as the elimination of pesticides. The result was that the interests of the health food industry became central to how the natural foods

FIGURE 6. Front cover of a 1973 booklet published by American Opinion, an affiliate of the John Birch Society. Opposition to Food and Drug Administration proposals to restrict vitamin sales made allies of groups usually at political odds. Reprinted with permission of The John Birch Society, JBS.org.

movement defined itself and its objectives. Opposing constraints on business, patronizing health food stores, and consuming health food products were key means to expression of a natural foods identity. In this way, the health food industry received economic and moral support that helped it expand and maintain its leadership in the natural foods movement.

At the same time that the health food industry was securing its right to sell vitamins, the number of natural foods followers was growing and diversifying. Joining the core constituencies of the past—the old and the sick—were the young and the healthy, brought into the natural foods fold through an upsurge in environmentalism and the counterculture. By the late 1960s, a more radical critique of how society produces, markets, and eats food could be widely heard, and new forms of natural foods production and distribution were innovated. Even following the vitamin victories, the battles with the FDA and medical authorities continued; their acceptance of natural foods lifestyles continued to lag behind popular interest. But by the time a new period of government enforcement emerged in the 1980s, the natural foods movement looked considerably different than it had even ten years earlier. The diversification and radicalization of the prior decade had paradoxically helped move natural foods closer to the mainstream.

CHAPTER SIX

Style

Identifying the Audience for Natural Foods

Few things capture the image of the contemporary natural foods field as well as a Whole Foods market, with its massive size, gleaming fixtures, huge selection of fresh and packaged goods that appeal to knowledgeable foodies, earnest descriptions of community and environmental impacts of products, and, at least for some items, premium prices. Yet, this institution, currently one of the dominant companies in the natural foods industry, could not be more stylistically different from the health food stores of years past. Gone are the small, disorganized, dingy spaces, the meager assortments of tired-looking produce, the displays targeting sickly and elderly customers, and the very term *health food*. Whole Foods' appearance, selection, service, clientele, and even its name represent a dramatic shift in the health food business as well as the cultural meanings and status attached to natural foods.

The elevation of natural foods' social status and the enlargement of the customer base for these goods were gradual processes that accelerated significantly beginning in the 1980s. This rise in its fortunes went hand in hand with the transformation of the category's style—that is, the aesthetic choices and symbols associated with the sale and consumption of natural foods. Since the natural foods movement's earliest days, adherents had struggled, generally unsuccessfully, to control the public image of natural foods and to alter the field's association with unappetizing items consumed by socially marginalized persons and sold by fanatics or charlatans. It was only in the 1980s—following a period of intense opposition by medical and government authorities, heightened mockery by outlets of popular culture, and the embrace of a new generation of

counterculturalists—that the health food industry, now starting to call itself the natural foods industry, found the means to dispel natural foods'
reputation as strange stuff that might be good for health but was unpleas-
ant to obtain and eat.

The use of style was central to these successes in marketing natural
foods. Health food entrepreneurs had always utilized specific imagery,
such as allusions to nature or science, in creating advertising, product
names, and labels. But style took on enhanced commercial importance in
the latter part of the twentieth century, a legacy of the acute consciousness, which developed in the 1960s and 1970s, of how style can be joined
to politics.[1] During these decades, the clothing people wore, the length
of their hair, the materials they used in home furnishings, and the mix of
food on their dinner plates were often intended as political statements: a
declaration of values and a judgment on dominant social practices.

Natural foods played a prominent role in the lifestyle politics of that
era; such food became widely recognized as symbolizing the rejection of
an artificial existence and the violence done to nature and human well-
being. What became known as the counterculture of the 1960s and 1970s
produced a large wave of new adherents, considerably younger in age than
had been typical of natural foods devotees of the past, and it intensified the
association of natural foods with antiestablishment values. These tendencies included a distrust of medical, government, corporate, and media authorities, and a revived do-it-yourself ethic, most fully realized in communal back-to-the-land ventures. While stereotyped images of granola-eating
hippies provided fodder for the continued cultural marginality of the field,
the combination of a vast new market for natural foods, a generation of
people looking for meaningful ways to make a living, and an industry open
to newcomers resulted in an influx of new businesses to the field, many
of them with explicitly political missions and some committed to alternative management and ownership structures. These new enterprises did not
replace but rather coexisted with older organizations to create a highly
diverse and dynamic health food industry.

While the social climate changed by the late 1970s and the counterculture faded, businesses remained aware of the importance of style for
asserting a personal identity, and they consequently used style in more directed and calculated ways to attract customers. Continued expansion of
the natural foods market now depended on reworking countercultural symbols and alternative ideals to fit mainstream sensibilities. A key factor in
achieving this expansion was the development of an aesthetic that, more

successfully than at any time in the past, erased most markers of fringe groups while keeping the concept of nature at the forefront. Design elements incorporated into elaborate—and resource-intensive—packaging and advertising displayed these aesthetics. Of particular importance was a major change in the look of health food stores. A Southern California chain, Mrs. Gooch's, was the most influential in spreading the new aesthetic. By creating clean, efficient, yet theatrical environments, founder Sandy Gooch built stores that were seen as less strange than traditional health food shops but that still promised an out-of-the-ordinary experience. In 1993, when Whole Foods acquired Mrs. Gooch's, it also adopted this style, and it turned the other outlets in its growing empire into glossy, upscale supermarkets that—far from communicating marginality—projected an image of sophistication and professional expertise.

Although the upscale natural foods market of the turn of the twenty-first century appears strikingly different from the countercultural food outlets that preceded it, the mainstreaming process that took off in the 1980s was actually an outgrowth of demographic and stylistic characteristics of the counterculture. For that reason, this chapter looks back on the 1960s and 1970s to show that rather than just being a colorful anomaly, these decades set the stage for the natural foods field to subsequently shed its marginal status. During this era, a number of social factors contributed to new ways of conceptualizing the meaning of natural foods and helped broaden the range of people taking an interest in this way of eating. These developments included a reaction against the conformity of post–World War II culture, which produced a search for greater "authenticity"; resentment of the large institutions that increasingly dominated society; the proliferation and heightened activity of a range of social movements; and a global outlook whereby Americans had more firsthand experience with foreign travel and more direct contact with immigrants settling in the United States.

In recounting the changes that took place in the natural foods field from the 1960s through the 1980s, I pay particular attention to the importance of the symbolic environment, both for furthering the fortunes of the health food industry and in helping to define movement goals. Numerous stylistic elements present in cookbooks, retail outlets, advertisements, newsletters, and other sites of cultural expression interacted with the social organization of natural foods production to shape assumptions about the field's values. A tone that stressed fun or seriousness, the attention given to exotic or familiar ingredients, and the use or absence of religious references all communicated something about the reasons for and purpose of adopting this way of life.

This time period saw considerable tension between competing understandings of a natural foods lifestyle. On the one hand, continuing an older tradition, natural foods stood for the simple life and a renunciation of the system of mass consumption. As Helen Nearing put it in her classic 1980 cookbook, *Simple Food for the Good Life*, "This book . . . is to be for simple-living people who have other things paramount on their minds rather than culinary concerns, than eating and preparing dainty and elaborate dishes. It is not for those who are interested in eating as such. This is for those frugal, abstemious folk who eat to nourish their bodies and leave self-indulgent delicacies to the gourmets. . . . Hundreds of homesteaders we know are raising their food and saying, 'Don't buy it; grow it. Use what you have instead of buying what you don't need'" (Nearing 1980, 8–9, 58).

On the other hand, there emerged a new way of thinking about natural foods that signaled an alternative hedonistic pursuit of culinary and consumer pleasures. In another classic, *The Vegetarian Epicure Book Two*, published in 1978, author Anna Thomas described her work as a cookbook for vegetarians who "don't intend to compromise on the satisfactions of really delicious food" (Thomas 1978, 5). Thomas's section on desserts, for instance, celebrated extravagance and found no conflict between consumer luxuries and a devotion to natural food: "Rich desserts, along with such things as great wines and rare spices, are certainly among the luxury items in the world of food, so one must dismiss all ideas of practicality in even thinking of them. It is fine to be practical when planting a lawn or cooking soup for the family on a cold day, but that is altogether the wrong attitude for choosing tickets to the opera, buying perfume or diamonds, or making a special dessert" (Thomas 1978, 323).

While both *Simple Food for the Good Life* and *The Vegetarian Epicure Book Two* remain in print almost forty years after their initial publication, it was Thomas's vision that ultimately triumphed. By the 1990s, the natural foods field had left behind most hallmarks of asceticism and voluntary deprivation in favor of the promise of novel experiences, extensive choice, and a secular ideal of sustainability. This way of thinking about the value of natural foods was no doubt a reflection of the tenor of the times, but it also indicated the influence of an industry seeking to expand its market. The natural foods movement remained committed to safeguarding personal health by respecting nature, reforming the agrifood system, and defying medical authorities. But it increasingly sought to do so in terms compatible with mainstream consumer practices.

New Approaches to Consumption

The enhancement of consumption opportunities and the development of a new consumer sensibility were actually, in part, spurred by certain kinds of ascetic practices and critiques of industrialism that gained a wide following in the 1960s and 1970s. These cultural ideals and practices laid the foundation for an openness to experimentation and a quest for quality among natural foods consumers that would become more fully realized in later decades. They also helped produce a consumption-oriented social consciousness that broadened and deepened the market for natural foods.

In the first place, a new environmentalist ethos supplied the natural foods field with a politics that increasingly resonated with many Americans. During this time, natural foods became more closely aligned with the environmental movement, as conventional agricultural practices came under scrutiny for their destructive effects on the earth. The focus on farming was a response to the growth of industrialized agribusiness, and especially to a massive increase in the use of pesticides during the years following World War II. As Robert Gottlieb (1993, 83) notes, "By the late 1950s, pesticides had fully supplanted all other pest control methods and insect eradication campaigns. Their use was of such magnitude that significant episodes of harm to wildlife and immediate health impacts on farmworkers began to be recorded throughout the country." The concerns that Jerome Rodale and others in the natural foods field had been discussing for years not only appeared more dire now but also had obvious parallels to other emerging ecological problems caused by unchecked technological development.

One landmark for both the natural foods and environmental movements was the publication of Rachel Carson's *Silent Spring* in 1962. In documenting the presence of the insecticide DDT and related chemicals in the food supply, Carson described both their adverse human health effects and the environmental disaster that such chemicals were causing (R. Carson 1962). Carson's book made a tremendous impact and helped spark interest among a wider public in the consumption of chemical-free foods. *Silent Spring* initiated a trend of periodic food scares connected to the use of pesticides, herbicides, or fertilizers, which would send sales of organically grown produce soaring. Whereas in 1961, Robert Rodale (Jerome's son) advised readers that so little organic food was available for purchase that "you still have to grow your own for the most part," by 1972, it was estimated that organic food sales in the United States had reached $500 million a year (R. Rodale 1961; R. Kotulak 1974).

At the same time that *Silent Spring* provided an incentive for Americans to explore natural foods, Carson's larger environmentalist message was given credence by those already committed to a natural foods diet. Underscoring *Silent Spring*'s popularity among natural foods followers, a health food distributor recalled, "We just sold thousands and thousands of that book."[2] Natural foods advocates were increasingly likely to find common ground between their critiques of contaminated food and environmentalist critiques of air and water pollution, or between a commitment to vegetarianism and a campaign to save the whales. This sympathy for ecological concerns was apparent in the pages of the trade journal *Health Foods Retailing*, which by 1970 periodically ran articles on environmental topics unrelated to the health food domain. Interestingly, Carson did not self-identify with the natural foods movement; it is likely that movement domination by the health food industry was a factor because she took pains to distance herself from all commercial interests (Murphy 2005, 45). Nonetheless, people in the industry perceived her as a champion of their cause and as so closely connected to the heath food industry's mission that its major trade association established an annual Rachel Carson Award, still given out to this day.

Environmentalism provided the natural foods movement with an ideology more accessible to consumers than the movement's prior rationales for revering nature. By conceptualizing a natural foods lifestyle as part of an effort to save nature and an endangered planet's natural resources rather than as giving oneself over to nature to be saved oneself, the natural foods movement could now offer an agenda that did not require wholesale personal transformation. At least in the less radical versions of environmentalist discourse, one need not give up the creature comforts of modern civilization as long as they were produced in an ecologically friendly manner. Thus, something such as a steak—if made from a cow raised on organically grown feed—could be acceptable to a natural foods diet.

Another significant development in the natural foods field was the adoption of philosophies and culinary styles from East and South Asia, which helped attract new followers who hoped to find both health and moral purpose through eating, and which added variety to commercially available natural foods. American natural foods advocates had long been aware that the Hindu and Jain religions had traditions of vegetarianism, but their influence on the American natural foods field remained fairly limited until the last third of the twentieth century,[3] as did the integration of Asian immigrants into the health food industry. (Perhaps the main exception was the Indian spiritual leader Paramahansa Yogananda, who was admired by American natural foods advocates as early as the 1920s[4] and whose Self-Realization Fellowship was operating vegetarian cafés in Southern California by the 1940s.) In the 1960s and 1970s, many Americans seeking spiritual and practical alternatives to mainstream culture turned to Asia as a source of inspiration; as part of that trend, real or imagined Eastern religious ideas regarding people's relationships to food and nature were incorporated into a natural foods ideology. In this respect, Japan proved to be an especially fertile source of beliefs, practices, and styles. American hostility toward Japan, which had stewed during World War II and the postwar occupation, moved in the 1960s more toward admiration of what Americans perceived to be distinctive and quaint Japanese traditions (Moeller 1996, 34). In line with this view, European-American natural foods followers, especially those weary of the Hollywood-centered appeal of such people as Gayelord Hauser, were now receptive to messages that promised a different path to fulfillment.

One organization that fit with these desires was the San Francisco Zen Center, which was formed in 1962 by Shunryu Suzuki Roshi, a Japanese Zen Buddhist priest. By the mid-1960s, the Zen Center was attracting large numbers of Americans intrigued by Zen Buddhist teachings,[5] and in 1967 it established a monastery, called Tassajara, on the secluded site of a former health resort near Carmel Valley, California. Subsequently, in an effort to become financially self-sufficient, the Zen Center started several businesses, most which ended up being related to food. This direction was more accidental than a direct outgrowth of Zen philosophy. In 1970, the head cook of Tassajara, Edward Espe Brown, published *The Tassajara Bread Book*, which gained a large readership with its practical instructions and narrative suggesting a meaningful, Zen approach to the process of baking. The popularity of the book, and of the baked goods served at Tassajara, inspired the establishment of the retail Tassajara Bakery in San Francisco in 1976. Three years later, the Zen Center opened Greens Restaurant, also in San Francisco. Other ventures included Green Gulch Farm, which grew organic vegetables, and Green Gulch Grocery.

In its early days, Greens, which is still one of the best-regarded vegetarian restaurants in the country, followed in the footsteps of an older generation of Christian vegetarian restaurateurs who saw spiritual value in serving vegetarian fare. However, Greens was also intended to show that vegetarian preparations could be as creative and high quality as any cooking style. The combination of missions at Greens produced an experience for diners that mixed mainstream and countercultural values. As one person affiliated with the restaurant said, "The whole goal was to have this feel like a very sophisticated place. In the beginning, though, we had Zen monks waiting on customers. I will honestly say it wasn't the speediest service in the world, and some of it might have been a little holier than thou." Despite their origins in a worldview that valued in-the-moment process over results-oriented professionalism and efficiency, both Greens and Tassajara Bakery (which closed in 1999) instituted professional standards and ended up providing models of natural foods establishments that could compete with conventional food outlets on the basis of taste and ambiance. A meal at Greens or a treat from Tassajara Bakery promised virtuous indulgence, something that no longer seemed a contradiction in terms.

Another mix of Eastern philosophies and cooking styles that opened up new adventures for consumers was macrobiotics. A set of principles borrowing from Zen Buddhism and Taoism, macrobiotics was developed by George Ohsawa in Japan and Europe. Two pairs of Ohsawa students, Michio and Aveline Kushi, and Cornellia and Herman Aihara, were most instrumental in introducing macrobiotics to the United States. The Kushis in Boston and the Aiharas in Chico, California, established study centers and publications (respectively, *East-West Journal* and *Macrobiotics Today*) to further knowledge about macrobiotics. Additionally, what became major—and competing—natural foods firms were set up under their auspices in the 1960s: the Kushis and Paul Hawken formed Erewhon, and the Aiharas and Bob Kennedy formed Chico-San. Both companies started as distributors of imported macrobiotic items from Japan and then expanded into domestic production. Erewhon also had several of its own retail stores in the Boston and Los Angeles areas.[6]

With much emphasis placed on proper food combinations, a macrobiotic diet favors simplicity of ingredients and features vegetable foods that are naturally derived, locally grown, in season, and in as whole a form as possible. The blend of seemingly simple instructions for eating and a broad philosophy of life produced large numbers of followers in the 1960s and 1970s. Macrobiotics's popularity alarmed natural foods opponents, who roundly condemned the school of thought and seized on followers' enthusiasm as evidence of macrobiotics's cultlike nature (Stare 1970; Dwyer et al. 1974a; Dwyer et al. 1974b). In popular culture, jokes about people subsisting on brown rice and seaweed were rampant, and for years, press coverage inevitably mentioned the single case, aberrant as it was, of a New York woman who starved to death on a macrobiotic diet.[7] Yet, as austere as the macrobiotic diet appeared to be, it helped expand the palates of natural foods followers, including people who did not adhere to its principles, by introducing new ingredients into the natural foods repertoire, such as miso, seitan, kombu, and umeboshi plum. Even after its popularity faded, macrobiotics also left the natural foods movement with a reinvigorated sense that diet is key not just to individual well-being but to restoring balance and harmony to the world in general.

Natural Foods in the Counterculture

These were themes that resonated with the 1960s and 1970s counterculture. The *counterculture* is the label given to various forms of expression and ways of living that were consciously intended as a rejection of mainstream assumptions about propriety and the good life. Although not identical with youth culture, the counterculture was most enthusiastically embraced by young people, many who turned the absence of material and career accomplishments into emblems of freedom and moral integrity. As Theodore Roszak recounted in *The Making of a Counter Culture*, America's youth were profoundly alienated from their parents' passivity in the face of a society subjugated by efficiency-minded technocrats. In contrast, "At their best, these young bohemians are the would-be utopian pioneers of the world that lies beyond intellectual rejection of the Great Society. They seek to invent a cultural base for New Left politics, to discover new types of community, new family patterns, new sexual mores, new kinds of livelihood, new esthetic forms, new personal identities on the far side of power politics, the bourgeois home, and the consumer society" (Roszak 1995, 66). Natural foods fit with the counterculture's rejection of slavish obedience to established authorities and industrial forms of organization, and they offered an answer to counterculturalists' quests for new, authentic experiences both sensual and spiritual. It would be a gross exaggeration to claim that the majority of those who identified with the counterculture adopted a natural foods diet. But counterculturalists were more open than the general population to trying natural foods, and many of the most visible counterculture institutions and philosophies embraced natural foods principles.

The counterculture's affinity for natural foods could be seen in publications such as *The Whole Earth Catalog*, the famous compendium of "tools" (i.e., books and other products for sale), which were considered appropriate for constructing an alternative lifestyle. The 1974 edition of

The Whole Earth Catalog included a fourteen-page section on food and cooking, plus other food-related listings scattered elsewhere in the catalog. Almost all the books and food supplies mentioned in these sections fell in the natural or health food category; also printed here were recipes from Adelle Davis and *The Tassajara Bread Book*, plus a long list of recommended vegetarian cookbooks. Reflecting the do-it-yourself outlook common to both counterculture and natural foods philosophies, the catalog included implements for grinding one's own grain and making one's own compost, along with sources of information on organic gardening, canning, and butchering meat (Brand 1974).

Another periodical coming out of the counterculture was the 1970s magazine *Natural Life Styles*, based first in New Paltz, New York, and then Felton, California, which aimed to provide guidance and reflection on achieving closer connections to nature, one's fellow human beings, and oneself. "REAL FOOD for the body and soul is our chief concern," proclaimed the inaugural issue.[8] A typical edition combined articles on natural childbirth, building one's own stone house, herbal body care, and federal policy on the environment with pieces on organic gardening, starting a co-op, whether to eat meat, and gathering mushrooms, as well as lots of recipes.[9] While *Natural Life Styles* was more food-focused than most, by 1970, it was common for countercultural newsletters to include regular columns devoted to obtaining and cooking with natural foods, or the occasional article denouncing conventional food production and eating practices.

The intersection of this time period's counterculture and the natural foods movement has been well documented by Warren Belasco in his valuable study, *Appetite for Change*. However, contrary to Belasco's argument, most of the nonconformist ideas and styles associated with a natural foods way of life in this era were not especially new. Instead, they were largely a continuation of cultural developments from earlier decades. For instance, the 1940s Nature Boys' stylistic legacy would carry over to the 1960s and 1970s counterculture as male hippies grew out their hair and beards, and men and women alike wore loose clothing and favored sandals or bare feet. (It is no mere coincidence that German-made Birkenstock shoes, which became emblematic of California hippies, were originally sold out of health food stores.) Similarly, 1960s and 1970s vegetarian communes and back-to-the-land ventures were often directly influenced by earlier experiments such as Helen and Scott Nearing's Vermont homestead. Indeed, it was the nonconformism and disdain for conventional authority found in the already existing natural foods movement that contributed to its appeal for the new generation of counterculturalists. The 1960s and

1970s counterculture certainly did shake up the natural foods movement and the health food industry, as I will discuss shortly. But the new followers did not create either the movement or the industry that served it. They merely, as one retailer told me, "put it on the map."

Perhaps the fullest expression of a countercultural natural foods lifestyle was seen in back-to-the-land endeavors that established rural communes from the mid-1960s to the late 1970s; the largest concentrations were in California and New England. These communes tended to embrace a pastoral ideal that saw rural living as an escape from and antidote to a corrupt society; for many participants, it included a commitment to creating a lifestyle that did without the consumer commodities and producer technologies of an industrial age (Berger 1981, chap. 4; Edgington 2008; T. Miller 1999). Often settling in isolated areas, communards attempted to be self-sufficient by growing their own food, sewing their own clothes, and making other items that they needed. However, members frequently found themselves in perilous conditions when crops or shelters were insufficient to sustain them through a winter. The difficulties of physically maintaining themselves and of harmoniously living together in such circumstances resulted in considerable turnover of residents, and most rural commune experiments did not last for long.

The failure of so many back-to-the-land communes could be understood as the predictable outcome of naïve individuals who, like the Fruitlands residents of the nineteenth century, had thoroughly unrealistic ideas about what was involved in living off the land. But the rural communes' demise meant something more for the natural foods movement in that it represented the final blow to large-scale efforts to achieve asceticism in the context of a natural foods lifestyle. The moral commitment to a way of life that eschewed dependence on varied and abundant consumer goods and that endorsed a diet of plain, simple food eaten in minimal quantities gave way to another tendency within the counterculture: the celebration of hedonism and indulgence. By the time the back-to-the-land movement was no longer a movement but rather a private lifestyle choice, expressions of ascetic self-discipline and self-denial were relegated to small corners of the natural foods field.

New Ideals, New Businesses

Former rural counterculturalists did not necessarily abandon the natural living ideal altogether even if they gave up on back-to-the-land dreams.

The experience of farming with minimal inputs, foraging for food, and fashioning meals from the food at hand instilled for many a lifelong interest in eating natural foods and, more immediately, propelled a number of them into market-based natural foods activities. There, they found other like-minded counterculturalists who were seeking alternative forms of work, consumption, and defining success. As the mission of a restaurant located on the campus of the University of California–Santa Cruz was described, "Whole Earth Restaurant is dedicated to the new sensibility of the Whole Earth and the restoration of kinship with the Whole Earth. Situated midway between the Wilderness and the Garden, the Whole Earth Restaurant takes part in that exodus from institutional bondage we are all called upon to enact" (P. Lee 1972, viii). Even if surrounded by the oppressive institutions of mainstream society, counterculturalists believed they could pioneer new ways of relating to nature and one another.

Several of the industry members I interviewed spoke about their roots in the 1960s–1970s counterculture and how it brought them into the natural foods fold. In some cases, informants simply referenced cities or neighborhoods in California as an explanation for how they were introduced to natural foods. Said one, "Well, I lived in the Haight [district of San Francisco] . . . So, hanging around the emerging hippie culture of the moment." "The short part is I came here [to Santa Cruz] in the early seventies," explained another. Being in these centers of countercultural life meant that people would at least encounter natural foods ideals.

One story, which I excerpt at length here, illustrates both the appeal of the health food industry for counterculturalists looking for a way to make the world a better place and the generational differences between old-style firms and those associated with the new counterculture. In stumbling onto a countercultural version of a natural foods trade show, my informant witnessed the challenge that a new generation was making to a health food industry that aspired to be accepted by the mainstream. And in learning to appreciate the contributions of natural foods advocates of both past and present, he discovered a means to simultaneously earn a living and engage in what he perceived to be a moral endeavor:

I actually was hitchhiking in June 1970 with a friend. And a car stopped finally, and there were two couples in it. Turned out they were from the Arcata food co-op. And they were on their way to a meeting of OM, Organic Merchants, which was an organization that was founded by Fred Rohe out of San Francisco. And we got to Shasta, and it turned out that this was like a trade show.

However, you had to hike to the alpine cabin and you'd better bring your tent and your sleeping bag. The folks who were there—and I can't remember now, maybe there were fifty, maybe there were a hundred people, maybe they were less—were folks that were running natural food co-ops in northern California. I was at a crossroads, trying to figure out what I was going to do with my life, and so I was going camping. But I sat on the periphery of this group and listened. And I listened to Fred and to them. But the thing that was really pivotal for me was when the folks from Loma Linda arrived. They walked up the mountain. They walked up in their wingtips and their suitcoats to address the group. And when they arrived, the group booed them. Most of those co-ops at that time in history were vegetarian, and of course Loma Linda was a vegetarian products company. But they made canned and dried meat analogs that the group felt was a transgression. You know, if you're a vegetarian, why would you be mocking meat? Why would you eat it? Why would you do that? So Fred went off on the group and gave them a lecture on Seventh-day Adventists, Loma Linda, Kellogg's. So, I was inspired. Because I was trying to figure out what I was going to do that would not contribute to what I considered to be the war machine, the military-industrial complex, rampant cannibalistic capitalism. Just a whole raft of things that I couldn't get behind. So I'm going to dare tell the guy that I hitchhiked up there with, I said, "I'm going back to L.A., and I'm going to open a natural food store."

And eventually, he did.

Thus, the counterculture not only expanded the clientele for natural foods in new ways, but it expanded the industry as well. For some counterculturalists, it meant taking jobs in existing health food businesses. But for many who desired to express an alternative style in the workplace, or who opposed the management techniques and profit orientation of conventional businesses, the preference was to start their own endeavors in partnership with like-minded fellows. The result was a profusion of new enterprises with nontraditional forms of organization or production methods. These included co-ops, buying clubs called "food conspiracies," communal farms, manufacturing collectives, and restaurants and bakeries that combined distaste for competitive capitalism with a pledge to use unprocessed, unadulterated ingredients. The desire to cultivate craft skills also found expression here as counterculturalists developed artisanal tofu, cheese, baked goods, and other food enterprises. Such entrepreneurs were attempting to create real alternatives to the conventional food industry and to explicitly join their politics with participation in the market. In this way, they hoped to usher in a new age in American society, one which was cooperative rather than competitive and which valued creativity over conformity.

These ventures were generally not singularly devoted to the natural health movement in the same way that an older generation of natural foods advocates was. Rather, the countercultural natural foods promoters identified with what came to be called "The Movement," which encompassed numerous left-leaning political expressions and which assumed a unity of purpose in changing society through and through. As a result, these businesses introduced a new kind of radicalism to the health food industry. Counterculturalists were not only, like their predecessors, combining the need to make a living with furthering a natural foods philosophy; their politics entailed not just challenging government, health, and agricultural authorities; and success was not simply measured by the ability to act independently in the shadow of large-scale corporate enterprise. The new radicalism was indeed about all these things, but in addition, countercultural entrepreneurs explicitly intended to challenge core principles of capitalist enterprise and the market by blurring or even erasing boundaries between worker and manager, and between consumer and producer.

The most visible form of alternative business devoted to countercultural ideals was the natural foods cooperative. Food co-ops, in which consumers share ownership and the work involved in distributing their food, had been an alternative to grocery stores since the 1920s. By members completing some or all of the labor themselves, and by buying food at wholesale prices but without the overhead of a traditional store, co-ops could provide members with food at a low cost. They were also a way to express a cooperative spirit, and indeed, in their early years, were often tied to labor or populist movements (Fowler 1936). But during the 1960s, food co-ops became closely associated with natural foods, an association that was more fully realized in the 1970s (Ronco 1974; Wickstrom 1974). Especially those counterculturalists who had moderate incomes were eager to experiment with alternative economic forms, and they extended the value of being close to one's food source and antagonism toward an industrialized food supply to the means of distributing food. Such values were also reflected in design elements of the co-ops, as sealed packages, with their plastic and paper coverings, were eschewed in favor of bulk bins that allowed direct contact with food, and as the modern look of the supermarket was traded for wooden fixtures and a ramshackle aesthetic reminiscent of the old country store.

Co-ops, like rural communes, depended on member commitment and required time-consuming interpersonal negotiations that were hard to sustain. By the 1980s, many co-ops were losing members and closing down or transforming to conventional management structures (Knupfer 2013, 138). On the other hand, what ended up being more enduring were businesses that began with typical capitalist ownership and management structures while still holding onto a countercultural identity and style. Like true collectives, such businesses were intended to demonstrate that the production and distribution of food could embody a more cooperative and nature-respecting sensibility than conventional enterprises did.

From Health Food Back to Natural Food

Countercultural enterprises wanted to differentiate themselves not just from conventional food firms but also from the existing health food industry. One of the most important differences between the newcomers and the established health food industry, especially in regard to retail stores, was counterculture enterprises' emphasis on fresh food and a turn away from supplements. Counterculturalists were certainly good patrons of health food stores, shopping for items such as honey and whole grains, but they found most such stores lacking. The irony that they often noted was that there was not much food available in a traditional health food store. Said one former retailer, "The health food store image that most people had was the image of just a bunch of pills. That image of the 1950s, early 1960s health food store was hardly any food. They were called a health food store, but they were mainly supplements. A person couldn't do their [regular] shopping in a health food store." For those counterculturalists who desired to avoid conventional businesses, the inability of the health food store to offer a viable alternate food outlet was dismaying.

There were some practical reasons why health food stores preferred pills to produce. Profit margins on packaged goods, especially supplements, were much higher than on fresh food. Furthermore, fresh food was difficult to stock. Much of it required refrigeration equipment; fresh foods spoiled quickly and needed frequent replenishing; and regular health food distributors did not supply these items. Simply finding reliable sources of organic produce, as well as natural alternatives to numerous other food staples, was a difficult and time-consuming project for shop owners. But a new generation of countercultural retailers, often oblivious to the barriers to carrying a full line of food, charged ahead, priding themselves on going into uncharted territory where they could make up the rules as they went along. When sources were unavailable, they encouraged friends to launch small farms or production facilities, or they did it themselves. And, no small matter, their principled indifference to the profit motive allowed them to be at least temporarily content with a meager income.

In line with these efforts, counterculture entrepreneurs desired to explicitly communicate their distinction from the old-style health food store. As a wholesaler explained, "So, when the movement started changing there, between maybe '73 and into the mid-'70s, stores started carrying everything that you needed to eat: a full line of produce and grocery items. At that point we started using the term *natural food stores* because it more accurately represented what our mission was." The shift in terminology, from *health food* to *natural food*, was not always recognized outside the industry; casual consumers tended to use these terms interchangeably for decades. Nonetheless, the change in language represented other important changes taking place during the 1960s and 1970s. It signaled a shift in the natural foods movement's political focus of the previous few decades, from an alternate way of conceptualizing health care to an environmentalist concern for the natural world. And it signified the strengthened economic potential of the health/natural foods industry since the category was now expanding to conceivably offer an alternative to every conventional food item the consumer ate. Indeed, the tide seemed to have turned by 1978 when, for the first time since health food industry sales were measured, the value of *food* sold by industry retailers was greater than the value of supplements, books, and other nonfood items (Spielman 1979).

The ability of newcomers to experiment, innovate, and make their mark on the business was partly because the health food industry remained relatively easy to break into. Demand for health and natural foods was growing fast; many neighborhoods and even entire cities lacked outlets selling such food; and with patrons accustomed to small, plain health food stores, capital requirements for opening an outlet were not very high. Moreover, the industry was still a culturally open place, with few social barriers to doing business and a high tolerance for people with little experience in the field. Continuing the tradition whereby devout Christians, bodybuilders, and nudists could all find a home in the health food industry, growth-seeking industry boosters welcomed anticapitalist crusaders along with those well versed in running a business. Practically speaking, it meant that established suppliers were willing to extend credit and advice to fledgling

FIGURE 7. Stanley Filipczak's Health Food Center, Dearborn, Michigan, 1969. This vegetarian restaurant represented an older style of natural foods provision that would soon be replaced. © Ed Haun/Detroit Free Press/ZUMA.

companies while nurturing sales. The low barriers to entry were reflected in the swift pace of new health food stores that opened during this period. In 1965, there were approximately 1,000 health food stores in the country. The number had doubled to almost 2,000 by 1971, reached 4,200 by 1976, and hit 7,100 by 1981 (Dunning 1965; Pacey 1972; Spielman 1979, 52; Simmons Market Research Bureau 1981, [iii]).

Still, the quick entry of so many counterculturalists, both as patrons and as business associates, could be unsettling to an older generation that now appeared staid by comparison (see figure 7). In a 1970 article, the trade journal *Health Foods Retailing* sought to instruct industry denizens about the new breed: "Young people, often the very young, often defect to Hippieland. They come from all walks of society—poor, middle-class and affluent families—and live in communes, which they call 'pads.' When it comes to food, anything goes, but they have a liking for natural foods. Many of the youngsters have been attracted to whole grain cereals, macrobiotic foods, etc., or, perhaps, foods which they think are different from those that The Establishment might eat" (Tonell 1970, 102). But after this acknowledgement of hippies' potential as customers, the reporter noted, "Unfortunately, the non-Hippie seldom attracts the attention of the news media, and we are apt to forget that there are millions of clean-cut, well-groomed youngsters in the U.S. On the other hand, just because a boy has long hair or a girl dresses 'mod,' doesn't mean that they are hopeless outcasts lost forever in Hippieland" (114).

Until young acolytes found their way back to a more conventional existence, the health food industry had to learn how to deal with them. To assist with this, *Health Foods Retailing* ran a two-part feature in 1970 reporting retailer answers to questions about "the so-called Hippie types as customers." In it, retailer Wilma Voge of Idaho Falls offered an almost clinical account: "We do have some of them in our store and we find them very interested in nutrition. Most of them seem to be in good health, they are very friendly and honest. We trust them, accept their California checks and, so far, they have not disappointed us. They buy mostly bulkfoods like grains, seeds, nuts and some vitamins. We treat all of our customers alike" (Brooks et al. 1970). Despite the liberal assurances of treating hippies the same as more long-standing customers, these and similar comments reflected anxiety about the potential for this antiestablishment group to turn against the health food businesses selling to them in the same way hippies scorned conventional businesses.

The culture clash was not just between senior industry members and young consumers. New countercultural enterprises coexisted with older industry institutions, occasionally with some friction. The story recounted earlier, about the visit of Loma Linda representatives to an Organic Merchants meeting, is one such example. In these cases, differences were often related to aesthetic or organizational styles (see figure 8). A former member of San Francisco's Rainbow Grocery, organized as a collective, spoke of older business associates being flummoxed by Rainbow's lack of hierarchy. A wholesaler confirmed that he found the grocery difficult to deal with then because he never knew who was in charge. Perhaps the time when the stylistic differences were most on display was at the annual industry convention. Said one manufacturer about the first show he attended, "My first sight was the 1980 natural foods convention in Chicago at McCormick Place. And my first entrance into there, I ran into people with long hair and wearing flowing robes and a lot of them had turbans on their heads. And I said, 'Oh my god! What the hell have I gotten myself into?' You know, I'm wearing a three-piece suit." Similar sentiments, but

FIGURE 8. Poster advertising Sunset Health Food Store, San Francisco, 1967. Screenprint in color on paper, 20 × 14 in. San Francisco was at the center of the countercultural style adopted by a new generation of natural foods businesses. Fried, Bob, Singing Mothers LSD Relief Society Studio, *Sunset Health Food Store*, Smith College Museum of Art, Northampton, Massachusetts. Reprinted with permission of Smith College.

from the opposite side, were voiced by a wholesaler: "I remember the first trade show that we went to. And there was a bunch of us counterculture types talking about organic produce or organic food. And dressed in our casual Levi's and sandals. And then there was a lot of people in suits from well-capitalized vitamin companies who had been kind of the foundation of the industry. And there was definitely at that point a merging of two cultures to really change the industry from the old health food industry to the new natural-organic industry." Although they learned to work together, the contrasting orientations underlying the health food–natural foods divide would cause industry rifts in years to come.

One early manifestation of this divide was the minimal affinity that counterculturalists felt for existing health food advocacy organizations. This lack of affinity extended to both citizen advocacy groups, such as the National Health Federation, and the trade associations, such as the National Nutritional Foods Association. As a result, counterculturalists formed their own, primarily regional, trade groups, such as Organic Merchants, formed circa 1970, and Regional Tilth, a northwestern organic farming group formed in 1974. It is significant that the formation of new industry organizations at this time occurred without a corresponding growth of new citizen advocacy groups. During the 1960s and 1970s, a natural foods diet was seen as simply one component of a countercultural lifestyle, and natural foods politics were understood as simply one expression of a larger environmentalist or anticorporate stance. Thus, support for alternative food practices could be exhibited through the design of everyday life and folded into the agendas of multi-issue advocacy groups. Indeed, in this era of intense social movement activity, only a handful of citizen advocacy organizations, not affiliated with business, were formed specifically to advance the natural foods cause, such as the American Vegan Society, founded by H. Jay Dinshah in 1960, the North American Vegetarian Society, also founded (in 1974) by Dinshah, the Institute for Food and Development Policy, founded in 1975 by Frances Moore Lappé and Joseph Collins, and the natural health–oriented Feingold Association of the United States, formed in 1976. On the other hand, the fluid boundary between countercultural producers and consumers of natural foods was creating a large group of people sympathetic to and knowledgeable about both political and commercial aspects of the field. When an upsurge of natural foods advocacy groups began in the 1980s, the participation of former counterculturalists reinforced an appreciation for market endeavors in organized efforts to spread natural foods ideals.

Revisiting the Image Problem

At the same time as the number of natural foods followers was growing in the 1960s and 1970s and the movement was achieving greater visibility, the field's public reputation was suffering. The long-standing association of health food with eccentricity was only heightened by natural foods' adoption by the counterculture, which was both mocked and demonized by mainstream institutions. An image of old people and bodybuilders swearing by their vitamins and blackstrap molasses was now joined and eventually replaced by an image of hippies and back-to-nature "freaks" rummaging through ramshackle stores for granola and alfalfa sprouts. In some cases, this image was a sinister one. During the 1970s, health professionals frequently noted with alarm the integration of natural foods "faddism" into the habits and worldviews of hippies, communards, and young people touched more peripherally by the counterculture (Dwyer et al. 1974a; Erhard 1973, 8). The counterculture's antiestablishment perspective, which deliberately turned upside down the usual standards of evaluation for behaviors and ideas, made more pronounced what had been a significant concern of natural foods critics from the very start: the way that natural foods followers did not accept mainstream sources of cultural authority but instead looked elsewhere for guidance regarding values and behavior.

Meanwhile, media outlets continued their tradition of ridicule. There were the bemused press reports explaining, for instance, how "Health-food stores are the meeting place for those two archetypes of South California, the little old lady in tennis shoes and the young, barefoot, bearded ex-radical" (Yergin 1973, 33).[10] But now other forms of popular culture increasingly took up the health food theme, encouraged, no doubt, by the large presence of natural foods followers among professional entertainers. References ranged from the whimsical, such as Neil Diamond's 1971 hit song "Crunchy Granola Suite" to satirical episodes in 1970s television situation comedies, such as *All in the Family* and *Fernwood 2 Night*, which got laughs by showing dizzy young people foisting onto family and neighbors unappetizing organic and health food along with peace symbols and antipollution politics.[11]

Yet, the popular association between natural foods and the counterculture masked the actual diversity in the health/natural foods market. To be sure, young people made up a significant segment of the market, especially compared to the past. But all age groups were now taking an interest in natural foods. By 1979, a survey by *Health Foods Business* found that 19 percent of health food store customers were younger than age 25, 37 percent were between 25 and 40, 30 percent were between 40 and 65, and 14 percent were older than 65. The same survey found customers skewing toward higher incomes, with 33 percent among the (undefined) "upper-middle" class and 49 percent among the "middle-middle" class. Only 9 percent were among the "lower-middle" class. At either end of the economic spectrum were 9 percent in the upper class and a mere 1 percent among the lower class (Spielman 1979, 55). Congruent with this profile, a 1975 market research report found that health food shoppers had much more formal education than the average American, with 40 percent being college educated (R. Hunt 1975; see also Licata 1981).

The shifting demographics were not entirely lost on critics, who frequently commented on the high levels of education among people interested in natural foods, as well as the middle-class status of many users. Seeing people with social positions that should enable informed choices go on to embrace natural foods was cause for considerable concern and puzzlement for those convinced that natural foods were worthless. Said one team of researchers, "Thus, to both nutrition and consumer behavior scholars alike, the apparent paradox of an irrational purchase behavior being maintained by people with normal, middle-American background characteristics presents a challenging enigma for study" (Saegert, Young, and Saegert 1978, 730). For those in the health food industry, this demographic was not seen as an enigma so much as evidence that with enough knowledge, people would choose a natural foods way of life. Regardless of their motivations, the enlarged base of consumers sent health food sales soaring. Retail health food sales went from about $100 million in 1970 to $1.94 billion in 1980.[12]

The heady increase in health/natural foods sales, and the interest shown by a well-educated and affluent population, held out the tantalizing possibility of continued growth if only the industry could overcome the lingering perception among most of the population that it sold strange and unappetizing food eaten by people with unconventional lifestyles. Two developments, one external and one internal to the industry, eventually allowed this hope to be realized. First, the cultural innovations and antiauthoritarian politics of the 1960s and 1970s counterculture produced large groups of people who, as they grew older and wealthier, left behind many of the more radical expressions of the counterculture while maintaining a keen interest in personal health and culinary adventures. Second, natural foods businesses learned how to take advantage of such interests and open up new arenas of consumption for a more mainstream audience. Entrepreneurs who themselves had identified with elements of the counterculture made efforts to rework countercultural symbols into a new set of cultural meanings that retained a sense of novelty and hedonistic pleasure, respect for individual autonomy, and an appreciation for nature without requiring immersion in a subculture or the renunciation of conventional values of orderliness and upward mobility.

Perhaps this transformation of cultural meanings was best seen in the development of a new aesthetic that characterized natural foods stores beginning in the late 1970s. Natural foods outlets started to grow larger, cleaner, brighter, and filled with well-organized and attractive displays of fresh produce and assorted packaged dry foods. Industry boosters had long been urging retailers to remedy the dim lighting in their shops, saying that a well-lit store is a modern store.[13] But in the 1960s and 1970s, health/natural foods retailers were also often scolded for their sloppy housekeeping and dingy appearance (Phillipps 1976; Gifford 1973). Although one might assume that the new attention to cleanliness came from a natural impulse for a more sanitary environment, it was in part a repudiation of the aesthetics of the counterculture. Whereas store decor that included sawdust on the floor, crude wooden shelving, and open barrels and bins of food was celebrated by those counterculturalists who desired to do away with artificiality and to increase the physical connections with their food, detractors simply saw disorderliness. Today, industry old-timers frequently compare the grubbiness of stores past to the cleanliness of those present, highlighting the former as an impediment to mainstream acceptance and the latter as a sign of progress. Commented one industry member, "At that time, natural food stores weren't the most pleasant place to shop. They smelled like brewer's yeast." In contrast, the standard now is for shops and the products they sell to look and smell pristine.

The person whom industry insiders credit with being most influential in changing the experience of shopping for natural foods—and, in the process, transforming practices throughout the industry—is Sandy Gooch. Gooch, a former schoolteacher, decided to open her own store after a natural foods diet helped her overcome severe health problems. The first outlet of her Los Angeles area retail chain, Mrs. Gooch's, opened in 1977. At almost five thousand square feet, it was not only far larger than the average health food store of the day but also showed meticulous, detailed care toward appearance and presentation of merchandise. According to one longtime industry member, "She designed stores that people would enjoy shopping in. She removed the dark. She removed the smell. She removed the disarray. She removed the inefficiency of shopping in a natural food store. She made them more like a grocery store. She called it 'food theater.' She made it an experience. She made it someplace that you would be proud to go into, that you could brag about the shopping experience."

As Gooch herself told me, several aspects of her stores were unusual for the time. The large space was kept immaculate. Not only were the surroundings without blemish, but so was the food. Gooch developed a grading system for organic produce that resembled what grocers used for conventional produce, with size, appearance, and freshness being taken into account. Farmers who wanted to do business with her had to conform to the highest standards. She also brought from her teaching days the concept of *realia*, meaning a theme that is visually represented in the classroom through the use of material objects. Throughout her original store, Gooch employed this idea by creating interesting things for children and adults to look at: for example, a little scene evoking a harvest placed on top of a display case. Similarly, rather than emphasizing price, her promotional material told stories about the farmers who supplied her produce, or how natural foods are produced differently from conventional food. In these ways, she made encounters with the store educational and entertaining.

While her stores stressed that good health would result from eating natural foods, Gooch also did much to show that a natural foods diet did not involve personal sacrifice. This achievement was seen in how she confronted head-on the perennial question of compromise in the health food industry. Ever since the industry's earliest days, natural foods supporters debated the kinds of deviations from a natural foods ethic that businesses could make to bring in more customers. Gooch decided to take a firm stance in this regard, and she developed a standard that pledged to keep out of her stores foods that were not natural (though her philosophy did not include vegetarianism): "It is our goal not to offer for sale any food, beverage, vitamin, cosmetic or household product made with refined flour or sugars, hydrogenated oils, artificial sweeteners, chocolate, caffeine, toxic preservatives, artificial flavors, or harmful dyes and additives."[14] Yet, rather than presenting this standard as a lack of selection that the consumer was forced to accept, Mrs. Gooch's framed it as a guarantee of trustworthiness, so that consumers could be secure about the quality of the goods being purchased. As the company grew, adding new outlets every two or three years

STYLE   165

to eventually become a seven-store chain, and as the company turned into a major customer for natural foods producers, the term "goochable" was used throughout the industry to talk about products that met Mrs. Gooch's standard. This phrase remained in place for years, even after the Mrs. Gooch's name was absorbed into Whole Foods, the company that acquired Mrs. Gooch's in 1993.

In the same way that a trip to Mrs. Gooch's promised entrance into a world of high quality, the store demonstrated that a natural foods lifestyle need not exclude luxury or indulgence. Along with the typical health food store's lectures on nutrition, Mrs. Gooch's sponsored numerous cooking classes at locations throughout the Los Angeles area on such topics as "Gourmet Vegetarian Cooking" and "Holiday Treats for Family and Friends."[15] Another innovation was to establish a gift department, integrating food with complementary nonfood items. By doing so, Gooch suggested that natural foods were something pleasurable that the consumer could share with others. Similarly, Gooch's methods fit with a newly emerging familial lifestyle that cultivated shared cosmopolitan tastes between parents and children. By sponsoring school tours for students and teachers, the retailer encouraged children to themselves become fans of Mrs. Gooch's and to join their parents in enjoying natural foods.

In all these ways, the store attracted, along with traditional natural foods followers, a more mainstream and affluent customer than had typically patronized health food stores of the past. As a journalist wrote, "Mrs. Gooch's made natural foods safe for the middle class."[16] To be sure, there were other large-format retailers that adopted the "supernatural" style in the 1980s, including Alfalfa's in Boulder, Colorado, and Bread and Circus in the Boston area. But Mrs. Gooch's was especially influential in altering the popular perception of natural foods and in providing a model for other retailers to imitate, owing to its rapid success as well as its location in Southern California, a cultural trendsetter for the country and the longtime center of the health food industry. The supernatural style helped effect a transformation in the image of natural foods, which by the end of the twentieth century communicated quality, cosmopolitanism, variety, and tastiness, traits that coexisted with older associations of good health and a direct connection to nature. Natural foods were still seen by the public as vaguely bohemian and an antiestablishment food choice. But at least in the sphere of consumption, to be antiestablishment was now more likely to be understood as hip than as subversive.[17] Natural foods' status was definitely on the rise.

Acquiring a Class Identity

In the 1980s, while retailers such as Mrs. Gooch's were cultivating a type of consumer who was affluent, conscious of how commodities fit into his or her lifestyle, and proud to be seen in the stores patronized, natural foods manufacturers were engaging in innovations of their own. Reversing a trend of the 1960s and 1970s, branded, packaged natural foods were on the rise, offering convenience to households no longer likely to have a full-time homemaker in place and assuaging fears about the defilement of edible products. The Tylenol scare of 1982—when cyanide-laced bottles of the pain reliever were sold in five Chicago-area supermarkets and drugstores, resulting in the death of seven people—was a watershed event in this regard. Although it did not actually augur a new era of illicit food and drug tampering, this incident, coinciding with heightened levels of suspicion toward strangers in general, elevated concerns about the safety of everyday objects. Natural foods were not immune from these fears. Concerns about safety and sanitation resulted in new FDA guidelines and state laws governing the sale of bulk foods.[18] While no-touch bulk bins, which allow items to fall from a bin directly into a bag, were developed to comply with the regulations, bulk food sales in general began to decline in favor of goods labeled as natural but encased in decidedly unnatural fortresses of plastic and coated paper.

These wrapped and boxed items looked and tasted different from packaged health food of the past. At the same time as the aesthetics of the natural foods store were changing, packaging was getting a new look. One natural foods wholesaler recalled, "The packaging started getting pretty, you started getting professional marketing people that came into the industry and knew how to make a nice-looking package [instead of] these dull, nondescript packages, that just, I mean, it looked weird." Nice-looking and professionally packaged food suggested a better-tasting product and reassured consumers that these goods were comfortably similar to conventional foods. Packaging serves more functional purposes as well, as it preserves items that will be shipped over long distances or that may sit on a warehouse or store shelf for a long time.

Corresponding to the new emphasis on attractive packaging was a new stress on the taste of natural foods. During the 1960s and 1970s, the assumption that healthy food tasted dreadful was widespread, with commentary implying that earnest, befuddled hippies found unpalatable food especially virtuous. "Granola's about as chewy as leather—and not quite as tasty," noted *Harper's Bazaar* in a typically dismissive article (Gittelson 1972, 32). Yet, it was the same willingness to try the unfamiliar that led natural foods advocates to experiment with unusual ingredients, flavors, and cooking styles, such as the Asian influences noted earlier. By the 1980s, "hippie" food, known for its blandness and lack of variety, had made common cause with "ethnic" food and certain gourmet trends, with the result that natural foods started to claim the mantle of good taste and tasting good.

A connection between good food and natural foods was furthered by figures from the culinary world who adopted some aspects of natural foods principles without adopting the identity. Such figures included Alice Waters, who founded the high-end Berkeley restaurant Chez Panisse in 1971. Chez Panisse became one of the most renowned restaurants in the country, known for using locally produced and extremely fresh ingredients. Although in later years Waters became a public advocate for sustainability, for many years she shied away from any mention of health, natural, or even organic food, concerned about their association with bad-tasting fare (Waters 1990, 115; Fromartz 2006, 121). Yet, the "California cuisine" that her restaurant helped popularize did much to make fresh produce and other minimally processed foods equivalent to gourmet.

As natural foods were increasingly associated with a high-quality culinary experience, they began to be perceived as the food choice of the affluent. It is important to recognize that a cultural connection between affluence and natural foods did not exist prior to this time. For most of the field's history, the indicators many observers today point to in order to suggest a fit between natural foods and an economically privileged population—the high cost of such items and the interest taken in them by a social elite—did not result in the popular perception of health food as something primarily consumed by the wealthy. Indeed, until the end of the twentieth century, the cost of a natural foods diet could vary tremendously, and the actual price of health food had only modest bearing on the social class of those who consumed it.

On the one hand, an ethic of asceticism and self-sufficiency could make natural foods less expensive than eating conventional food, and indeed, many advocates of the past promoted a natural foods diet by highlighting how it allowed one to economize. As they noted, because of the high price of meat, adopting vegetarianism could save a household money. And the processing, packaging, and transportation costs of conventional factory-produced food tended to make it more expensive than food one grew or prepared oneself (Cooper 1917; Latson 1902; Borsodi 1933, 14). On the other hand, purchasing health food was frequently more costly than buying conventional products. The price differential was largely because the venues that sold health food—health food stores—had higher markups on their products than did conventional grocery stores. Such was the case at least from the 1930s, when supermarkets entered the American retail landscape. By 1972, a US Department of Agriculture study found that the difference in price for a standard market basket of goods at a supermarket was $11.00, compared with $21.90 at a health food store (R. Hunt 1975). However, this did not mean that health food stores were exclusively patronized by the wealthy. Opponents of health food frequently expressed astonishment that so many people of limited means, especially the elderly, continued to shop at health food stores.

Just as historically the cost of acquiring health food did not signal that it was a lifestyle for the affluent, the fact that social elites were often at the vanguard of adopting a natural foods diet did not turn health food into an emblem of upward mobility. From the transcendentalist intellectuals who followed Sylvester Graham, to the prominent visitors to John Harvey Kellogg's sanitarium, to the Hollywood film and television stars who embraced health food, natural foods had frequently been taken up by a cultural aristocracy. Still, belying any "trickle-down" theory of fashion and status (Veblen 1953; Simmel 1904), the consumption of natural foods did not accord ordinary consumers any reflected status, and this lifestyle remained unfashionable among the majority of the middle class. It was only at the end of the twentieth century, when the style in which natural foods were marketed and consumed changed to fit with other aspects of an upper-middle-class lifestyle, that this cultural association became solidified.

Sociologists have paid considerable attention to the ways that food choices correspond to social class; many, following Pierre Bourdieu, describe the attempt to achieve distinction through demonstrating socially superior tastes in food (Alkon and Agyeman 2011; Johnston and Baumann 2007; Warde 1997). It is not discrete consumer goods that set their users apart but rather an entire style of life, based on a set of tastes or what Bourdieu (1984) referred to as "dispositions," that is granted deference. Celebrities of the 1940s and 1950s might have inspired middle-class Americans to consume the occasional health food. But the legitimation of natural foods as a way of life occurred only when the style of natural foods promotion, by industry and by citizen advocates, changed to coincide with an emerging consumer lifestyle. The aesthetics and experience of purchasing and consuming natural foods then matched the preferred values and deportment of a group of people who aspired to a lifestyle of hedonism, cosmopolitanism, autonomy, authenticity, and appreciation of nature—and who had the income to support this lifestyle. It was at that point that natural foods gained a reputation as a category of goods associated with an affluent, educated, worldly population.

With this transformation, price itself took on a new cultural meaning. The high cost of health food shifted in popular perception from signifying irrationality on the part of health fanatics to indicating a special discernment for the finer things in life and a commendable attention to self-care. As the natural foods industry cultivated an expanded audience by investing in more sophisticated marketing and outfitting large stores in high-rent districts, new costs were incurred. But the industry discovered that a price premium could actually work to its advantage. Said a manufacturer of soy products, "Well, yeah, it's a premium issue. I always want to be forty cents higher than competition. But we always have to be better if that's what we're going to do. So that's how I justify it." For this manufacturer, price serves to communicate that his product is of higher quality than others on the market and consequently directed toward consumers with discriminating sensibilities. In this way, the industry realized the economic and cultural benefits to be had in shifting the primary audience for natural foods to one more capable of paying higher prices.

Thus, by the twenty-first century, we see the gourmet foodscape described by Johnston and Baumann (2010), where distinction is gained by consumption of foods whose organic, local, ethnic, and artisanal qualities signal their sustainable, ethical, exotic, and authentic virtues. Such virtues may appear self-evident to the numerous patrons of Whole Foods markets or farm-to-table restaurants, but the foods and their associated lifestyle so celebrated today were not given credence until they became connected to cultural styles, first developed in the counterculture and then modified by 1980s affluence.

When the natural foods lifestyle became perceived as a viable and respectable alternative to mainstream eating practices, the associated movement to spread this way of life also became a more credible political and cultural force. But at the same time as the movement was exercising its newfound clout, it had to grapple with the mixed blessings of enhanced legitimacy. Not only was the clientele of natural foods more mainstream than in the past, but the conventional food industry discovered the profit potential in selling natural foods. This development led to new tensions as the natural foods industry and movement found people with highly diverse motivations in their midst. Not surprisingly, mainstreaming has been accompanied by a modification—some would say a watering down—of many of the political ideas, philosophies, and symbols that had previously been so important to the movement. It is these sets of conflicts that I discuss next.

CHAPTER SEVEN

Drawing the Line

Boundary Disputes in the Natural Foods Field

By the turn of the twenty-first century, with ever-increasing numbers of people adopting at least parts of the natural foods lifestyle, the natural foods industry had become a serious economic force, generating sales of $15.5 billion in 1997 (Hartman and Wright 1999, 7).[1] The enlarged interest in natural foods was certainly furthered by the movement's cultural victories; as the years passed, the public image of devotees was less and less about spaced-out, sandal-wearing hippies who found virtue in bad-tasting food, and more and more about hip, affluent professionals who wanted to eat well and do good for the environment at the same time. Claims of health problems associated with a diet heavy in meat and processed foods were now being substantiated with scientific evidence, and the notion that people might genuinely prefer food within the natural foods repertoire no longer seemed outlandish. The movement was poised to achieve additional successes as well; schools, workplace cafeterias, hospital kitchens, and other mainstream institutions would soon start to integrate natural foods into their offerings.

On the other hand, the movement's ability to affect public policy and reform the conventional health care and food production spheres was more mixed. The medical profession was taking nutrition more seriously than ever before, but it still jealously guarded its prerogatives and looked askance at natural foods proponents' attempts to bypass medical authority and conventional drug regimes. Government agencies were less likely than in the past to campaign against natural foods advocates and businesses (though crackdowns occasionally took place), but public policy still favored the conventional agrifood sector. And while that latter sector was now making efforts to court the natural foods market, production and distribution of most food were still dominated by industrial methods that created great distance between nature and the products that the majority of Americans ate.

The growth in sales, number of followers, and legitimacy of natural foods, combined with the resistance to radical change on the part of medical and food institutions, also intensified several conflicts internal to the natural foods field. Many of these divisions coalesced around disputes over boundaries within the natural foods arena. They concerned the line dividing what counts as natural from that which is not, the line differentiating which consumers and businesses are movement insiders from those who are outsiders, and the question of who has the authority to determine where these boundaries lie. Such conflicts had been present in the natural foods field since the health food industry was first established, but they became more pronounced as the potential market for natural foods grew and consumption of such food became more mainstream.

The question of where to draw boundaries differentiating what is internal from what is external to a field is a problem faced both by field participants and by scholars who study them. In their useful work setting out a theory of fields, Fligstein and McAdam recognize that the scholar's desire for clean analytical categories may not always match the perspective of participants regarding membership in a field; nonetheless, Fligstein and McAdam favor less inclusive membership criteria and propose that a field requires "an agreement about who the players are and what positions they occupy" and "consensus regarding the rules by which the field works" (2012, 216). While this formulation may make it easier for the analyst to specify the contours of the field, it directs attention away from the boundary negotiations that tend to hold considerable meaning for participants in and around a field; indeed, how actors handle boundary disputes has consequences for the field's activities and the direction in which change occurs (Zietsma and Lawrence 2010).

As Fligstein and McAdam note, a field is often destabilized by the "invasion" of outsiders who act as challengers to existing incumbents and often transform the field in the process of being absorbed by it (2012, 99). As shown by my account of counterculturalists who entered the health food industry, this process can be observed in the natural foods field. But the case of natural foods suggests that it is not just active challengers who are a destabilizing force. More passive groups of newcomers, who are viewed as potential constituents for challengers and incumbents alike, also act to trigger boundary disputes and turmoil within the field. Precisely because of these newcomers' indifference to preexisting positions and rules, any such influx into the ranks of the audience or mass membership of a field threatens established boundaries even more than active challengers do.

Throughout the history of the natural foods field, an expanding consumer base for natural foods products and an expanding constituency that identifies with the movement have created incentives to accept a looser understanding of the natural foods category, one which is inclusive of a greater range of consumer and political tastes and one which gives businesses more discretion in how to cater to those tastes. However, stretching the definition of a natural lifestyle can also endanger the integrity of the concept. People working in the industry and participating in advocacy efforts confront the trade-off between strictly adhering to basic principles, which is likely to lessen choice and dampen the appeal of the category, and making principles more flexible—and less meaningful—to attract new followers and spread ideals as widely as possible. As I show in this chapter, these tensions have provided a constant backdrop to natural foods promotion from the 1960s to the present.

Three issues in particular, which exemplify these tensions and the attempts to resolve them, are discussed here. The first, exemplifying ambiguity about the line dividing the natural from the nonnatural, concerns the status of vitamins and other supplements. Supplements are principal revenue generators within the industry and are also often a gateway product for consumers new to the natural foods lifestyle. Thus, they are key to continuing economic growth and expanding movement support. Furthermore, for much of the past one hundred years, many of the mainstay firms in the industry have been supplement companies. These companies have been major backers of trade associations, of legal battles defending the right to sell and consume health food, and of publicity efforts to improve the public image of natural foods. But supplements are also seen by some members of the field as not really qualifying as either natural or a food. Additionally, perennial scandals involving misrepresentation of supplement ingredients and effectiveness threaten to derail the legitimacy gains that the field has achieved. For these reasons, some advocates would like to push supplements out of the natural foods category altogether.

A second issue, highlighting uncertainty about the boundary between movement insiders and outsiders, concerns the entry of major corporations into the natural foods field. Since the 1980s, there has been considerable consolidation in the natural foods industry, especially in retailing and wholesaling, as companies merge in order to gain capital and neutralize competition. At the same time, whether it be through acquisition or starting their own lines, conventional food companies at both the manufacturing and the retail level have decided to serve the growing natural foods market. For those with an ethical commitment to natural foods, this has been a worrisome development. While it represents success in the sense of lifting natural foods out of the economic margins, it is also emblematic of the industrialization of natural foods, with producers and distributors being drawn into many of the same kinds of practices that natural foods advocates have criticized since the early twentieth century. This process blurs the line between a conventional and a natural foods company.

The final area of debate discussed here, exemplifying conflict about who has authority to resolve boundary disputes, involves *certification*, the process whereby items are given a stamp of approval guaranteeing that they have met standards related to organic, humanely raised, sustainable, fair trade, or other attributes. This codification of standards is seen as a way to restore integrity in a field that has become too large and unwieldy to be regulated by less formal measures. Certification is intended to increase public confidence in natural foods and to make explicit the boundaries separating natural foods from the nonnatural. But this process also embodies certain contradictions as it reverses the movement's tradition of eschewing institutionalized authority and a standardized approach to health and food. In place of seeing nature—both the natural environment that sustains life and each individual's natural body—as the ultimate authority, and instead of measuring a product's purity according to how closely it corresponds to a condition found in nature, negotiated rules administered by the state or other bureaucratic agencies regulate determinations about what has moral worth and what is healthy. Ironically, in the attempt to clarify the line between natural and conventional, certification exacerbates the industrialization process and further undermines the original natural foods ethic of self-reliance.

In a situation in which the natural foods movement and industry are intertwined, each of these issues raises the question of how to separate out supporters of the movement's ideals from people who simply want to profit from them. In the past, when this movement was small and marginal, people who identified with it were confident of their abilities to distinguish friend from foe. The standard used to differentiate the truly committed from the poseur was the consistency of one's engagement with natural, and shunning of industrial, processes and products. Choices of natural food products were limited, and therefore, the touchstones were obvious: whole grains, organically grown fresh produce, and a limited array of items designated as health food. Similarly, the people who produced and sold natural foods were few in number and knew one another, by name if not personally, through the small network of publications, trade shows, and distributors. While there were heated disagreements and internal lines dividing movement participants—vegetarians from consumers of animals raised without chemical additives, or proponents of health food from those who condemned any manufactured product—the gap between the world of natural foods and the conventional food system was wide and clear. But after commercial opportunities expanded and newcomers poured into the industry, the dedication of people claiming to champion the reform of society's food and medical sectors became far more suspect. In this context, disputes over boundaries took on heightened importance.

Packing Nature into a Pill

The uncertainty about whether vitamin supplements should be considered a natural food goes back to when vitamins were first identified as important for nutrition. Natural foods proponents regarded the discovery of vitamins as further evidence for the importance of maintaining a healthy, vegetable-rich diet. But the notion of supplementing the diet with isolated vitamin products provoked more debate. Natural foods leader Otto Carqué was one who early on opposed the promotion of any substance not a whole food. He noted that "many volumes have been written on vitamins, and commercialism has taken advantage of this situation by unduly exploiting the vitamin theory. Specially prepared vitamin foods, in different shapes and forms, are now widely advertised, claiming miraculous effects, and they seem to find a ready sale to a credulous, misinformed public" (Carqué 1925, 79). Carqué's advice to turn away from such substances did not prevail in the health food industry, however, and vitamin supplements were commonly sold in health food stores by the late 1930s. Promoters of vitamin supplements argued that a purely natural diet was not possible in urban society and therefore supplements were a necessity for those who sought good health. This was especially the case, they argued, for the general public, who had not yet learned how to stop consuming conventional food. As Ada Alberty, another health food leader, wrote in a promotional booklet for her products in 1939, "As a result of over-processing and re-finement of our foods, plus a faulty selection of the foods that constitute the daily diet, there seems to be ample evidence of an ever increasing con-dition of vitamin deficiency in the average diet."[2]

Despite the association of vitamins with nutrition, it was not the case in the early decades of vitamin sales that vitamin supplements were defined as a health food in the same way that wheat germ or blackstrap molasses or kelp was. Indeed, most vitamins were manufactured by drug compa-nies, and conventional drugstores dominated the vitamin market through the 1940s (Apple 1996, 68). Department stores and grocery stores sold them as well. But the vitamin supplements sold in health food stores were often different from vitamins sold elsewhere, and that difference helped reinforce the idea that a pill could be a natural food.

The difference came down to natural versus synthetic vitamin supple-ments. So-called natural vitamins are simply concentrations of vitamin-rich food. Synthetic vitamins, on the other hand, are derived from a variety of sources, such as petrochemicals or bacteria, which are chemically manipu-lated to get a pure vitamin with the same or similar molecular structure as one derived from food. This process allows for vitamins to be manufactured far more cheaply than naturally derived vitamins. For many scientists, a vi-tamin is a vitamin, and the source is irrelevant. But the health food industry has always viewed supplements like other foods and insisted that chemi-cal processing methods and unhealthy fillers or additives make synthetic vitamins inferior to their natural counterparts. Therefore, natural vitamin manufacturers would frequently list the food source of their vitamins; for example, rose hips for vitamin C, or brewer's yeast for vitamin B, or wheat germ oil for vitamin E.[3]

Thus, the defense of vitamin supplements in the health food industry was always twofold. It was about defending the value of supplements in general, something not universally accepted within the natural foods field. And it was about defending the superiority of natural vitamins over syn-thetic varieties, something that most natural foods advocates accepted.

Within the health food field, vitamins became the focal point for de-bates about the boundaries of the natural foods category, overshadowing skepticism about other concoctions that were also clearly manufactured rather than plucked from nature. This focus on vitamin supplements was related to their taking pill or capsule form, resembling a medical drug—the exact thing that those following a natural health regimen were trying to avoid. The concern about imitating the practices of conventional medicine helps explain why other packaged or processed foods sold under the health food umbrella could look acceptable by comparison. For instance, in 1945, Loma Linda Foods, the manufacturer of canned meat substitutes, could scornfully dismiss the craze for vitamins, urging: "Make this a challenge to you, United States consumer. Get wise to good food and good cooking. If you are in excellent health, well selected good food in sufficient quantity will provide your nutritional needs much more economically than pills. If you are ill, let a responsible doctor prescribe for you."[4] For mid-twentieth-century supplement defenders, on the other hand, naturally derived vitamins were akin to herbal and other natural folk remedies that preceded the pharmaceuticals of conventional medicine. But even proponents understood that vitamins were something of a concession. Relying on their seeming health-giving properties was a concession to living in a society where a truly natural lifestyle was not possible. And their revenue potential was a concession to the difficulties of running a profitable business in which most of the goods for sale were unappealing to most consumers.

As discussed in chapter 6, the counterculturalists who entered the industry in the 1970s were especially vocal about the contradictions of promoting health foods that were adjuncts to the diet rather than the main course, and they successfully reoriented the industry toward providing more actual food. But the counterculturalists did not succeed in eliminating supplements from the natural foods mix. On the contrary, vitamins remained a symbol of health food and were often the product that drew new consumers into the natural foods orbit. In other words, vitamins were key to recruiting followers, especially those who were culturally mainstream, to a natural foods lifestyle. After people entered a health food store in search of vitamins, they might engage in conversation with the proprietor about natural health or come across other products they were willing to try. Vitamins represented an easy first step to experimenting with alternative health practices.

Over time, vitamins accounted for a smaller proportion of total supplement sales, while enzymes, plant and fish oils, fruit and vegetable concentrates, and other supplements took a larger share. (Once the Dietary Supplement Health and Education Act of 1994 was passed, the legal definition of a *dietary supplement* became "a vitamin, mineral, herbal, botanical, or amino acid ingredient used to supplement the diet.") Along with an expansion in the assortment of and demand for available supplements came a greater temptation for manufacturers to give nature a boost by surreptitiously adding unauthorized ingredients. Precisely because they are not straightforward foods, supplements have always been prone to misrepresentation and adulteration. But the incentives to introduce decidedly nonnatural components into their formulas was heightened after supplements caught on within physical culture circles in the mid-twentieth century. Bodybuilders, weight lifters, and other athletes were intensely interested in increasing strength, endurance, and body mass, and especially those who competed at an elite level faced considerable pressure to find a regime with proven results.

It was in the 1950s that some athletes began experimenting with anabolic steroids, which are synthetic hormones that resemble testosterone. Despite alarming side effects, steroids became more common among elite athletes during the 1960s. Health food manufacturers did not lace their products with steroids at this time, but some producers were probably complicit with steroid use. Randy Roach has argued that supplement sales in the 1960s benefited from steroid use since athletes would not admit to taking steroids and instead attributed their successes to diet and supplements. Admirers of the athletes, hoping to achieve similar physical feats, then flocked to the endorsed products (Roach 2004, 33).

However, as the health food industry grew—with a widened customer base, new entrepreneurs entering the market, and more abundant sources of capital available for developing new products—some supplement manufacturers were directly involved in using ingredients produced in a lab. In such cases, they created products that resembled pharmaceuticals more than substances harvested from nature. Problems with misrepresentation in supplements are persistent, with bursts of public attention whenever some new class of ingredients that cross the line dividing benign botanicals from dangerous drugs comes to light. Substances that mimic steroids periodically crop up, such as androstenedione, which the US Food and Drug Administration (FDA) ordered companies to cease distributing in 2004.[5] Until recalled by the FDA in 2013, so-called workout supplements containing DMAA, a stimulant found in a type of geranium but actually produced synthetically for commercial use, put users at risk of increased blood pressure and appeared to contribute to at least two deaths (Singer and Lattiman 2013a, 2013c, 2013b; Singer 2013). Along with supplements marketed to athletes, products promoted as assisting weight loss and libido gain are most susceptible to problems (Bond 2011). Safety concerns do little to dampen the demand for such supplements, though. Consumers who seek out products that promise bodily enhancements are less than satisfied with the bodies that nature gave them; finding nature lacking rather than intrinsically superior, these consumers are less wary than other health food followers are of supplements that resemble drugs.

More widespread than the marketing of hazardous chemicals are practices related to adulteration. In the 2010s, studies found that numerous supplements substituted cheap fillers—such as soy, wheat, and rice, or even potentially toxic materials—for the expensive herbs that are the products' calling cards. One 2012 estimate was that up to one-quarter of the supplements on the market were adulterated (O'Connor 2013; Marshall 2012). The tendency for the discovery of potential health properties in relatively rare plants to generate rapid, intense demand contributes to the problem. Easily harvested plants are often soon depleted, and as the ingredient becomes harder and more expensive to source, the resulting price of a supplement puts off otherwise eager consumers. Unwilling to lose business, suppliers simply substitute in some cheaper material.

Since their origins, deceptive practices were perceived as a problem by members of the health food industry; many members feared that such practices would further health food's negative reputation, and the large number of industry members truly committed to a natural ideology were dismayed by synthetic goods masquerading as something natural. However, in an industry that is no longer a small network of people who are personally acquainted with one another, with ingredients now regularly sourced from all over the world, and with many more avenues available for selling products than in the past, the ability of the industry to effectively self-police is greatly diminished. In this way, the growth of the supplement market has undermined attempts to preserve the boundary between a natural food and a nonnatural substance. The disruptive role of supplements goes even further, though, as efforts to control lucrative supplement sales have also affected power relations within the natural foods field and have been a catalyst for redefining the field's core activities.

Supplements and Market Strength

Despite periodic scandals, the population's consumption of supplements has increased since the late twentieth century. According to the trade group the Council for Responsible Nutrition (2014), 68 percent of all American adults took supplements during 2014. A market research group, the Natural Marketing Institute, reports even higher penetration, with 84 percent of Americans claiming supplement use in 2014.[6] Although natural products merchants account for a minority of supplement sales—37 percent in 2015 (Kvidahl 2016)—supplements have remained a significant product category for natural foods retailers. Since the 1970s, supplements have accounted for, on average, 30 to 45 percent of natural and health food retailers' sales, though that share diminished somewhat by the 2010s. According to industry figures, supplements made up 27.5 percent of sales of natural products stores in 2015 (Huth 2016).[7] With higher profit margins resulting from larger markups than on grocery items, supplements keep many retailers—and wholesalers—solvent.

As supplement sales grew in the second half of the twentieth century, the financial strength and reach of purveyors of supplements was felt throughout the natural foods field. Supplement companies have long been a major source of funding for industry institutions, such as trade publications (via advertisements) and trade shows (via exhibits). Furthermore, many of the most popular spokespeople for health food have had a direct interest in supplement companies. But what has been especially divisive within the industry is the clout achieved by particular companies that have cornered portions of the supplement market.

One company that exemplifies the natural foods movement's ambivalence about the place of supplements in the field is GNC. David Shakarian, who came from a family of Armenian yogurt producers, founded a health food store called Lackzoom (a name later replaced by the more staid General Nutrition Centers, now known as GNC) in Pittsburgh in 1935. The store's inventory expanded along with the industry, and for some decades, it carried a full line of available health food. In the 1950s, the retailer added private-label vitamins to its selection of brand-name supplements, a common practice among health food stores then and now. As the health food market grew in the 1960s, General Nutrition, propelled by Shakarian's aggressive marketing efforts, expanded into a chain. The company saw massive growth in the 1970s; in 1971 alone, it more than doubled in size from the seventy-two outlets with which it began the year. Ten years later, it reached over a thousand outlets, and it kept growing, helped by an infusion of capital when the company went public in 1980.[8]

Throughout this period, GNC stores carried a large selection of natural and organic foods as well as supplements, including both natural and synthetic vitamins. But a growing emphasis on supplements was perhaps signaled in 1979 when the company began manufacturing its own vitamins. By then, others in the health food industry were accusing General Nutrition of unfair competition, including opening new outlets in close proximity to existing health food stores, and bait-and-switch advertising. Critics noted that GNC would announce heavily discounted prices on the most popular brands of supplements but actually stock few of them; instead, customers were steered to the retailer's own private-label items. In 1985, General Nutrition settled two lawsuits, one with supplement manufacturer William T. Thompson Co. and one with retail chain Nature Food Centres, both of which had charged General Nutrition with trying to monopolize the health food industry.[9] The lawsuits had many supporters within the industry, who agreed that General Nutrition posed a threat to other businesses and who denounced GNC for betraying the values of natural foods. David Ajay, the president of the National Nutritional Foods Association (NNFA), was quoted in the press as saying, "Ours is a business built on quality and integrity, and the chains are concerned only about price" (Minsky 1979).

Despite legal and business setbacks in the mid-1980s, GNC recovered and, beginning in 1988, found new avenues for expansion by selling franchises (Ansberry 1988). It also continued to cultivate its reputation as a discount retailer of health food in the same way that chains in other fields, such as Waldenbooks or Toys 'R' Us, were establishing themselves as low-cost and low-service merchants. At a time when most natural foods retailers were moving toward a fuller line of food, GNC increasingly focused on supplements and pursued a customer base of athletes and bodybuilders rather than natural foods devotees. By 1984, vitamins and other supplements made up 70 percent of General Nutrition sales, compared with 31.3 percent of sales of the average independent health food store.[10] GNC was also frequently the target of FDA and Federal Trade Commission (FTC) investigations into unauthorized health claims for its products, and it was often slow to discontinue items found to contain adulterated or dangerous ingredients.

Quick to capitalize on whatever nutritional finding was in the news, employing marketing campaigns that emphasized performance instead of natural qualities, and frequently called out for a lack of purity in its products, GNC has hovered at the margins of the natural foods field, neither fully in nor out of it. But its presence cannot be ignored. One wholesaler remarked, "GNC is kind of a sterile place. Even the franchisees, I don't find them to be gung-ho health food people. They could just as well have a Quiznos submarine shop franchise, I think." After agreeing with him, his coworker noted, "We used to always complain about them, but they helped to bring health foods to the mass just by doing so much advertising." More than any other health food or natural foods retailer, GNC successfully turned itself into an accessible merchant of (some) health food, serving a public more interested in the technical advancements of an industrialized society than in the unvarnished purity of nature. In the second decade of the twenty-first century, GNC remains a major player in the industry. In 2016, GNC had 4,456 outlets and accounted for 3.3 percent of all sales of natural and health food stores in the United States (Huth 2016, 31).

While GNC pursued a mainstream image and clientele early on and adopted a vertical integration strategy that allowed it to work largely independent of the rest of the health food industry, many other companies dealing in supplements were more invested in a natural foods identity and in sustaining relationships in the natural foods field. The supplement business was integral to cementing some relationships, while at the same time exacerbating tensions with industry members who viewed pills as a violation of natural foods principles. This situation is best seen in the wholesale sector where, for many years, the control of supplement sales gave a handful of firms a dominant position in the industry. Wholesalers play a key role in any consumer products industry characterized by numerous dispersed small retailers and suppliers who otherwise would have to manage a continuous stream of small, unstandardized orders. For most of the twentieth century, health and natural food stores tended to rely on wholesalers to provide much of their inventory, and from their origins in the 1930s through the late 1970s, the same eight wholesalers dominated the industry.[11] How these distributors handled delivery schedules, pricing, minimum purchase policies, the extension of credit, and the vetting of new products could make a major difference in a retailer's business as well as which items the retailer promoted to consumers. And with only one or, in a few places, two wholesalers controlling a given territory, retailers had little choice but to accede to the distributors' terms. As one manufacturer said, "The distributor, he laid the law down."

Even during the industry's expansion years of the 1960s and 1970s, small distributors found it difficult to compete because the large wholesalers made deals giving them exclusive rights to distribute popular brands of products. As interview respondents working during that time told me, the most important products distributed in this way were supplements produced by Schiff Bio Food Products and Plus Products. Remarked a wholesaler, "It was interesting because in order to be a major distributor—there were [lots] of minor distributors—you had to have Schiff and Plus, the two vitamin lines, of which there was eight distributors, or whatever the number was, that had them. . . . Schiff and Plus were happy. They were growing as fast as they could handle. They didn't want to rock the boat either. So a lot of small companies could not really get involved in becoming major distributors." This level of control by the major distributors caused considerable resentment, not just because growth ambitions were curtailed but because that ambiguous natural food, the vitamin, was the key to developing a sizeable business. The major wholesalers' market strength provided added reason to advocate for an understanding of natural foods that was less pill-centered.

With no possibility of becoming a major player, most distributors in the 1960s and 1970s had to settle for developing specialized niches. One such niche was frozen food, something the large health food distributors did not carry but which was developed by Tree of Life, a Florida wholesaler. Another niche was reaching the countercultural natural foods stores that had little interest in supplements and whose cultural styles were distinct from the older health food generation. Chico-San, for instance, formed the Spiral Foods Distributing Company to distribute macrobiotic food to natural foods stores (Milbuty 2011). Another firm with a countercultural orientation was Mountain Peoples Warehouse, which started distributing fresh produce, especially to co-ops. By 1982, there were an estimated 122 health/natural foods distributors in the United States, most of which did not carry a full range of available products.[12] The result was a more diversified industry, in terms of food options, and new companies, such as Tree of Life and Mountain Peoples Warehouse, that were growing powers in distribution.

Efforts to diminish the centrality of supplements in the industry had implications for natural foods politics as well. While the old guard prided itself on maintaining purity by keeping conventional food companies at arm's length, the younger generation chafed at what they saw as hypocrisy in claiming to maintain natural standards while pushing questionably natural supplements. Said one person who was part of the generation critical of health food, "They were opposed to some of the things that we were trying to do. Like clean up the vitamin part of the business. We couldn't trust what those products were because they wouldn't come clean with what they were. They didn't want to accept the fact that all these artificial ingredients and preservatives and stuff needed to be moved out. One was natural and one was health. And the health part didn't have the same standards as the natural products." These tensions came to a head in the 1981 election for the president of the National Nutritional Foods Association.

The health food wing backed Rosemarie West, a retailer from Richmond, Virginia. The natural foods wing supported Hank Bednarz, Jr., owner of an Ann Arbor, Michigan, store called Arbor Farms. What was at stake in the election was in part the symbolism of who controlled organization leadership. But what also mattered was the form of advocacy in which the trade association would engage. For most of the natural foods movement's history, relations with government and other centers of institutional power were reactive and defensive, with natural foods advocates trying to preserve the right to engage unimpeded in their lifestyle in the face of efforts to marginalize or criminalize it. The issue of supplements embodied this reactive stance, as proponents sought minimal oversight by government and the exclusion of medical authorities from decisions about supplement consumption. A more active and positive form of advocacy, though, would enlist the state to mandate that natural foods principles be applied more broadly. The supplement-focused trade associations may have endorsed positive goals such as legal restrictions on preservatives and pesticides or state financial supports for organic agriculture equivalent to those available to commodity agribusiness, but the trade groups did not actively pursue such goals.

After West narrowly won the NNFA election,[13] the natural foods wing directed its restiveness into building new trade associations. These organizations tended to be small and narrowly defined, focusing especially on organic food. In this way, members could draw precise boundaries around their particular conceptions of natural foods and ensure greater affinity among themselves, though at the expense of the fragmentation of the industry and the movement as a whole. An important exception to this fragmentation trend was when Doug Greene, publisher of the trade journal *Natural Foods Merchandiser*, founded a new trade show, Natural Foods Expo, in 1981. It was meant to be a more inclusive gathering than the NNFA annual convention and one where supplements did not dominate. Industry members identifying with the newer natural foods orientation were immediately drawn to Natural Foods Expo for both political and stylistic reasons. As one participant said, "The show was hip. At an NNFA party they had big band music; at the Expo they had rock 'n' roll." The new show was highly successful, attracting 3,500 attendees in its first year.[14] Before long, the health food wing, including supplement companies, started attending it as well, and the NNFA convention faded to a small gathering focused mainly on policy issues instead of being an occasion to do business. Natural Foods Expo remained an annual (and later, biannual) event that brought together all parts of the industry and created opportunities for new alliances and new players to be discovered.

While the generation that grew out of the counterculture applauded this development for allowing for a more central role for food, some health food people saw a field that was now open to opportunists who were more interested in making money than in spreading natural foods values. Said one wholesaler, "The NNFA wouldn't allow these mass-market people into their conventions. The NNFA would not let these people become members, the drug store chains and the supermarkets. Didn't want them there. Until these guys, Natural Foods Merchandiser, came on the scene and started their own shows and opened it up. And that's when it exploded. They've taken it over. And they don't have the rules and restrictions. It's big business now." In trying to reclaim the concept of natural from the supplement-heavy health food wing, advocates inadvertently helped open up the industry to a huge range of manufactured products sold by an equally diverse range of companies including, as I will discuss shortly, some of the largest food corporations in the world. In 2015, 71,000 industry members attended what is now called Natural Products Expo West, with 2,700 exhibitor companies.[15]

In the transition from health food to natural foods, the industry and movement did renew a commitment to promoting a comprehensive diet composed entirely of natural foods. But this transition did not resolve questions about the definition of a natural diet. Supplements remain a key part of many individuals' natural foods repertoire. Packaged, processed, and prepared foods—made with natural ingredients—appeal to consumers craving convenience. Natural sweets and snack foods proliferate so that indulgence can be a routine occurrence. Proponents of a natural foods lifestyle certainly debate whether these types of foods belong in a truly natural diet. But a desire to expand the consumer base for natural foods creates pressures to accept a flexible understanding of the natural foods category. It also creates incentives for the natural and conventional food industries to join forces.

The Industrialization of Natural Foods

As I have been arguing throughout this book, the natural foods movement has for more than a hundred years been led by the health/natural foods industry. In this situation, aspirations for achieving profits and realizing philosophical ideals informed each other so that spreading a natural foods way of life became synonymous with creating consumer demand for relevant products. This convergence between economic and political goals was always subject to some dispute but generally accepted as long as the health food industry remained starkly different from the conventional food sector in terms of personnel and ways of doing business. However, managing the inherent tension in this situation became much more difficult after the natural foods industry underwent intensive industrialization in the latter part of the twentieth century. To speak of the industrialization of a preexisting industry may sound tautological. But, following other scholars (Fitzgerald 2003; Barlett 1993),[16] I am using the term *industrialization* in a more specific way to refer to the ability to engage in truly mass production and distribution. That involves large-scale operations, standardized facilities and procedures, an intensive division of labor, and frequently the use of machinery and other technologies. While each of these dimensions matters for the natural foods industry, what has been most emblematic of industrialization in this field is the entry of big corporations.

Julie Guthman has argued that in the realm of agriculture, a focus on scale or size as an indicator of industrialization and an assumption that smallness is equivalent to virtue are misguided. In her view, these perspectives are rooted in a conservative sentimentality that overlooks how labor has been exploited on so-called family farms; moreover, she claims, there is nothing inherent in bigness that makes it incompatible with alternative agricultural practices (Guthman 2004, 12, 174–75). However, while Guthman is correct that small-scale operations are perfectly compatible with exploitation, it is not simply because of romantic illusions about the past that so many economic actors—whether workers, managers, or consumers, and whether in agriculture, manufacturing, or distribution—find bigness alienating. With bigness often comes an impersonal work environment, an ever-changing cast of exchange partners, and the monotony of specialization. But beyond implications for the work experience, the existence of large-scale enterprises has important consequences for the concentration of economic power. It corresponds to efficiencies and economies of scale that make it very difficult for other players to compete. And it gives the big considerable influence in shaping the terms of market exchange. But growth is a double-edged sword; while it grants large firms significant competitive advantages, it also erodes their independence as it compels them to do whatever is necessary to attract a large enough market to support them.

Since the 1970s, the natural foods movement has had to confront the presence of large companies in its midst. Some companies have been home-grown, some are the product of mergers, and some represent conventional food corporations or diversified conglomerates that have entered the nat-ural foods field. In many cases, a combination of these three processes are at work. This development has caused considerable controversy as natural foods followers debate whether large firms are as committed to the values of their movement as are smaller companies. Almost everyone I interviewed had mixed feelings about bigness in the natural foods field, including people who themselves held top positions in large companies. Many were appreciative of large firms' ability to grow the market, and many also see bigness as an inevitable outcome of an industry that has finally matured. But most were at least somewhat critical of the outsize clout of big companies, though they tended to direct their criticism not at their own companies but at larger competitors or at the big suppliers and customers on which they depend. Thus, retailers criticize big wholesalers, wholesalers criticize big manufacturers, growers criticize big retailers, and so on. Commented a retailer:

> Say there's one big company in the area. And the founders are really committed to what they were doing. Made a fortune, sold out their company. Think that the only way that things can get better in this world is if *they* get bigger. They're re-ally committed to that concept of them getting bigger. And yet, they're flying in stuff from New Zealand and China and elsewhere because they can't get enough ingredients here. And they almost exclusively can only deal with giant farms at this point. And I don't want all that. I'm part of the local movement. I don't want all this control in a very few people, even if they're decent, good people.

The first signs of industrialization surfaced when conventional grocery stores started to show serious interest in health food in the early 1960s. At first, supermarkets carried selected items integrated with other products. But in 1970, supermarkets in California took this practice a step further by developing separate sections to showcase health food.[17] Supermarket personnel were not highly knowledgeable about health food; all they knew was that customers were now asking for the products. To cultivate business, health food wholesalers offered to serve as *rack jobbers*, mean-ing that they did most of the work of maintaining the health food sections by monitoring sales, handling stocking, and tagging and arranging mer-chandise. In this way, supermarkets did not need to invest in developing expertise about a seemingly peculiar domain that was parallel to the conventional one they knew.

The move toward placing health food in conventional markets greatly angered health food store owners, who worried about a loss of business resulting from the convenience of one-stop shopping offered by supermarkets and the big grocers' ability to charge lower prices. The retailers considered it a lack of solidarity when health food producers or wholesalers sold to conventional grocers. To manage the antagonism, manufacturers sometimes carried two lines of the same or similar products—the traditional brand sold to health food stores and a different label sold to supermarkets.[18] Similarly, the wholesaler Kahan & Lessin set up a subsidiary in 1965 called Best Brands to serve conventional grocers separately from the health food stores. Using a separate distribution facility and separate trucks, the distributor could claim that its principal business was dedicated to the health food stores. The wholesalers tried to show their loyalty in other ways as well. One said: "We had some enlightened self-interest, so we protected the little independent stores by not bringing certain brands into those [conventional] stores. And those grocers started getting calls for certain brands, and we would give them excuses why they couldn't buy it. And actually it was trying to protect the core business, which was the independent operators." Despite such efforts, health food retailers remained angry. They threatened boycotts, and in some parts of the country, they tried to set up their own distribution arms to cut out the faithless wholesalers. A flyer announcing a 1971 organizing meeting of the Independent Natural Food Retailers Association, based in Jersey City, asserted:

> For many years now we have purchased all our merchandise from these distributors and watched them grow from small business to giant corporations with a life and death hold on the HEALTH FOOD industry here in the metropolitan area. For many years now we have watched the rest of the country enjoy a HEALTH FOOD boom and now, when it has finally reached New York the big distributors, who we put in business, are going to the big chain stores and putting them in direct competition with us [which] has stumped [sic] the growth of our business. . . . If we organize now, we can fight this influx of big business into our industry.[19]

In the retailers' view, the transition from small to large company represented a moral as well as a size change, foretelling a ruthlessness in business relations and a weakening of commitment to a natural foods way of life.

As it turned out, supermarkets did not become the lethal threat that health food stores feared. The conventional grocery stores stocked a limited number of health food items and could not offer the advice about naturopathic health that interested many health food followers. With uneven success in selling such products, the supermarkets' forays into natural foods were erratic. When they didn't produce anticipated profits, the grocers would pull back and then try again some years later. Even with a division dedicated to serving conventional groceries, supermarkets made up only about 15 percent of Kahan & Lessin's sales by 1979.[20] Still, the supermarkets did breach what had been a firm divide between the conventional and natural foods sectors and gave natural foods further legitimacy in the public eye. Supermarkets became a more important destination for natural foods customers beginning in the 1990s. But by then, the corporate world had made other significant incursions into the field.

It is fitting, remembering the split between John Harvey Kellogg and his brother Will over the cornflakes business, that one of the first attempts by conventional food companies to create their own lines of natural foods occurred with breakfast cereal. Granola, the preparation that helped launch John Harvey Kellogg into the health food business in the nineteenth century, made a comeback during the 1960s, with both homemade and commercial varieties eaten by natural foods devotees and experimenters alike. Impressed—and concerned—by the popularity of granola, conventional food companies decided to get into the act. Between 1972 and 1974, several major food corporations, including Pet, Quaker Oats, Kellogg, and General Mills, developed their own lines of granola-like cereals for the mass market, though these products tended to have a lot more sweetener than health food varieties did.[21] Ralston Purina went even further, in 1972 bringing out not just granola but twenty specific items categorized as health food (Pacey 1972). The natural breakfast cereal market proved especially lucrative, and gradually conventional food companies stopped thinking of natural foods as laughable and instead decided to cautiously invest in them. Because it was such unfamiliar territory for the conventional food companies, success usually depended on acquisition rather than producing their own lines.

Early interest in acquiring health food companies actually came not from the major food corporations but from other conglomerates and investors who saw opportunities in a growing market. One of the first major acquisitions was in 1968, when the venerable natural vitamin company

Schiff Bio Foods was purchased by Iroquois Industries, a diversified conglomerate whose only holding in food was a brewery.[22] Another milestone was the 1970 acquisition of the Seventh-day Adventist company Worthington Foods by Miles Laboratories, the maker of Alka-Seltzer, One-a-Day vitamins, and other conventional health products. Miles was less interested in pursuing a natural health market than in acquiring Worthington's technological expertise in creating fabricated foods such as textured vegetable protein, used as a meat substitute. In this way, one of the oldest health food companies helped lead a conventional consumer product company into sophisticated processing activities.[23]

It was not until the 1980s that the major food companies looked to acquire natural foods manufacturers. The pace of acquisitions picked up over the next two decades when the owners of many natural foods companies reached a crossroads. Some company heads wanted to retire and had no in-house successor. Some had growth ambitions and needed more capital to fulfill them. Some simply saw that the time was right to cash out and profit from their years of labor. It was now clear that natural foods were not a passing fad, and by the first decade of the twenty-first century, most major food companies felt obliged to respond to the growing segment of consumers concerned about the relationship between food and health. Since then, natural foods companies have been drawn into a whirlwind of acquisition, merger, and divestment activity.[24] Some of the best-known natural foods brands have come under the ownership of General Mills, Kellogg, Kraft, Coca-Cola, and other major food companies.

Just as supermarkets did not always understand how to profitably merchandise natural foods, conventional manufacturers sometimes falter in negotiating what is still a niche market and may sell off or discontinue their natural foods lines. Perhaps the company that best illustrates the dance between natural foods and conventional food companies is Hain, a health food outfit that started in the 1920s and that became the largest manufacturer in the health food industry. Although Hain underwent some ownership changes earlier, its tenure under conventional food company ownership began in 1982, when it was sold to Ogden Food Products, maker of Progresso soups. In 1986, Ogden sold Hain to Pet, and then in 1994, Pet sold it to Kineret, a public specialty foods company run by Irwin Simon. Under conventional food company ownership, Hain was a neglected oddball subsidiary. But Simon decided to focus his business, now called the Hain Food Group, on the natural foods market and showed how growth could be accomplished by borrowing the techniques without the actual ownership of the major food corporations. Employing practices typical of any growth-minded corporation, Simon directed capital derived from being publicly traded into an aggressive acquisition strategy that snared many established natural foods concerns and into extensive marketing that helped land Hain products in both natural and conventional food outlets. Hain's numerous deals included a merger with Celestial Seasonings in 2000, at which point the company's name was changed to Hain Celestial. By 2014, Hain Celestial had achieved worldwide sales of $2.2 billion on more than fifty-five brands incorporating thousands of natural foods and personal care products.[25]

Hain Celestial, the brands controlled by the conventional food companies, and some other large independent companies now account for most natural foods sold. As the trade press reported, "Large manufacturers (greater than $15 million in revenue) make up only 3 percent of all natural product makers, but they gobble 85 percent of market share, according to the Natural Products Marketing 2015 Benchmark Report by SPINS and Pure Branding" (Marshall 2015). What this means is that there are huge numbers of small producers with small, often exclusively local, sales existing side by side with a group of natural foods giants that have often had, currently or in the past, some relationship with a conventional food company. These giants include not only makers of packaged food but also organic produce growers, such as Earthbound Farm, and organic dairy producers, such as Horizon; those two companies were brought together in 2014 when Horizon's parent, WhiteWave Foods, acquired Earthbound.[26]

The large natural foods manufacturers both do and do not resemble conventional food producers. They all achieve financial gains by pursuing the mass market, but natural foods companies do so by developing alternatives to the many packaged and convenience foods of the conventional food industry. What allows these alternative products to claim the natural foods title is usually their ingredients, which may be organic or lacking in artificial preservatives or other additives. But their status as healthy food can be rather questionable since, like conventional products, they are often high in fats, sugar, and sodium to enhance tastiness. The big natural foods companies also distinguish themselves by professing a commitment to environmental stewardship. But their products may combine ingredients sourced from all over the globe. And their processing, transportation, and storage involve considerable resource use since many different elements have to come together in a manufacturing facility and then go out again in individual packages to far-flung distributors and retailers.

In all these ways, natural foods production has undergone considerable industrialization and has helped move the concept of natural foods even further away from something that is as close as possible to its natural state, is produced with minimal impact on the environment, and allows the consumer an intimate connection with nature. However, the industrialization process has not occurred just at the level of production. It is also in distribution and retailing that the lines separating the natural and conventional foods industries have been blurred.

The Chaining of Natural Foods

The greatest amount of consolidation in the natural foods industry has actually been in the distribution sector. In the 1980s, with other supplement manufacturers on the rise, the once dominant Schiff and Plus brands lost market share and no longer could make or break a distribution company. Instead, economies of scale became key to a wholesaler's success and set in motion a wave of mergers that eventually subsumed the old distributors on which the industry had depended for so many decades. The wholesale companies that came out ahead ended up being from the generation that had been forced to look beyond supplements for goods to sell. One of those, Tree of Life, was acquired by the Dutch company Wessanen in 1985. With Wessanen's capital behind it, Tree of Life acquired Balanced Foods in 1986 and suddenly became the largest natural foods distributor in the United States, but with a more varied line of food than the older major wholesalers had. In 2010, Tree of Life was sold to KeHE Food Distributors, a specialty food wholesaler that had moved more into natural foods in the first decade of the twenty-first century. KeHE solidified its position as one of the two largest natural foods distributors in the country when it acquired one of the last independent natural foods wholesalers, Nature's Best, in 2014.

Meanwhile, another important merger occurred in 1996 when Mountain Peoples Warehouse joined with Cornucopia Natural Foods, a similar-sized wholesaler on the East Coast, to form United Natural Foods Inc. (UNFI). UNFI went public that year and began a string of acquisitions that turned it into the country's largest natural foods distributor by the beginning of the twenty-first century. UNFI and KeHE became the main gatekeepers to the natural foods consumer market, since any producer who wanted widespread access to retail outlets would likely need to first get his or her goods accepted by one of those two distributors. The shrinking number of wholesalers also helped spur the growth of another type of intermediary, the broker, who specializes in convincing distributors and retailers to carry a manufacturer's product.

Although not nearly as concentrated as distribution, the retail landscape has also seen striking consolidation since the 1990s. Certainly the most visible success story in the natural foods industry is Whole Foods Market.[27] This retail giant, like so many other businesses in the field, grew out of an expression of a countercultural lifestyle. John Mackey, a young man who had lived in a vegetarian co-op and worked for a natural foods store, cofounded his own shop in Austin, Texas, in 1978, called Safer Way (a play on the name of the Safeway supermarket chain). In 1980, the store was merged with another Austin retailer, Clarkesville Natural Grocers, and was renamed Whole Foods. After opening a handful of additional outlets in Texas, the company started acquiring natural foods stores elsewhere around the country, helped by an infusion of capital when it went public in 1991. Being especially interested in large outlets that sold a wide range of natural foods, Mackey purchased several regional chains that had developed the "supernatural" format, including Bread & Circus of Boston, Mrs. Gooch's in Southern California, Maryland-based Fresh Fields, and Harry's Farmer's Market of Atlanta. (Paumgarten 2010; Biddle 1992; L. Lee 1996; Zwiebach 2001.) The 1993 purchase of Mrs. Gooch's, by then a seven-store chain, was especially important to Whole Foods' future because Mrs. Gooch's provided expertise in style, service, and selection that was used to guide other Whole Foods outlets. Whole Foods' most contentious merger came in 2007 when it acquired Wild Oats, its major national rival at the time. The FTC initially opposed the merger on the grounds that it would reduce competition. After two years of court battles, a settlement was finally reached whereby Whole Foods agreed to sell off some outlets in exchange for the regulator's approval.[28] The deal solidified Whole Foods' standing as the country's largest natural foods retailer. By 2014, Whole Foods had 387 outlets and 28.8 percent of all natural foods store sales (Marshall 2015, 20).

Whole Foods is viewed with great ambivalence among natural foods supporters. As one producer said, "Whole Foods is the biggest problem in the industry right now, in addition to being one of the biggest good things." On the one hand, it is admired for attracting so many new consumers, for compelling its suppliers to adhere to high standards for ingredients, and for elevating the status of natural foods. On the other hand, it is viewed as a ruthless competitor that has put countless small stores out of business while remaking natural foods into the quintessential good for affluent consumers with a conscience. The company also has considerable power within the field. After noting how Whole Foods has "grown the industry substantially" because of the quality of its food and the attractiveness of its stores, a retailer said:

> They have a lot of clout. A *lot* of clout. . . . Everybody in the industry will feel it. Manufacturers will feel it by the amount of product that Whole Foods buys. And the distributors feel it the same way, by the amount that gets ordered through the distribution center. . . . When you try to put a line of products at Whole Foods—and this is not just Whole Foods, it's the other chains as well: Sprouts out in Arizona, Sunflower—they all want a free case of everything to put up on the shelf and get started. And they want advertising on top of that. It costs a lot of money. Smaller, little boutique manufacturers can't afford it.

Whole Foods helped stimulate the proliferation of new natural foods products by creating such a massive amount of shelf space to fill. But it also gave an advantage to the big distributors and producers who could meet the chain's demands to efficiently and consistently deliver large quantities of goods, along with providing the discounts and other financial incentives that Whole Foods expected.

As the foregoing quote illustrates, Whole Foods is not alone among the supernaturals. Sprouts and Vitamin Cottage, for instance, are two regional chains that seek to offer a full selection of food items. Additional competition comes from online dealers, especially in the area of supplements. And there are still several thousand independent natural foods retailers left in the country. While many small-scale and alternative retailers have not been able to survive since Whole Foods' ascendance, farmers markets have mushroomed, as well as Community Supported Agriculture arrangements, in which consumers prepay a farmer for a weekly supply of goods during the growing season. Even co-ops, which declined after the new style of natural foods store came on the scene in the 1980s, made a comeback in the twenty-first century (J. Robinson and Hartenfeld 2007; Jablow and Horne 1999; Haedicke 2014; Thompson and Coskuner-Balli 2007). Nevertheless, the natural foods chains remain especially successful, in part because of the economies of scale they can employ. Additionally, they construct environments that appear more alluring and easy to use than smaller stores, and they transform a qualitative approach to consumption—the purposeful seeking of personal and environmental health—into greater quantities of consumption. Retailers such as Whole Foods work to assure customers that they have put into place the mechanisms that allow people to consume both responsibly and without restraint.

It is easy, of course, to demonize Whole Foods. The grocer replicates a story that has been played out in so many other industries, from books to hardware to office supplies, wherein a giant retailer enters the scene and drives out many small independent shops, amassing enormous power in its industry in the process (L. Miller 2006). And Whole Foods has been faulted for its antiunion stance (reflecting Mackey's libertarian politics) and its blatant appeal to status-conscious affluent shoppers. But the picture is more complex than that of simply a ruthless corporation out to make a profit at any cost. Those who founded and manage Whole Foods sincerely believe in the superiority of natural foods. They have won over new natural foods enthusiasts and have enhanced the legitimacy of a natural foods way of life. They have set standards for quality and reliability of products that others in the industry need to follow. Whole Foods thus embodies both the peril and the promise of growth.

While many aspects of Whole Foods' operations straddle the line between conventional and natural sectors, other retailers, such as Trader Joe's, do so even more. Indeed, natural foods have been so widely diffused that it is hard to find a specialty "gourmet" shop or upscale grocery that does not emphasize items that fall into the natural foods category. Equally significant, the mainstreaming of natural foods has inspired mass market retailers to enter the field— not just regular supermarkets but even the formidable Walmart, whose discounted prices make it extremely difficult for other retailers to compete.

The result of all this activity is heightened ambiguity over who qualifies as a bona fide member of the natural foods field. Yet, this activity occurs at the same time as the anticorporate rhetoric of natural foods advocates gains wider currency. Condemning agribusiness, profit-obsessed multinationals and an industrialized food supply is easy to do in the abstract. But with so many parties claiming to support the values of natural foods, identifying the movement's specific opponents is not such a simple task. As one longtime natural foods advocate said, "The eagle that flies over the very large organic farm who is selling directly to Walmart doesn't care. The water's fresh, the land has some pests to attack. The farmer's happy that the eagle is eating the ground squirrels or the moles. And labor may not care. But the consolidation of that farm and the impact on farmers, they do care. So it's a tough one." Another advocate said, "I don't know where this is all going to end up. If it all ends up with the Whole Foods and the Walmarts run by the Earthbounds, I don't think we've changed anything other than there's less chemicals. I don't think it's really changed a lot." In his view, social change is defined as encompassing more than the environmental or health goals of removing chemicals from the food supply. But taking a broader view of social change means going beyond the easily reached consensus that natural is best. When considering the larger context in which natural foods are produced and used, specifically the scale and methods of operations, the sources of industry power and influence, and the economic and cultural motivations of consumers and producers alike, identifying the most important values connected to natural foods is much more subject to conflict.

Defining Standards

It is to resolve such questions about the line differentiating desirable from suspect products that the natural foods movement and industry have developed standards to codify a range of values, which can then be certified as present or not in a good. Standards translate general and vague principles into a set of explicit indicators whose presence can be empirically verified and which can be applied to all cases claiming to embody a value. Standards represent a rational, technical solution to the problem of achieving trust in a field that has grown too large and dispersed for people to be personally acquainted or to be able to regulate one another through informal means.

The move toward codifying standards has been most fully realized with organics. The problem of deception, in which sellers claim produce is organically grown, even if conventional fertilizers, pesticides, or herbicides have been used, goes back at least as far as the 1960s, when organic fruits and vegetables started to gain popularity. In 1972, an editor of Rodale's *Organic Gardening and Farming* magazine estimated that 50 to 70 percent of organically labeled food was not actually produced under organic conditions. Rodale Press began the first certification effort in 1971 in California, a center of organic production. Rodale's inspectors visited and took samples from farms to test for humus content and the presence of heavy metals, pesticides, and other contaminants. The following year, the program also included meat production, and expanded to the eastern United States.[29]

In 1973, the idea of organic certification was further developed with the formation of California Certified Organic Farmers (CCOF), a group of small organic growers who wanted to create a meaningful definition of *organic* that customers could trust. CCOF gradually attracted more members, who were certified as conforming to the organization's standards, and some became active in pushing for a state law that would specify organic standards for all of California. This law, passed in 1979, was limited by having no provisions for enforcement, but it nonetheless provided encouragement for other states to pass similar legislation and for crafting a federal law that would bring uniformity to how organic standards were applied. In 1990, the Organic Foods Production Act was passed, mandating the establishment of the National Organic Program under the US Department of Agriculture (USDA). Developing the actual standards took a decade longer, and the final version was approved in 2000, though there continue to be periodic updates. The law not only instituted specific standards but required that third-party agents do the actual certifying, which involves inspections of farms and facilities and checking the paper trail a producer keeps to track multiple aspects of his or her operations. The intention of the law was that certifiers be independent of producers, though in practice, there are often close ties between certifying agencies and the producers using their services.[30]

While many advocates of organic food supported the concept of an official seal certifying a product's organic qualities, the devil is in the details, and there was and is continuous disagreement over the content of the standards. For example:

1. How many years must soil be free of added chemicals before it is considered organic?
2. Can produce be called *organic* if it is cleaned in chlorinated or otherwise chemically treated water before packaging?
3. Can a manufactured food be organic if made with a synthetic thickening or stabilizing agent?
4. How much of a cow's feed needs to be organically grown for the resulting milk or meat to be considered organic?
5. Can confined livestock who eat organic feed but do not graze on pasture be considered organically raised?
6. Can wild fish, whose feeding habits cannot be controlled, ever be certified as organic?
7. How should new technology, such as genetic engineering or nanotechnology, be treated?

Each of these questions and many more have been debated at great length by the National Organic Standards Board, the body responsible for defining organic standards, with input from organic producers and nongovernmental organizations. Answers appear in technical language but are necessarily political in nature.[31] What is constantly being weighed is the extent to which stricter standards, which speak to a notion of purity, would disrupt existing practices of some growers and manufacturers and would raise the cost of compliance.

Standards have helped many small farmers, who can receive premium prices for certified organic products, yet standards have also aided in the industrialization of organic agriculture. In the first place, trade across territories becomes easier because protocols pertaining to organics are uniformly applied. One supporter of standards explained, "We don't have to worry about different laws in individual states. Or if we're exporting to the Pacific Rim or European Union, everyone understands what the products are grown by. The standards being consistent have made it easier to sell more products to a broader marketplace." Furthermore, the complex and costly bureaucratic procedures involved in certification can disenfranchise small players who may scrupulously adhere to organic principles but do not follow codified rules. The process of gaining organic certification can be so time-consuming and expensive that many farmers do not bother, instead calling their produce "no-spray" or something similar.[32] Moreover, standards act as a moral leveling device. Whether it be a large or small grower, or an independent or conglomerate-owned manufacturer, if they adhere to the standards, they appear to produce equally organic goods, which gives such diverse producers equivalent moral credibility in the eyes of the public.

Organic regulations represent the place where there has been the greatest amount of cooperation between the state and the natural foods industry. The motives of Congress and the USDA in developing the standards were not about paving the way for organic to be the norm in the food system but rather to facilitate trade in a growing economic sector. It is perhaps for this reason that organic standards have been a major source of division within the natural foods field. There is considerable debate about how strict the rules should be and considerable suspicion about the commitment of some of the players involved in developing the regulations. Tensions became especially acute during the ten-year period when the National Organic Standards Board was writing the federal standards and during the five-year period following issuance of the rules, when a Maine farmer named Arthur Harvey sued the USDA for allowing practices that he claimed violated the integrity of the organic law.[33]

During these years, organic proponents became divided into factions roughly corresponding to their social positions in the natural foods field. These factions included farmers, represented by groups such as the Northeast Organic Farming Association; environmentalists, represented by organizations such as the National Coalition Against the Misuse of Pesticides (later called Beyond Pesticides); consumers, represented by groups such as the Pure Food Coalition (which evolved into the Organic Consumers Association); and processors, manufacturers, and retailers, represented primarily by the Organic Trade Association. The Organic Trade Association in particular became alienated from other groups as it was viewed as trying to dilute the standards for the benefit of its large corporate members that were muscling their way into the field. Yet, the divisions were not as clean as a simple typology makes them out to be. There was some overlapping membership among groups, and many of the people who now found themselves at odds had cooperated with one another in various efforts during years past. There were also internal disagreements within particular organizations about the best course of action to take.

In my interviews with people who had been participants in these events and who were on opposite sides of the split over organic regulations, it was clear that they all believed very strongly in the value of the organic ideal; none of them were cynically trying to use the organic label as a form of greenwashing. But a fundamental difference had to do with where people stood on questions of size and scale—that is, whether the integrity of the organic concept was endangered when in the hands of big companies and whether allowances should be made for the sake of growing the market. Those who had supported looser or more gradually introduced standards believed that compromises were necessary to attract more entrepreneurs into the industry and to create enough diverse and affordable products to lure fickle consumers. For those who wanted stricter standards, the point of organic agriculture was first and foremost to "emulate nature" (K. Stewart 2003, 74), and industrial practices do not accomplish that goal. Organic standards may have made the legal definition of *organic* explicit, but they did not resolve questions about the priorities of an organic movement.

Although the USDA has some rather vague guidelines regarding how the word *natural* and a few related terms are to be used with reference to animal products (United States Department of Agriculture, Food Safety and Inspection Service 2015), no natural foods standard other than organic is administered and regulated by government agencies. Instead, a bewildering number of certification programs are offered by a range of trade associations, natural foods companies, advocacy organizations, and for-profit third-party agencies. Some of these certifications include a seal that is meant to inform and guide the consumer. Some are intended to communicate to industry buyers that a product or ingredient meets certain specifications. Among available certifications are GMP (good manufacturing practices) developed by the Natural Products Association for supplements; Natural Personal Care and Natural Home Care standards for cleaning products, also developed by the Natural Products Association; the Non-GMO Project, which verifies the absence of genetically modified or engineered substances; the Fair Wild standard for the sustainable collection of wild plants; the CarbonFree Product certification for reducing and offsetting a company's carbon emissions; the Marine Stewardship Council seal for sustainable fishing; various animal product certifications including guarantees that an animal was humanely raised, cage-free, or grass-fed; and numerous other seals certifying that a product is gluten-free, kosher, whole grain, and more. Many producers also seek fair trade certification (Brown 2013; Linton, Liou, and Shaw 2004) as an indication of fair labor practices associated with their goods' production.

All these certifications contribute to the cost of doing business, which is at least in part passed on to consumers. Producers who want a seal of approval generally need to invest in expensive new equipment, inputs, procedures, record keeping, and contracts with third-party certification agencies that monitor producer compliance. One 2010 estimate of the cost to a manufacturer in obtaining and maintaining several certifications put it at more than a million dollars a year (Agin 2010). While the natural foods industry, with its libertarian streak, has resisted heavy-handed government regulation for so many years, it has created a tangle of private red tape to assure consumers that the process of making natural foods is tame and orderly. The result is additional layers of intermediaries who stand between nature and the consumer.

While consumers do show signs of certification fatigue, as they are required to weigh the merits of products crowded with various seals of approval, it is important to remember that consumers are not the only customers for certified goods. Retailers also consider standards in merchandising decisions. Whole Foods, for instance, uses several sets of standards when determining whether to stock particular products, and it incorporates certifications into its marketing efforts. Some are preexisting programs, such as the USDA organic seal, some are developed in-house, such as Whole Foods' "Eco-Scale" for rating household cleaning products, and some are developed externally with Whole Foods sponsorship, such as the Global Animal Partnership that covers meat-animal welfare. Because of Whole Foods' enormous buying power, natural foods producers will frequently design their goods to meet Whole Foods' standards, which then get diffused throughout the industry. Whole Foods has often been commended for setting the bar higher than was previously typical in the industry. But it is another way in which the company achieves considerable control over what happens in the rest of the industry, and over the dietary practices of natural foods consumers.

The busy arena of standards and certifications can be understood as an attempt to reconcile the desire for a natural life with a modern, urbanized existence. Natural values are broken into discrete measurable pieces, but the aggregate may not produce the outcomes that advocates of a close connection to nature had in mind. Supplements and complex packaged foods, which appeal to consumers' desires for health, convenience, variety, and taste, are designated as just as natural as the raw ingredients with which they are made. Moreover, standards do not truly solve the problem of differentiating natural foods movement insiders from outsiders. Standards provide a blueprint that even the most politically indifferent for-profit business can follow to enter the market. And by innovating products that catch on with natural foods followers, that business may help define the future direction of the natural foods movement.

Unresolved Dilemmas

The growth in the number of people who believe in the merits of natural foods, along with the growth of the industry that serves them, mean that the natural foods movement is much less focused than in the past on achieving cultural legitimacy for this lifestyle. Instead, efforts are directed toward gaining state support and institutionalizing natural foods practices in places where food is produced and consumed. But as such practices have spread, so have uncertainties about who has the right to claim membership in the natural foods movement. In the past, relatively few people would profess an attachment to natural foods unless they actually were committed to reforming the dominant agrifood system. Today, the economic and cultural rewards for being recognized as part of the natural foods field are great enough that motivations are much more diverse.

The problem of how strictly to draw and police their boundaries is one faced by many social and cultural movements dealing with growth. Efforts to maintain a narrow and more orthodox understanding of movement ideals may preserve a movement's integrity, but they make it more likely that there will be fewer participants. For some movements, remaining small is an acceptable price to pay for staying true to core beliefs. But conventional wisdom generally assumes, rightly or wrongly, that social change is more likely to occur with a mass movement, creating internal pressure to grow. The desire for growth is all the more intensified when financial incentives are present, which in turn open up the movement to a wide variety of consumers and businesses, levels of commitment, and interpretations of movement goals.

In the natural foods movement, what is new is not the question of whether business should play a role; that was affirmatively answered long ago when John Harvey Kellogg combined the health food business with the religious ideals of food reform. Rather, the issue today is how to manage the large businesses that increasingly dominate the field and that cater to new waves of consumers unfamiliar with the natural foods field of old. While the movement can consider it a victory when natural foods are so popular that supermarkets stock them and conventional food companies manufacture them, these successes threaten to erase the distinction that separates natural from conventional foods and that previously gave the natural foods movement a vision of an alternate way of producing and consuming food.

Growth has changed both the social relations of the natural foods field and the field's unity and coherence. The industry has become less freewheeling than in the past and more subject to standard business practices. Many old-timers I spoke with expressed a sense of loss for an industry that was once small and intimate enough that everyone seemed to know one another and that generated a sense of common purpose in the face of ostracism and social repression. While nostalgia no doubt makes the past look rosier than is warranted, the current fragmentation of the field is evident in the profusion of businesses and advocacy groups, many of which focus on narrowly defined concerns. Yet, as I will argue in the next and final chapter, that fragmentation has not ended the leadership of industry in the natural foods movement.

CHAPTER EIGHT

Cultural Change and Economic Growth

Assessing the Impact of a Business-Led Movement

The dominant narrative in accounts of the modern natural foods movement holds that alternative food practices and a radical worldview
arose out of the counterculture and related social movement activity of
the 1960s and 1970s (Belasco 1989; Cox 1994; Schurman and Munro 2010).
These alternatives ranged from small-scale artisanal businesses to economic practices meant to exist outside of an exchange or for-profit context.
Consumer co-ops and "food conspiracies," back-to-the-land communes,
free food distribution endeavors, and other experiments that put, as the
slogan says, "people before profits," embodied a vision of how food could
be produced and consumed in an equitable and environmentally conscious
way. In this narrative, commercial forces exerted a corrupting influence as
alternative practices became reintegrated back into an industrial capitalist framework (Belasco 1989; Fromartz 2006).

This narrative is not completely wrong. But the long view of the natural foods movement points to a different way of understanding the movement's trajectory. If our starting point precedes the 1960s, we see that there
was never a linear progression from an economically disinterested movement to one whose politics were abandoned after the profit motive gained
ascendancy. Instead, the natural foods movement and industry have been
tightly intertwined since the late nineteenth century, with those connections reinforcing some of the radical tendencies of the movement and even
helping to give rise to the alternative experiments of the 1960s and 1970s

as well as to present-day innovations, such as Community Supported Agriculture and the spread of farmers markets. Furthermore, the long view reminds us that the natural foods movement has only rarely been opposed to the system of free enterprise and private property that characterizes capitalist relations, despite the anticorporate rhetoric heard in the 1960s and in the present era and despite the fact that some of the movement's most eloquent spokespeople, such as Otto Carqué, whose words opened this book, were incisive critics of capitalism. Rather than the movement's history being a simple tale of sabotage by market forces, the participation of individuals and organizations representing the natural foods industry both contributed to the natural foods movement's successes and affected the very understanding of what success means for the movement.

A survey of the social and cultural landscape of the contemporary United States shows that those successes have been considerable. There is now more cognizance and acceptance of the benefits of producing and consuming natural foods than at any other time in American history. The options for and availability of natural foods have grown enormously, making it perfectly normal to find quinoa at the supermarket and organic vegetables at Costco. Mockery of health food "nuts" has waned while sizeable portions of the population seek to integrate whole grains, fresh organic fruits and vegetables, herbal supplements, and packaged preparations made without synthetic additives into their diets. Many consumers draw connections between their food choices and a desire to engage in alternative health practices, and more people than ever before are consciously committed to sustainability, protection of the natural environment, and a belief in the value of a short line from food source to table. Science has confirmed some of the natural foods movement's claims about the dangers of processed food and synthetic inputs to agriculture, while the medical establishment pays heightened attention to nutrition as a factor in health. Government is as likely to support the natural foods sector as crack down on it. And mainstream institutions, from corporate cafeterias to public school systems, develop partnerships with the natural foods field.

Yet any such summary of transformations in food provisioning can be offset by an equally long list of areas where natural foods ideals have not triumphed. The practices of a dominant agrifood sector and the eating habits of most Americans continue patterns that the natural foods movement has long condemned, including a reliance on processed food, a meat- and sugar-heavy diet, and the use of synthetic fertilizers and chemical pesticides and herbicides in agriculture. Genetically engineered plants are so entrenched in soy, corn, and other crops that even the most careful organic farmer cannot prevent contamination. Food technologists are given wide latitude to create new edible substances that are as much a product of the lab as of nature. Industrial practices that mass-produce food cheaply (in part, because of government subsidies) create financial incentives to maintain and patronize the conventional sector. With consumers delighting in the array of choices made possible by a system in which neither season nor climate nor geographic distance need be an impediment to procuring items, food tends to travel hundreds or thousands of miles to reach its final destination.

For all these reasons, a natural foods movement oriented toward reforming prevailing food practices continues. And while there are more visible signs of strain than in previous eras, the movement is still tightly intertwined with the natural foods industry. That relationship helps explain many of the changes that have taken place in the natural foods movement. What remains central is a notion of the inherent goodness of nature and its restorative powers as compared to the physically and spiritually degrading effects of an existence dependent on artificial substitutes. However, this reverence for nature is now incorporated into a secular worldview that welcomes material abundance rather than a religious framework that teaches asceticism. Similarly, while a belief in the healing qualities of natural substances remains, natural foods are for most followers less a coherent philosophy and way of life with strict mandates than a set of individual consumer choices that are justified by reference to personal preference and that are easily taken up and put aside depending on the situation.

In this final chapter, I reflect on the evolution of the natural foods field, especially the consequences of commercial enterprises having played such a central role in the natural foods movement. In doing so, I provide some answers to the questions that have guided this book: What allowed natural foods ideals and practitioners to gain cultural legitimacy? How have movement goals and the meanings that underlie them been altered by the participation of people with an economic stake in movement activities? This analysis is meant to further an understanding of what the natural foods case can tell us about the intersection of private industry and social movements more generally.

When I first began my research, I too expected to find a fairly straightforward relationship between industry incursion and the progressive deradicalization of the natural foods movement. By radical, I am not referring to any particular political philosophy but to positions that shake up core beliefs and systems of social action. As discussed in chapter 1, the question of deradicalization has been a concern of numerous analysts of the natural foods movement, some who link deradicalization to institutionalization. This notion of institutionalization grew out of the application of organizational theory to social movements. While scholars vary in how they define it, *institutionalization* generally refers to movement activity that becomes routinized and subsumed in formal, often bureaucratic, organizations where activity is directed by a professional staff. Potential outcomes of institutionalization include the moderation of a movement's demands and tactics, or even co-optation into established political channels (David Meyer and Tarrow 1998).

The process of institutionalization is especially pertinent to the natural foods movement because of the development of trade associations, certification agencies, and corporations involved in the field, as well as cooperative endeavors with state regulators (Tovey 1999). Yet, as Nicola Edwards notes, institutionalization happens not just at the level of organizations but also through what she calls "normative institutionalization" (2013, 73)—that is, the mainstreaming process that makes movement values or goals culturally legitimate. The question is then whether that mainstreaming process necessarily includes the moderation of challenges to fundamental cultural ideas and practices that previously were taken for granted in a society. In her study of Indonesia's organic agriculture movement, Edwards argues that organizations that develop some aspects of institutionalization, such as a hierarchical structure and active engagement with the market, do not necessarily relinquish radical objectives and tactics. She claims that "institutionalization does not directly correlate with any particular values, conventional or otherwise" (Edwards 2013, 85).

As I have shown in my history of the natural foods field, industry leadership has drawn movement activity into formal organizations, such as companies and trade associations, and has found ways to further the mainstreaming process, especially through glamorizing symbols of an unconventional lifestyle. Yet, this history also demonstrates that these aspects of institutionalization do not invariably lead to movement deradicalization. After all, the natural foods industry existed for a century before the state and the conventional food and health sectors stopped denouncing the field as a threat to public welfare. To explain why (contrary to my initial expectations) a linear story of deradicalization in the natural foods field is not adequate, as well as to highlight those tendencies for moderation that do appear with a movement's engagement with private industry, I suggest we shift the focus away from institutionalization per se and toward particular aspects of capitalism that exist independent of the routinizing characteristics that affect any formal organization. Those aspects of capitalism include the imperative for growth (growth being what some have argued gives rise to institutionalization in the first place: Jenkins 1977, 569) and the imperative for flexibility and innovation. By looking more carefully at these pressures that come from competing in a market environment, we can better understand the often contradictory cultural and organizational effects of industry involvement in a movement.

My argument here is twofold, taking into account, first, the moderating influence of the allure of growth, which affects any social movement as well as any business, and second, the destabilizing, even radical influence of flexibility, which is a characteristic especially rewarded by the market. As scholars of institutionalization have shown, movements often respond to growth by formalizing or rationalizing existing organizational activity. But equally important for movement dynamics is to anticipate growth. The desire to attract a broader constituency acts to make movement advocates reluctant to push goals or tactics that could offend or that make strenuous demands on potential members. And while this deradicalizing process affects any movement that looks to draw in new participants, commercial enterprises attached to a movement have added incentives to see the movement, and hence their customer base, expand. But while businesses are especially loath to squander opportunities to broaden their appeal, this does not mean that they always choose a moderate course of action. In the quest to create new products and cultivate new markets, a capitalist environment encourages organizational innovation and a flexible approach to meanings and symbols that can be transformed in the service of stimulating demand. This flexibility is potentially radical in its willingness to dismiss cultural certainties and undermine cultural authorities. However, it is not only mainstream ideals that are up for grabs; a flexible stance also militates against ideological rigidity within a social movement allied with private enterprise.

When assessing the impact of capitalism's bias toward growth and flexibility on the natural foods field, it is worth considering organizational and cultural effects separately. On the organizational side, the desire to cultivate new markets leads to organizational innovation, such as the religious collectives of the past or the Community Supported Agriculture endeavors of the present. But when efforts to reach a wide public take on momentum, so does the pressure to adopt conventional organizational forms that can efficiently handle large-scale operations, which may include outright absorption into the conventional agrifood sector itself. Partially counteracting that trend, growth and flexibility have also led to considerable differentiation in the field, with greater specialization among proliferating businesses and advocacy groups alike.

It is on the cultural side that we see even more complex results. The combination of the desire for growth and a flexible approach to movement values creates an inclination to make compromises to appeal to people leery of ideas and forms of expression that appear extreme or outré. This inclination was manifested most strikingly in the move away from a stern asceticism, which marked natural foods advocates as rigid and peculiar, to a flexible hedonism that fit with the cultural zeitgeist of the late twentieth century. Similarly, a view of the importance of living close to nature, which required a retreat from modern life, was transferred into an ideology of environmental stewardship that was congruent with an urbanized and consumption-centered existence. While this represents a moderation of the movement's challenges to conventional society, the same flexible approach to cultural certainties has exerted a radical force through the field's indifference to the cultural authority of the medical-scientific establishment. Despite the deference usually given to professional expertise, and despite punitive measures taken by government, the natural foods industry has consistently encouraged movement followers to be skeptical of institutional claims to authority and demands for conformity regarding how people manage their own bodies.

The propensity of businesses to undermine existing sources of authority and be compatible with cultural change while at the same time upholding the basic framework of a free market system is in keeping with how many others, going back to Karl Marx, have described the capitalist enterprise. As Marx explained, capitalism is an economic system always in flux, with new production techniques constantly being innovated and once-powerful capitalists continuously being displaced by newly ascendant entrepreneurs. From this perspective, it becomes understandable how the natural foods industry, by proposing a substantially different approach to food production, has threatened the conventional food sector, though not the stability of a system of private enterprise. Furthermore, Marx, like other more contemporary scholars, such as (from divergent political positions) Marshall Berman and Tyler Cowen, noted that the dynamism of capitalism extends to the cultural realm, with the effect that tradition no longer holds sway and certainties can quickly fall (Marx and Engels 1978; Berman 1988; Cowen

2002). Such cultural ferment cannot be fully controlled by the actors setting it in motion; thus, it comes to pass that natural foods companies deliberately undermine the cultural authority of established medicine and
the political authority of the state that protects professional medicine,
while at the same time inadvertently undermining the religious and philosophical ideals that provided the movement's original foundation. What
the natural foods case reminds us is that it is a mistake to assume that the
influence of industry is singularly conservative or radical, to view it as
either accommodating a movement to the status quo or confronting the
establishment with a revolutionary torch. Rather, businesses play a more
varied and complex role in social change, and one that simple left/right
distinctions cannot capture.

Growth and Its Discontents

The growth of the natural foods field can be understood in terms of the
development of a progressively more outward-looking orientation over
time. That outward orientation enabled the field's expansion, but it also
lessened the field's coherence and heightened the boundary disputes I discussed in chapter 7. In the first part of the nineteenth century, the natural
foods movement laid the foundation for the creation of a natural foods
market by developing a distinct oppositional identity.[1] When commercial
activities intensified in the late nineteenth and early twentieth centuries,
they were still primarily aimed at serving a small population that identified with the natural foods movement. During this time, the field continued to be disconnected from the conventional food sector and mainstream
respectability, and it was able to engage in considerable economic and cultural innovation. But as possibilities for significant growth emerged in
the mid-twentieth century, those innovations were, haltingly at first but
swiftly by the 1980s, made palatable to a broader audience. At that point,
in the throes of major expansion, the field became vulnerable to being
swallowed by the mainstream and splintered by internal differences.

While control by conventional food companies poses obvious risks to
the field's integrity, the influx of new followers also threatens the movement's identity and purpose. One informant, a person who had been involved in both natural foods businesses and advocacy organizations,
noted the possibility that the commitment to fomenting social change can
become diluted after a broad segment of the population accepts natural

foods. He remarked, "And we're talking about going from social movement to commercial movement and now sort of saying, the benefit is
mainstreaming. And how do we get the social movement back into it?
And really, in my mind, if you want to distill this down to one thing, it's
when people really realize that they have a personal interest in the health
of the earth. Then you either got denial or activism." As he suggests, a
movement often depends on people perceiving a cause that is linked to
but is still bigger than their own individual welfare. Yet, polls consistently
bear out that consumers are more likely to choose natural foods for reasons of personal health and well-being than because of any larger belief
system. In October 2008, for instance, a market research study found that
only 16 percent of Americans surveyed purchased organic foods because
of philosophical, religious, or political reasons (Mintel International Group
2008, [18]).[2] There are moments, such as in the early 1970s and, arguably,
the present era, when greater numbers of consumers have a politicized
critique of the conventional food industry and see their consumption
choices as a means to further social change. But especially as natural
foods become more mainstream, most people who integrate such products into their diets do not consider themselves to be members of a movement. Indeed, Andrew Szasz has argued that consumers engage in the
"opposite of social movement" by making individual purchases, such as
organic products, to ward off hazards instead of taking political action
to demand social change (2007, 3). Moreover, as a wholesaler suggested,
many people believe that if natural foods are so widely available, the political struggles associated with them must have been won: "So it's not a
simple answer, yet the easiest answer for me to say is that the average consumer today buys it not because they want to change the world, but because they think the world has already changed, and they're reaping the
benefits of it."

Since the 1980s, the natural foods industry has actively courted consumers who remain tentative in their acceptance of the benefits, personal
or social, said to come from these goods. To attract those customers who
eat some natural foods but without making them central to a full-fledged
philosophy of life, businesses try to avoid making demands that such consumers conform to standards of purity as the price of entry. The concept
of purity has long had special relevance in the natural foods movement.
As Julius Roth points out, purity is what natural foods followers hope to
achieve by excluding that which is artificial and morally degrading: "Purify means to clean from material defilement and imperfection, to free

from anything alien, corrupting, or otherwise damaging. It also means to free from moral blemish. All of these meanings are directly relevant to purist natural healthers since they are concerned with freeing the body from pollution and also with purifying their mental and spiritual state" (1977, 13). However, the natural foods industry has helped replace the quest for purity with the pragmatism of flexibility. As one producer said in an interview, "It's, I think, a mistake to try to tailor the production of the food for the general natural foods industry simply based on my philosophical outlook on life. . . . The marketplace is our boss. And even though we have a certain philosophical bent, if there aren't enough people that agree with us on the way we want to do things, so that they will buy the products that we will produce at the price it takes to keep us in business, we are out of business. And so they're the boss. They're the boss." Unlike organizations dedicated exclusively to political activity, where adherence to specific values is more likely to be carefully policed, businesses assure consumers that no one is keeping score, and individuals can create a natural foods lifestyle to fit their own preferences. This approach by businesses perhaps helps explain why vegetarianism, once the driving force of the natural foods movement, receded to an optional behavior practiced by a minority of natural foods followers. In contrast, the term "flexitarian," coined by the Food Channel in 1998 to refer to "meat-eating semi-vegetarians who determine eating preference based on mood, rather than health, lifestyle or philosophical reasons,"[3] encapsulates the current spirit of personal choice and an absence of dogma.

For religious groups, such as the Seventh-day Adventists who denounced John Harvey Kellogg for not putting the religious mission of the church before the health food business, and for citizen groups, such as the nineteenth- and twentieth-century vegetarian organizations that insisted on strict adherence to diets without meat, ideology is the driving force of collective action, and the rewards of physical, spiritual, and moral purity depend on staying true to the message. To water down that message to accommodate the partially committed appears self-defeating in that the end goal is compromised to the point of being unrecognizable. In contrast, groups oriented toward expansion often sacrifice purity in the name of tolerance and flexibility since purity demands a level of engagement and discipline that many sympathizers are unwilling to undertake. Roth notes, "Success leads to a desire for more success. While the movement is small and embattled, the leaders may be more concerned with ideological purity than with increasing their numbers at the expense of doctrine. Once a substantial increase in numbers has occurred, however, they see the vision of finally triumphing over current orthodox doctrine, and to promote this aim, they strive to win still wider support and membership. Such an effort almost certainly signifies a willingness to compromise on doctrine on the part of at least some movement members" (1977, 48–49). Once set in motion, the allure of growth, with its promise of increased political clout and cultural legitimacy, is hard to resist. For that reason, a movement that wishes to remain "pure" may have to hope for continued obscurity. While this dilemma affects all types of movements, the economic incentives attached to market growth make the issue of purity especially difficult for a movement closely connected to private enterprise to navigate.

Holding a Movement Together

Despite the active involvement of conventional food companies in the natural foods field and the industry's growing dependence on an apolitical consumer base, the natural foods industry has not completely left behind its oppositional identity. Even in the current era of corporatization, people who make natural foods the means to their livelihood still commonly describe their work as serving a moral purpose that cannot be reduced to profit making, and they frequently use the language of being part of a movement. Such entrepreneurs reference commitments to building businesses that support the health of the human body, preserve the environment, and demonstrate compassion for animals; in this way, they see their work as leading to the betterment of society. Indeed, several founders of natural products companies have penned books outlining a moral philosophy. The titles of their books are telling in this regard, such as Tom Chappell's *The Soul of a Business: Managing for Profit and the Common Good* (1993).[4] Yet, these commitments do not necessarily mean that industry members understand their actions as mimicking more self-evidently political activity. In interviews, the same people who used the language of advancing a "movement" often said that they had never belonged to an advocacy organization or even a trade association. Instead, they were committed to achieving widespread social change through their day-to-day work, which many, especially an older generation, saw as standing outside of politics. For these members of the natural foods industry, the mundane tasks of confirming an ingredient's purity with a supplier or educating customers about the merits of their products were the means to articulate values and push this diffuse movement forward. Everyday work routines helped advance their cause and in some circumstances, such as when opposed by government regulators, could also be acts of defiance.

Thus, it is not the case that newcomers entering from the outside have removed the movement from the industry. Another question is whether, in the face of movement growth, the industry has been removed from the movement. Movement activity through collectivities formed exclusively to agitate for social change is vigorous, but it is marked by intense fragmentation, as hundreds of natural foods advocacy organizations have been formed since the 1990s, most of them small and regionally focused, many short-lived, but some becoming players on a national level.[5] The number of organizations that describe themselves as dedicated to sustainable farming, organic agriculture, permaculture, local food production, farmers markets, co-ops, Community Supported Agriculture, community gardens, school gardens, urban farming, homesteading, seed saving, heirloom plant cultivation, anti-GMO (genetically modified organisms), antipesticides, anti-irradiation, health freedom, local food sovereignty, food security, raw food, slow food, vegetarianism, veganism, and farm animal rights indicates a field that is both vibrant and fractured beyond recognition from the vantage point of those nineteenth-century advocates who formulated the ideals and precepts that gave rise to these various issues.

While this last list may suggest that what we now have is a mix of separate and unconnected movements, the natural foods industry continues to act as a coordinating and binding force. Most of these various strands depend on a commercial sphere, still distinct from the conventional food sector, for acquiring and selling the material goods that define their politics. Moreover, just as it has done over the past hundred years, industry continues to provide an arena where the ideas and practices of these various tendencies can be amplified. And at the same time that the number of specific advocacy groups has skyrocketed, more often than not, their organizations include representation from groups or individuals with experience in natural foods businesses. Thus, industry retains a leadership role in defining and acting on the range of issues connected to natural foods advocacy.

The most active and well-funded advocacy organizations are still formal trade associations. The Natural Products Association, Organic Trade Association, American Herbal Products Association, and Council for Responsible Nutrition engage in lobbying, educational and public relations activities, and they also spearhead litigation aimed at protecting the rights and privileges of their members. Because they are open only to the trade and are explicitly dedicated to improving market conditions for their members, many natural foods advocates do not consider these organizations representative of their concerns. But precisely because they have the backing of industry, they are especially stable and well resourced. While advocacy groups that insist on a complete absence of industry ties have also been involved in educational and legislative efforts, they have been few in number, and their ability to influence public opinion or public policy has, with some exceptions,[6] been limited.

Consistent with the history of dense links between the natural foods industry and the natural foods movement, most advocacy organizations today are actually composed of a combination of unaffiliated citizens and people with direct ties, past or present, to natural foods businesses. Recent staff or boards of directors of national advocacy groups, such as Beyond Pesticides, Cornucopia Institute, Food & Water Watch, Organic Consumers Association, and Food Democracy Now, include people involved in farming, manufacturing, retailing, or restaurant enterprises. Some organizations explicitly describe themselves as coalitions bringing together like-minded citizens and industry representatives, especially farmers. Through these connections, consumers, activists, and representatives of private enterprise can develop an identity of interests. This coalescence does not always occur smoothly. As one informant told me, well into the 1970s, environmental groups were distrustful of working with organic farmers because all agriculture was assumed to be by definition destructive of the environment. But with few visible endeavors for producing and distributing food that stand outside of commercial relations, for-profit enterprises dedicated to natural foods ideals came to represent the alternative for which activists defining themselves as environmentalist or anticorporate were striving. Indeed, the natural foods industry has helped make some forms of capitalism palatable to people who are largely critical of the capitalist system. Thus, the lines of conflict that have emerged in the natural foods movement are less about advocacy groups in opposition to businesses than about differences regarding the presence of *big* business and competing priorities for what the movement is trying to accomplish.

Mainstreaming and Its Limits

Perhaps the most striking change that has taken place in the natural foods field since the 1970s is the extent to which it has gained cultural legitimacy.

This, of course, has always been one of the natural foods movement's principal goals, as it is for most movements. Through the practices of movement adherents, according to Gusfield, "actions, beliefs, and ideas that have been outside the realm of the normal are now portrayed as undergoing the possibility of being transformed into the normal" (1980, 300). In the contemporary United States, eating practices that were widely viewed as weird a generation ago have indeed become normalized into something unremarkable.

The process of legitimation is recognized by many scholars as key to achieving not just social acceptance but also institutional change. Analysts tend to conceptualize the quest for legitimacy as highly strategic and aimed at winning favor with those elites who initially dismiss insurgents (Habermas 1975; Stryker 1994; Suddaby and Greenwood 2005; Archibald 2010). It is perhaps because movement actors are viewed as so strategic that social movement scholars often reduce the cultural dimension of movement activity to framing, and overemphasize discourse as the means through which legitimation takes place. With framing, movement actors create new or foreground existing interpretive schema that lead others to understand events in a similar manner (Snow and Benford 1992). The problem with this perspective, though, is that movement credibility is often seen as the outcome of adopting the right logic that will resonate with people not initially inclined to be sympathetic to the movement. Framing an issue in a compelling way is certainly one important factor in gaining acceptance. But cultural processes involve more than discourse or logics; they also involve modes of expression, such as style and aesthetics, which make practices and material objects, not just ideas, meaningful.

The ability to move from the cultural margins to the mainstream can, as in the case of natural foods, take place through bypassing elite opponents rather than by winning them over or replacing them altogether. Natural foods proponents did not achieve legitimacy at the end of the twentieth century by convincing established medical experts or government officials that their cause had merit. Instead, acceptance by such elites, which still remains incomplete to this day, followed only after portions of the public—particularly an affluent, educated middle class—started using natural foods alongside conventional eating and health practices.

Furthermore, what made natural foods appealing to that class of consumers was not that such foods were situated in a conventional conceptual framework. On the contrary, it was the ability to glamorize and stylize marginality that lifted natural foods from something mocked and relegated to the old and infirm to something admired and seemingly avant-garde.

Beginning in the mid-twentieth century with images of bodybuilders and Hollywood celebrities, and culminating a generation later with the hip and sensuous environment of the redesigned natural foods store, consumers were vividly shown how natural foods could be associated with fashionably bohemian lifestyles that embraced new experiences and valued the fit and beautiful. In the process, the sacrifices that were previously viewed as necessary when adopting health food—abstaining from indulgences and doing without the conveniences of packaged or prepared foods—no longer applied as new products emphasizing flavor and convenience were developed. Indeed, not just the values of asceticism and self-reliance but also the directive to live one's life with as few unnatural aids as possible were now seen as optional. With the process of mainstreaming, style became detached from ideology. One could adopt a natural foods lifestyle without adopting the philosophical ideas that underlay it.

Yet, even with these changes, the natural foods field is not fully ensconced in the mainstream. It is precisely because the dominant agrifood sector and the medical establishment are not completely accepting of natural precepts that mainstreaming is not complete, and conflict with both these institutions as well as the state continues. Health professionals are much more receptive to natural foods principles than they used to be, so much so that the "healthy" diets now promoted by the American Medical Association look much like the advice offered by natural foods proponents over the generations. Still, tensions exist over claims made about health properties of natural substances or alternative therapies, and any suggestion that physicians be excluded from decisions regarding health care is strongly resisted; medical doctors continue to fiercely protect their authority against noncredentialed challengers. Similarly, even with the gains in legitimacy made by the natural foods movement, conflict over what is seen by the natural foods field as excessive and discriminatory government regulation continues. For instance, rules requiring costly equipment or tracking technologies, such as that used with livestock, can be prohibitively expensive for small producers, many of whom claim that since it is an industrialized food system that makes foodborne illnesses so difficult to contain, small-scale production and local markets eliminate the hazards those rules are meant to combat.

One issue that exemplifies how the contemporary natural foods field battles the coordinated opposition of health professionals, the conventional food sector, and government has to do with restrictions on the right to sell raw dairy products. Raw milk is roundly condemned by public health officials and the conventional dairy industry, which insist that pasteurization is necessary to destroy pathogens.[7] Most raw milk enthusiasts counter that if produced and handled under the right conditions, which exclude large-scale operations where contamination easily occurs, the milk is safe, as well as healthier and tastier than pasteurized products. Raw milk proponents denounce paternalistic decrees concerning what individuals may or may not ingest and try to subvert legal restrictions with illicit distribution schemes.

As this example suggests, the natural foods movement continues to be characterized by a lack of deference to those experts, especially professional medicine, who propagate a rational-technical worldview. Such experts are cultural authorities insofar as they are looked to for guidance about what a society values and how individuals should conduct their lives. The natural foods movement undermines the legitimacy of these cultural authorities, who claim specialized knowledge in domains related to the care of the body, by unfavorably comparing them to a more virtuous and disinterested nature.

Harry Collins has argued that because modern systems of communication expose the scientific process to public scrutiny, professional science has lost much of its social prestige, and the public now believes it has equivalent expertise in matters on which citizens once deferred to scientists. For Collins, this development represents an unfounded and dangerous self-confidence that has led to unwarranted skepticism about climate change and a sacrifice of the population's herd health as parents forgo vaccinating their children due to erroneous beliefs about vaccines' safety. Because "integrity is built into the very nature of science" (Collins 2014, 127) and the scientific community aspires to discover the truth rather than be driven by personal interests, Collins believes that science deserves to regain its elevated position in society. This argument is echoed today by many others alarmed by people who refuse to acknowledge overwhelming scientific evidence for climate change or evolution, or evidence against a link between vaccines and autism. But the concern over indifference to science is not altogether new. Since the early nineteenth century, the selective way in which natural foods followers accepted and rejected the pronouncements of science has, for critics, shown a high level of delusion on the part of laypersons about their powers of judgment.

To be clear, I myself agree that there are real problems when a population ignores the logic and evidence of science, both in terms of setting individuals and public policy on a harmful path and of exacerbating an anti-intellectual disregard for reason so pervasive in the United States.

But it would be a mistake to dismiss the natural foods movement's lack of trust in the institutions of medical science as simply an irrational refusal to acknowledge the explanatory power of science. Indeed, the natural foods philosophy shares with science an interest in understanding the so-called laws of nature, though unlike the scientific enterprise, which has been harnessed to technical achievements, the natural foods philosophy holds that nature can rarely be improved on. The natural foods movement has not so much dispensed with science and scientific knowledge (after all, so many proponents have tried to couch their arguments by reference to science) as much as it takes issue with the system that determines who does or does not have expertise in the intersection of human and natural affairs. Congruent with Collins's argument, natural foods proponents do not believe that nature is hidden from view of the ordinary person. Professional medicine is an authority to be rejected not only because it presents itself as a realm of expertise that stands above individuals' own relations with nature but also because it is *not* disinterested. Instead, it is viewed as subject to ulterior motives and as forming alliances with other social interests, such as the conventional agrifood industry.

The natural foods industry has reinforced this inclination of the movement to see professionals as never disinterested and almost always protective of their privileges and social status. Natural foods industry members only have to look to their struggles for legitimacy to highlight the ways that legislators and government agencies have been tightly allied with professional medicine, enhancing the latter's prerogatives and accepting its advice on matters of policy and regulation. Natural foods proponents also remember the scientific certainties that have been overturned throughout the decades, such as the supposedly benign effects of processed foods and chemical pest controls, positions which cast doubt on medical science's immunity from prevailing cultural assumptions. And the very real financial benefits that accrue to health professionals who convince a population to regularly take drugs and submit to complex medical procedures are seen as an indication that professionals' demands to trust their directives can never be fully separated from their economic interests. Those natural foods advocates who greet medical science with skepticism perceive that no proponents of a worldview, not even the most well-meaning scientists, are completely disinterested. Perhaps it takes people who explicitly mix economic and moral considerations to understand that reality the best.

When medical professionals are believed to be influenced by economic, status, and political motivations, they may be viewed as having no more legitimacy than the merchants of natural foods, or than individual natural foods followers themselves who choose to combine philosophical, religious, or political commitments with scientific evidence. Hence, in leveling cultural authority, the natural foods movement embraces a form of individualism that puts great faith in individuals' capacity to understand their own needs and calculate their own individual risks when assessing how to live. This is not to say that the natural foods movement rejects cultural authority in all spheres of social life. It is on questions of lifestyle, especially the ability to make choices regarding the care of the individual body, that natural foods followers find a professional health care system overstepping its legitimate authority.

Rethinking the Role of Business in Arenas of Dissent

The active presence of the private sector has in many ways been an asset to the natural foods movement, as long-standing firms facilitate movement continuity and visibility. Indeed, one of the more noteworthy aspects of the natural foods movement is its longevity. Few social movements last so long, tending instead to burn out, declare success and dissipate, or transform into something unlike their original incarnations. The longevity that characterizes the natural foods movement owes a lot to the existence of businesses in its midst, some of which have been run by the same families for several generations. The natural foods enterprise may be subject to the whims of the market for survival, but since it provides its owners with a livelihood as well as a moral cause, it does not have to rely on volunteers' free time and goodwill simply to exist, as do so many social movement organizations.

While the active role of industry provides a certain amount of institutional stability over time, it also promotes considerable variability in the meanings and expression of a natural foods lifestyle. The natural foods movement, founded in the turmoil of the Industrial Revolution, disputed an assumption that technical innovation and industrial methods are equivalent to progress. That critique of an industrial order has not disappeared, but over time it has been softened as industry players sought to increase productivity and expand operations by employing those very techniques that had been the subject of criticism. Moreover, entrepreneurs strive to develop new products, services, and market niches to gain an edge over competitors. Consumers today have a range of choices in how to pursue a natural foods lifestyle that would have been unimaginable a hundred years ago.

In this way, industry has helped lead the natural foods movement away from an emphasis on asceticism and simple living and toward a valuation of indulgence and material comforts. In the most general terms, the goals of the natural foods movement have stayed the same since its earliest days: to bolster the health of humans and the natural environment by promoting food production and eating practices that alter nature and the fruits of nature as little as possible. But instead of instructing followers to purify the body by removing all but the most basic nourishment and purify the mind through self-discipline, the natural foods industry grew to celebrate the pleasures of gastronomy, which are enhanced by a multitude of ingredients and culinary styles. Correspondingly, the industry downplays the notion that the adoption of a natural foods diet requires the fortitude to stick to an invigorating routine and instead presents this diet as akin to embarking on a fun adventure. However, these kinds of adventures rarely happen without assistance; commercial enterprises are needed to lend a hand.

Beginning with Sylvester Graham's exhortation to bake one's own bread, the natural foods movement elevated the value of self-reliance by encouraging people to cook at home with as many raw ingredients as possible. With the invention of health food, manufactured canned and packaged preparations started to make inroads into a natural foods diet, but advocates still stressed the ideal of cooking with fresh ingredients obtained from a reliable source. In the second half of the twentieth century, the promotion of backyard garden plots, home baking, and food preservation activities were seen as ways to revive skills lost in a consumer society and to achieve greater control over one's food. However, with the explosion of packaged and prepared natural foods so readily available, consumers increasingly opted to pay for the convenience of a meal in a box or take-out container and for the stimulation of the elaborate surroundings and packaging in which these items appear. In the twenty-first century, even DIY (do-it-yourself) efforts are market opportunities for entrepreneurs who sell equipment, such as kits for raised gardens, beekeeping, or chicken coops, along with the usual how-to books and manuals. Natural foods retailers are encouraged to offer educational classes and lectures to DIYers; if shops are not the actual source of material goods, they can still remain the source of expertise and advice (Sarnoff 2015). Whereas the original natural foods philosophy held that ordinary people are best able to direct their own health and well-being, the natural foods industry sets itself up as the indispensable facilitator of this lifestyle. Thus, movement followers' dependence on the market continues to deepen.

It is because of the scale of commercialization so evident in the field in recent years that many observers see the natural foods movement as in danger of being tamed and depoliticized by the invasion of market forces. As I have argued, this way of understanding the movement ignores just how long ago that "invasion" occurred, and it overlooks the political activities in which industry participants have been so heavily involved. Industry members have helped undermine government-backed food production and distribution techniques that harm human health, degrade soil and water systems, and contribute toxins to the environment. They have pressed for using public mandates and funds to encourage the use of natural foods in institutional settings, such as schools, or with specific populations, such as low-income communities. Through these efforts they have put the conventional agrifood sector on the defensive. Yet, it is also the case that as a result of the industry's leadership since the late nineteenth century, the movement's political agenda has foregrounded goals that benefit the economic interests of the industry.

These various issues raise the question of what broader lessons can be learned from the natural foods movement's relationship to private enterprise. At least until recently, social movement scholarship tended to focus on actors standing outside of those institutions, such as for-profit firms, that symbolize the dominant power structure. This preference shows an affinity for groups who have been clearly disadvantaged by prevailing social arrangements. But as the natural foods case demonstrates, a social movement is not by definition antibusiness, just as businesses are not by definition equivalent to mainstream centers of power. Natural foods industry members were ridiculed, ostracized, and sometimes jailed for their beliefs. For most of the industry's history, they had few defenders in government. Their precarious status confounds any assumption that business owners are always equivalent to elites. Rather than ignoring the divergent interests that exist within the business world, a more nuanced understanding of how business actors differently relate to the market, the state, and the communities in which they do business helps us understand how profit-minded entities can sometimes be in opposition to one another and sometimes make common cause with, and even lead, citizens involved in efforts at social change.

All contemporary social movements are faced with establishing some relationship to capitalism, and most depend on the services of private enterprise in some way, from legal assistance, to specialized information for sale, to suppliers of Internet applications. What this suggests is that all movements represent potential markets for enterprising businesspeople. And in a society so thoroughly infused with capitalist market relations, even those movements that start by trying to oppose commercialization are likely to find themselves interacting with and depending on market forces. But an actual identity of interests between industry and movement, such as that which exists in the natural foods case, is much more likely with lifestyle movements. As discussed in chapter 1, a lifestyle movement is oriented toward spreading cultural values represented in choices about everyday life. Since consumption is so important to the expression of a lifestyle, such movements are prone to develop especially close connections to the market. These movements usually require various material goods to support a special way of life and therefore can be closely aligned with the commercial interests selling those goods.

The natural foods movement presents an especially good case for seeing this process, as the movement has been intertwined with private industry for such a long time. But other movements, especially but not only those related to consumption, also exhibit close relationships to industry. Environmentalism has given rise to recycling and renewable energy industries. Marijuana reform is now tightly bound up with efforts to legally cultivate and sell it. The home schooling movement increasingly depends on commercial producers of educational materials. In each of these cases, the choices of and ways in which material goods are integrated into private life become not just symbols of a movement but the very substance of what the movement is about. Such choices are not made by individuals or groups standing outside of a market context but are in part shaped by relations with those actors producing and selling them goods. And in many instances, consumers and producers of these goods move back and forth between their roles, as people try to combine their lifestyle choices with the urgent need to make a living.

Despite its seeming distance from the world of work and the halls of government, lifestyle is not trivial. The cultural values that mark patterns of everyday life may feel intensely private, but they are actually supremely public. And as issues such as gentrification, the place of extracurricular activities in the competition for college admission, and the red state–blue state trope demonstrate, lifestyle differences have become central to marking larger social divisions. It is perhaps marketers who have long understood this connection the best, as they seek ever more precise ways to target consumers. But this insight is not monopolized by market cynics hoping to exploit gullible consumers. It is precisely because lifestyle can be a vehicle for broad cultural change, change that is seen as enhancing the social good, that it is subject to sale by those who make their paid work an expression of a moral cause. By understanding these entrepreneurs' moral commitments, we see how economic action is actually never just about economics but is always wrapped up in cultural ideals about the natural order of things.

Source Abbreviations

The following abbreviations are used to denote sources of unpublished material that is cited:

AAS   American Antiquarian Society, Worcester, MA

AMA   American Medical Association Historical Health
                 Fraud Collection, Chicago

BENTLEY   Bentley Historical Library, University of Michigan,
                 Ann Arbor, MI

FENTON   Shiloh Community Papers, Fenton Historical
                 Society, Jamestown, NY

LA SIERRA   Heritage Room, La Sierra University, Riverside, CA

LOMA LINDA   Heritage Research Center, Loma Linda University,
                 Loma Linda, CA

MILLER   Personal collection of author Laura J. Miller

MSU   Papers of John Harvey Kellogg, Collection 13,
                 Michigan State University Archives and Historical
                 Collections, East Lansing, MI

SCHLESINGER   Schlesinger Library, Radcliffe Institute, Harvard
                 University, Cambridge, MA

STANFORD   Naturopathy collection, M0759, Department of
                 Special Collections, Stanford University Libraries,
                 Stanford, CA

STARK   H. J. Lutcher Stark Center, University of Texas at
                 Austin
STOLTZ   Personal collection of Garth "Duff" Stoltz, Battle
                 Creek, MI
WILLARD   Willard Public Library Local History Collection,
                 Battle Creek, MI

Notes

Chapter One

1. "Natural Stays on Perennial Path to Growth," *Natural Foods Merchandiser* 33, no. 6 (June 2012): 23. Definitions and methods of calculating sales have changed over time, making these figures not entirely comparable. The 2011 number includes a variety of retailers, whereas the 1979 figure is limited to health food stores. The 2011 number also includes a larger share of nonfood items, such as body care products and household cleaners, than do earlier estimates. Another survey, which left out such nonfood items, found that natural and organic food and drink sales came to more than $39 billion in 2010. "Natural, Organic Food Sales Outpacing Conventional," *Whole Foods* 34, no. 8 (August 2011): 9. Despite their inconsistencies, these figures do serve as a useful indicator of how extensively sales in the natural foods category have grown over a forty-year period.

2. Frank Fuller, Appt., v. Barton Huff et al., 104 F. 141 (2d Cir. 1900), Lawyers Reports Annotated at 332; Battle Creek Sanitarium Company, Limited, v. Fuller, 134 O.G. 1299, Decisions of the Commissioner of Patents, The Supreme Court of the United States and the Court of Appeals of the District of Columbia in Patent and Trade-Mark and Copyright Cases 370 (D.C. Cir. 1908). The first instance I could find of Seventh-day Adventist use of the term *health food* is in 1888: Advertisement, Sanitarium Food Company, *Good Health* 23, no. 4 (April 1888): 161.

3. For an influential statement proposing this type of focus, see McAdam, Tarrow, and Tilly 2001.

4. On the cultural dimensions of social movements, see Gusfield 1980; J. Goodwin and Jasper 2004; Polletta 2008; Kurzman 2008; Armstrong and Bernstein 2008.

5. One can contrast the lifestyle movement with subcultures, whose denizens do not desire to recruit a larger population but whose politics of style still undermine the legitimacy of mainstream lifestyles. See Hebdige 1979.

6. Nor can a lifestyle movement be reduced to only consumption. In this way, I am talking about something broader than what has been called ethical, political,

alternative, or socially responsible consumption. See R. Harrison, Newholm, and Shaw 2005; Micheletti 2003; Bevir and Trentmann 2007; Soper, Ryle, and Thomas 2009. For arguments that discount the potential of consumption movements to challenge at the system level, since they leave the foundation of capitalism or structures of economic inequality untouched, see Chasin 2000, 23–24; Ransome 2005, 113.

7. On the problems with equating radical movements with particular ideologies, see Calhoun 2012.

8. On pure food crusades, see DuPuis 2002; Smith-Howard 2014; L. Goodwin 1999.

9. Belasco's book is probably the best-known account of the transitional years when the natural foods concept began to be picked up by conventional food companies. For another good, though nonscholarly, history of the natural foods movement in Britain and the United States, see Griggs 1986. Despite being more comprehensive than most other histories, Griggs's highly partisan defense of a natural foods philosophy can detract from her analysis. For an account of health foods by an industry insider, see F. Murray 1984. See also the publications of the Soyinfo Center, accessible online at http://www.soyinfocenter.com/bibliographies.php.

10. See also Fligstein and McAdam 2012 for an account that joins together social movement and organizational perspectives on fields.

Chapter Two

1. Bible passages cited by the Bible-Christians in support of vegetarianism included, among others, Gen. 1:29, Gen. 9:4, Prov. 23:20, Isa. 66:3, Rom. 14:21, Num. 11:33, 1 Cor. 8:13 (Maintenance Company 1922, v–vi).

2. "Bread," *Journal of Health* 1, no. 18 (May 26, 1830): 278, 277. On the *Journal of Health*, see Nissenbaum 1980, 76; Horrocks 2008, 77–82.

3. Iacobbo and Iacobbo 2004, 42; "Catalogue of Living Vegetarians," *American Vegetarian and Health Journal* 1, no. 5 (May 1851): 93–94.

4. The literature on Sylvester Graham is extensive. See, e.g., Bobrow-Strain 2012; Carson 1957; H. Green 1986; Gusfield 1992; Iacobbo and Iacobbo 2004; Nissenbaum 1980; Schwartz 1986; Shyrock 1931; Tompkins 2012; Whorton 1982.

5. Philathropos, "To Dr, John C. Warren—of Boston," *Rhode Island American and Gazette*, August 31, 1832, [1]; B, "Dear Brother," *Rhode Island American and Gazette*, February 21, 1832, [2].

6. Advertisement, C. & G. Coit, *Norwich Courier*, May 16, 1832, [1]; advertisement, Abraham Barker & Co., *New Bedford Mercury*, January 15, 1833, [3]; advertisement, E. Williams & Co., *Daily Atlas* [Boston], June 30, 1836, [3].

7. See American Physiological Society, *Record Book, 1837–1839*, AAS.

8. "Physiological Market," *Graham Journal of Health and Longevity* 1, nos. 2 and 3 (April 18, 1837):21.

9. "Physiological Society's Provision Store," *Graham Journal of Health and Longevity* 1, no. 25 (September 26, 1837): 200; "Physiological Society's Provision Store," *Graham Journal of Health and Longevity* 1, no. 26 (October 3, 1837): 208.

10. For descriptions of the Boston Graham Boarding House, run by David Cambell, see S., "The Graham Boarding House," *Liberator*, June 16 1837, 4; "History of a Graham Boarding House," *Graham Journal of Health and Longevity* 3, no. 25 (December 14, 1839): 398–99.

11. On the water cure movement, see H. Green 1986; Weiss and Kemble 1967.

12. Advertisement, Fancher & Miller, *Water-Cure Journal and Herald of Health* 29, no. 5 (May 1860): 78; advertisement, Fancher & Miller, *Water-Cure Journal and Herald of Health* 30, no. 1 (July 1860): 14.

13. Advertisement, Miller & Browning, *Herald of Health* 4, no. 1 (July 1864): 145.

14. Advertisement, Our Home Granula Co., *Medical Brief* 16, no. 5 (May 1888): 204.

15. "Our Home Granula Co.," *Dansville Advertiser*, April 12, 1883. This article appears to be the source of Gerald Carson's claim, in his *Cornflake Crusade*, that Granula was invented around 1863. Carson's work is the basis for almost all published accounts of Granula. In contrast, a guide issued by General Foods in the 1940s puts the start of Granula in 1875. See Conklin 1971, 154. The 1875 date was dismissed by Conklin as inaccurate, but I believe there is a good possibility that it is correct.

16. Advertisement, Hall & Fairweather, *St. John Daily Evening News*, March 11, 1869; Hoblyn 1865, 269.

17. E. Murray 1873; "Murray's Granulated Wheat," *Farmer's Cabinet*, April 15, 1874, [2].

18. For example, advertisement, M. B. Adams, *Progressive Batavian*, July 25, 1873; advertisement, Darrell & Co., *Bee-keeper's Magazine*, December 1875, inside back cover.

19. "Frank Fuller Dead; Utah War Governor," *New York Times*, February 20, 1915, 5.

20. *The Health Food Company*, (New York: Health Food Company [1878]), Miller; " 'What Shall We Eat?' " *New York Times*, February 17, 1877, 2.

21. See, e.g., Dodds 1886, 110; Dodds recommends cold-blast flour, one of Fuller's products, for some of her recipes.

22. Hall's Journal of Health, "Granulated Wheat Biscuit," *Deseret News*, August 25, 1875, 15; advertisement, Health Food Company, *New York Medical Eclectic* 3, no. 3 (July 15, 1876): 22; *Health Food Company*; M. Henderson 1885, 26–30.

23. According to Strasser (1989, 30), branding became an attribute of successful marketing starting in the 1850s.

24. "Our Home Hygienic Institute, Dansville," *Dansville Advertiser*, November 4, 1880; "Our Home Granula Co.", *Dansville Advertiser*, April 12, 1883; "Health

Resort Became Best in the Business," *Genesee Country Express* 1976, 9; Bunnell [1902?].

25. See Numbers 1976, 128–37, for an examination of other reformers' influence on White.

26. For extended discussions of White's health philosophy, see D. Robinson 1965; Numbers 1976.

27. Schwarz's work remains the best-documented account of Kellogg's activities. I have relied on it for my understanding of Kellogg and for directing me to some original sources. Also useful for understanding Kellogg's food-related activities in particular is Carson 1957. Carson's research is excellent, but his mocking tone helped establish the image of Kellogg as a buffoon.

28. See, e.g., Deutsch 1961; Boyle 1993. For a serious treatment of Kellogg's views on sexuality, see Numbers 2003.

29. The Sanitas Nut Food Company, Limited vs. Carl A. Voigt, Elizabeth Voigt, Frank A. Voigt, William F. Hake, and Charles P. Pepins, The Supreme Court of the United States for the Western Division of Michigan, Southern Division, January 22, 1904, Box 8, Folder 10, MSU; State of Michigan, John Harvey Kellogg, The Kellogg Food Company, and Sanitarium Equipment Company vs. Kellogg Toasted Corn Flake Co., W. K. Kellogg Cereal Co., Kellogg Laboratories, Incorporated, Will K. Kellogg, and John L. Kellogg, Supreme Court Record, [Lansing: 1920?], Volume 2, p. 364, Box 21, MSU.

30. Advertisement, *Health Reformer* 11, no. 12 (December 1876): inside front cover.

31. *Fuller*, 104 F. 141 (see chap. 1, n. 2).

32. John Harvey Kellogg et al. vs. Kellogg Toasted Corn Flake Co. et al., Vol. 2, p. 367, Box 21, MSU; John Harvey Kellogg, The Kellogg Food Company, and Sanitarium Equipment Company vs. Kellogg Toasted Corn Flake Co., W. K. Kellogg Cereal Co., Kellogg Laboratories, Incorporated, Will K. Kellogg, and John L. Kellogg, Supreme Court Record [Lansing: 1920?], Vol, III, p. 851, Stoltz.

33. Advertisement, Sanitarium Food Company, *Good Health* 23, no. 3 (March 1888): 126; advertisement, Sanitarium Food Company, *Good Health* 23, no. 4 (April 1888): 161.

34. *Fuller*, 104 F. 141; *Battle Creek Sanitarium*, 134 O.G. 1299 (see chap. 1, n. 2).

35. John Harvey Kellogg et al. vs. Kellogg Toasted Corn Flake Co. et al., Vol. 2, pp. 368–69, Box 21, MSU.

36. "Nut Foods Sold," Box 8, Folder 2, MSU.

37. R. H. Cadwalader, auditor, to W. Ray Simpson, manager, 7 December 1900, Box 8, Folder 2, MSU.

38. "How to Get Fat," *Modern Medicine and Bacteriological Review*, January 1896, Advertisements-10.

39. John Harvey Kellogg, Arthur S. Kellogg, Herbert C. Jeffers, and Will K. Kellogg, of Battlecreek, Michigan, Assignors to the Sanitas Nut Food Company of

Battlecreek, Michigan, "Process of Hulling Seeds," Patent No. 791,473 dated June 6, 1905, Application No. 83,647, filed Nov 25, 1901, Box 6, Folder 9, MSU; John H. Kellogg, of Battle Creek, Michigan, Assignor to the Sanitas Nut Food Company, Limited, of Same Place, "Process of Preparing Cereal Cakes," Patent No. 634,003 dated October 3, 1899, Application No. 693,284 filed October 12, 1898, Box 6, Folder 7, MSU.

40. John Harvey Kellogg et al. vs. Kellogg Toasted Corn Flake Co. et al., Vol. 2, pp. 648–49, Box 21, MSU.

41. "Recommendations with Reference to General Sales Policy of the Battle Creek Sanitarium Co., Ltd., and Sanitas Nut Food Co., Ltd.," 1907, Box 8, Folder 6, MSU.

42. "Recommendations with Reference to General Sales Policy of the Battle Creek Sanitarium Co., Ltd., and Sanitas Nut Food Co., Ltd.," 1907, Box 8, Folder 6, MSU.

43. Ibid.

44. *The Kellogg File: Closed 1907, Reopened 1986*, Willard; Schwarz 1970; Wilson 2014, 85–93.

45. Summary of letter from Dr. Herbert Ossig, Gland, Vaud, Switzerland, 27 June 1907, Box 4, Folder 7, MSU.

46. "Special Petition for Consideration of Various Matters Pertaining to Sanitarium Food Co. Interests and Work—April 24, 1900," Box 8, Folder 2, MSU.

47. Agreements, Box 8, Folders 4, 7, 8, 9, 15, MSU.

48. "Health Food Fakirs," Folder: Lectures & Speeches 1902 Jan, Box 4, John Harvey Kellogg Papers 1832–1965, Bentley.

49. For example, *The Battle Creek Food Idea* 1(1) January 1901:3.

50. Financial records, Box 8, Folder 4, MSU.

51. Even serious investigations of natural foods followers can take this route. See, e.g., Whorton 2002; Hamilton et al. 1995.

Chapter Three

1. Quotations that are not footnoted all come from interviews I conducted, as explained in chapter 1.

2. On reverence toward nature in American thought, see Albanese 1990. On the relationship between reverence toward nature and food, see Eder 1996.

3. For a brief account of the rise of the food processing industry, see Levenstein 1988, 30–43.

4. On naturopathy, see Kirchfeld and Boyle 1994; Whorton 2002.

5. Cody 1996, 8; "Biographical Sketch of Dr. Benedict Lust," *Benedict Lust Permanent Memorial*, Cornerstone Laying Ceremonies program, Stark.

6. Kennedy (1998) brings together much material on the connections between

German immigrants and natural living. Unfortunately, Kennedy's work suffers from poor attribution of sources. I have tried as much as possible to find and cite the original sources for his otherwise useful and engaging account.

7. See, e.g., "Bengamin Gayelord Hauser," *Journal of the American Medical Association* 108, no. 16 (1937): 1359–60.

8. On *lebensreform*, see Hau 2003; Meyer-Renschhausen and Wirz 1999; Eder 1996, 152–53; Kennedy 1998.

9. On the connections between ideologies of natural living and eugenics in Germany, see Weindling 1989; Hau 2003.

10. "The Vegetarians," *Los Angeles Times*, February 2, 1894, 6; "Fighting the Flesh," *San Francisco Chronicle*, May 12, 1885, 5.

11. Hine 1953; Colman 1933; "The Grass-Eaters," *Los Angeles Times*, June 20, 1890, 3; "Grass Eaters: The Anaheim Curiosities in Trouble," *Los Angeles Times*, June 18, 1890, 3; "Queer Spirits of Vegetarian Sect," *Los Angeles Times*, June 2 1901, C3; "The Societas Fraterna," *Los Angeles Herald*, May 8, 1879, 3; "The "Societas Fraternia," *San Francisco Chronicle*, June 1, 1879, 1.

12. "A Vegetarian Colony," *San Francisco Chronicle*, November 11, 1883, 1.

13. See advertisement, Health Science School, *Los Angeles Times*, November 19, 1922, XI25, for what may be the first announcement of Inner-Clean for sale, just a little more than a month after Ehret's death.

14. Little information on Carqué's early biography is available, but immigration records confirm that he previously resided in Germany.

15. See, e.g., "Nature Boy," *Life* 24, no. 19 (May 10 1948): 131–35.

16. Display advertisement, *American Vegetarian* 7, no. 8 (April 1949): 6.

17. "Loma Linda Foods Marks Eightieth Anniversary," *Adventist Review*, November 6 1986, 27; "Worthington Foods, Worthington, Ohio," *Health Foods Retailing* 40, no. 12 (December 1976): 152; *Pacific Union Recorder*, March 5, 1990, 7, Document File 3108: Battle Creek Food Company (1915+), Loma Linda.

18. Loma Linda Foods file, La Sierra.

19. George T. Chapman, "Loma Linda Food Company: Statement from Report of General Manager at Recent Constituency Meeting," 1942, p. 2, Loma Linda.

20. Diverse soy products were pulled into the health food orbit following World War I. See [Kellogg] 1918; Lager and Jones 1963, 5.

21. "MSG—What Is It?" *Chopletter* 9, no. 3 (May 1956): 3, Loma Linda; see also "Tongue Twister," *Chopletter* 2, no. 1 (March 1949): 3–4, Loma Linda.

22. Jack T. Ericson, Field Trip to Shiloh, April 29, 1968, Fenton; Dennis Pritchard, "The Shiloh Story," *Jamestown Post-Journal*, Oct 6, 1962, Fenton; T. Miller 1998:180–81.

23. "New York Jews' Feast," *Vegetarian Magazine* 21, no. 2 (February 1922): 10.

24. See Douglas and Saenz 2008 for a discussion of how this concept is less useful when applied to more recent immigrant groups.

25. Pleiner's Health Food Store (San Francisco), *Catalogue and Price List Season 1937–38*, Miller.

26. Ruth's Health Food Stores (San Francisco), *Catalogue of Natural Foods*, ca. 1936, Miller; Health Food Distributors (New York), *Health Guide and Catalog 1935–6*, Miller; Brownies Natural Food Products (New York), *Catalog of Natural Foods*, 1938, Miller.

27. Vegetarian Pure Food Cafe menu from April 2, 1906, James C. Whitten Ephemera Collection on the History of Vegetarianism, 1844–2001, Box 1, Folder: Menus California, Michigan, NY, London, Schlesinger.

28. "A Constant Growth," *The Nut Cracker* 1, no. 5 (Thanksgiving Number 1901): 77.

29. Naturade Products Co., "Naturade Products for All the Family from Nature's Laboratory of Vitamins and Minerals," (product guide), 193?, Miller.

30. Health Foundation of California (Los Angeles), "The Curse of the Age: 'Wrong Diet' Vegetrate Brings You Life Anew" (product guide), ca. 1930s, pp. 13, 12, Miller.

31. Health Food Distributors (New York), *Health Guide and Catalog 1935–6*, pp. 3–4, Miller.

32. Testimony of W. E. Goff, State of Michigan, John Harvey Kellogg, The Kellogg Food Company, and Sanitarium Equipment Company vs. Kellogg Toasted Corn Flake Co., W. K. Kellogg Cereal Co., Kellogg Laboratories, Incorporated, Will K. Kellogg, and John L. Kellogg, Supreme Court Record, [Lansing: 1920?], Volume I2, pp. 648–49, Box 21, MSU.

33. "Unfermented Grape Juice," *Los Angeles Times*, August 19, 1906, VI15.

34. "Leading U.S. Health Food Stores Selling Health News," *Health News* 6, no. 17 (September 9, 1938): 8.

35. "Health Show Made a Good Beginning," *California Health News* 1, no. 12 (July 15, 1933): 5; "Health and Trade Show Under Way," *Los Angeles Times*, June 27, 1933, A5.

36. "Health Industry to Protect Self," *California Health News* 1, no. 14 (August 15, 1933): 1, 9.

37. "Food and Health Show Opens Here Tomorrow," *Chicago Tribune*, May 21, 1937, 16.

38. "The Health Food Racket," *Dr. Shelton's Hygienic Review* 1, no. 4 (December 1939): 81.

39. "The Health Food Store," *Dr. Shelton's Hygienic Review* 5, no. 1 (September 1943): 14.

Chapter Four

1. Ray Van Cleef to Jesse Mercer Gehman, 2 August 1949, Jesse Mercer Gehman Collection, MRC-11 Top Drawer, Folder: American Vegetarian Convention Correspondence, Stark.

2. "Nut Foods Sold," Box 8, Folder 2, MSU.

3. Advertisement, Sanitas Nut Food Co., *American Monthly Review of Reviews* 20, no. 119 (December 1899): 150.

4. *Battle Creek Vegetable Entrees* [n.d.], Document File 3108: Battle Creek Food Company (1915+), Loma Linda.

5. Battle Creek Food Co., *Good Eating for Health* [n.d.],; Battle Creek Food Co., *You Will Enjoy These Modern Recipes*, ca. 1940s,; Battle Creek Food Co., "Different and Tempting Menus Prepared with Protose and Savita," ca. 1930, all in Miller.

6. "Under the Postmark," *Chopletter* 8, no. 1 (February 1955): 2, Loma Linda.

7. "Going to the Dogs," *Today's Food* 3, no. 4 (Winter 1958): 8.

8. *Chopletter* 10, no. 4 (July 1957), insert, Loma Linda.

9. "Laboratory Check on Products," *Chopletter* 1, no. 1 (April 1948): 1, Loma Linda.

10. *California Health News* 1, no. 12 (July 15, 1933): 1, 3, 4.

11. *Los Angeles Times*, September 17, 1932, A3.

12. See, e.g., "Prof. Bragg Will Bring You Back to Health Nature's Way" (brochure), Box 337, Folder 0337–14, AMA.

13. See, e.g., Hauser's magazine, *Diet Digest*, published in the 1940s and 1950s.

14. "Announcing the Opening of a New Nature Food Centres Health Food Store at 114 North Dearborn St." (circular), 1957, Box 336, Folder 0336–14, AMA.

15. On Macfadden's life and career, see Ernst 1991; W. Hunt 1989; Adams 2009.

16. "Health Letter Prizes Offered," *American Vegetarian-Hygienist* 16, no. 5 (May 1959): 15.

17. See., e.g., Bragg Health Products and Self-Help Books (catalog), ca. 2010, Miller; and Bragg 1985.

18. See, e.g., advertisement, *Better Nutrition*, January 1965, 14; "Live Food Products, Desert Hot Springs, Calif.," *Health Foods Retailing* 40, no. 12 (December 1976): 143–44.

19. Advertisement, Health Center, *Los Angeles Times*, April 5, 1925, K26.

20. See, e.g., Bragg 1928; Hirsch 1928a; advertisement, Bragg's Health Center, *Los Angeles Times*, December 30, 1928, J29.

21. Advertisement, Bragg Foods, *Eat for Health* (Pavo's Natural Dietetic Foods), Spring 1940, inside back cover, Miller.

22. "Guide to Booths and Exhibitors," *Health Foods Retailing* 30, no. 8 (August 1966): 24–25. The other exhibitor with extensive floor space was wholesaler Kahan & Lessin.

23. Ida Jean Kain, "Movie Star Originates Novel Bridge Luncheon," *Home Digest* 1, no. 12 (November 1927): 7, Battle Creek Food Company [Miscellaneous Printed Items], Folder: Home Digest, Bentley.

24. Hauser 1944; Kerr 1984; Deutsch 1961; Lehman 1951; Dun & Bradstreet report, May 9, 1936, on Modern Health Products, Inc., Milwaukee, Box 323, Folder 0323–09, AMA. The company's name was changed again, from Modern Health Products to Modern Diet Products, and then finally to Modern Products.

25. *Diet Digest*, no. 24 (1949): 50.

26. "Meet Diet Columnist," *Chicago Daily Defender*, May 1, 1971, 1, 24.

27. For example, "On the Cover," *Health News* 6, no. 16 (August 26, 1938): 6. *Health News* (originally called *California Health News*) was renamed *Let's Live* in 1942.

28. "Health Girl," *Chicago Daily Tribune*, August 31, 1944, 5.

29. See, e.g., the July 1946 cover with Elyse Knox and the September 1951 cover with Mitzi Gaynor.

30. "Films to See," *Let's Live* 13, no. 10 (October 1945): 1.

31. See, e.g., the April 1942 cover of *Eat to Live Journal of Health* with Maureen O'Sullivan, and the August 1953 cover of *Better Nutrition* with Susan Hayward. In earlier years, the name of *Better Nutrition* varied according to the retailer selling it.

32. Rodale 1965, 64; Rodale and Adams 1954, 199; Dougherty 1986; "Catching Up to Rodale Press," *Time* 97, no. 12 (March 22, 1971): 71.

33. "Health Food Store Sells 1100 Copies of Book at Party," *Publishers' Weekly* 188, no. 23 (December 6, 1965): 50–51.

34. *The Steve Allen Show*, April 19, 1963.

35. "Blackheads," *Sta-Wel Magazine of Health*, July 1948, 19.

36. Mrs. Frank Koch as told to Gerel Rubien, "Nutrition Builds Four Beauties," *Journal of Living*, December 1942, 208, 209.

37. "Our 'Cover Girl' Is Philadelphia Outdoor Beauty," *American Vegetarian-Hygienist* 12, no. 11 (November 1955): 2.

Chapter Five

1. "Doctors: An Editorial," *National Health Federation Bulletin* 13, no. 1 (January 1967): 11; emphasis in the original.

2. However, note that thousands of chemicals approved for use in food have never undergone rigorous toxicological testing. See Neltner et al. 2013.

3. See Enticott 2003 for a discussion of how people's food choices are influenced by lay theories that privilege their own individual health experiences, and Roth 1977, 77, for how the privileging of individual experience undercuts the scientific credibility of natural foods proponents.

4. For more general discussions of lay challenges to expert knowledge, see Gaventa 1993; Wynne 1996.

5. For examples from two periods, see, on the one hand, Beeuwkes 1956; and, on the other hand, reports on an American Association for the Advancement of Science conference panel: R. Kotulak 1974; Nelson 1974.

6. United States v. Kordel, 164 F.2d 913 (7th Cir. 1947).

7. See Aronson 1982, 52, on these groups' struggles to gain social recognition.

8. Murphy 2005, 95–96; Stare 1992, 1996; *Health Frauds and Quackery, Day 3*,

Hearings Before the Senate Subcommittee on Frauds and Misrepresentations Affecting the Elderly of the Special Committee on Aging, 88th Cong. 288 (1964) (testimony given on March 10). Many of Stare's views are contained in Whelan and Stare 1975.

9. *Health Frauds and Quackery, Day 3*, 289.

10. Ibid., 292–93, 299–305; Boston Nutritional Society, Inc. v. Frederick J. Stare, 342 Mass. 439 (1961); National Nutritional Foods Association; David T. Ajay, d/b/a Dave's Diet And Nutrition Foods; Sid Cammy, d/b/a The Diet Shop; and Max Huberman, d/b/a Natural Health Foods against Elizabeth M. Whelan, Sc.D., and Fredrick J. Stare, M.D., 492 F. Supp. 374 (S.D.N.Y. 1980); F. Murray 1984, 178–80. A similar libel case, but not involving Stare, was filed in 1967 by a New York health food store against Time, Inc., for a book that carried a photo of the store in a chapter on food fads and frauds. This case too was dismissed. All Diet Foods Distributors, Inc. v. Time, Inc., 290 N.Y.S.2d 445 (1967).

11. The following discussion is based, in part, on my own examination of relevant portions of the investigation department files. I am grateful to the AMA for providing access to them.

12. Abramson 1970, 99; P. White 1958; "Food Faddism," *Journal of the American Dietetic Association* 34, no. 11 (1958): 1266, 1268.

13. Health Foundation of California (Los Angeles), "The Curse of the Age: 'Wrong Diet' Vegetrate Brings You Life Anew" (product guide), ca. 1930s, Miller.

14. Advertisement, *Better Nutrition*, July 1959, 20.

15. Advertisement, *Healthful Living* 32–33 (1959): 60.

16. See. e.g., material collected by Radio TV Reports, Inc., Box 338, Folder 0338–06, AMA.

17. J. W. Davidson, Special Agent, San Francisco, to Dr. C. B. Pinkham, Board of Medical Examiners, San Francisco, 10 May 1932, Box 337, Folder 0337–14, AMA.

18. Robert A. Youngerman to Oliver Field, Memo, Legal and Socio-Economic Division, July 17, 1963, Box 338, Folder 0338–01, AMA.

19. See membership cards, memos, and reports in Box 529, Folders 0529–06, 0529–07, and 0529–08, AMA.

20. Helen S. Mitchell to Dr. Frank J. Clancy, Bureau of Investigation, 12 January 1937, Box 337, Folder 0337–11, AMA.

21. Beeuwkes 1960, 80; "Food Faddism," *Journal of the American Medical Association* 167, no. 17 (1958): 2088–89; *Health Frauds and Quackery, Day 2, Hearings Before the Senate Subcommittee on Frauds and Misrepresentations Affecting the Elderly of the Special Committee on Aging*, 88th Cong. 230 (1964) (testimony given on March 9).

22. Oliver Field to Reuben M. Dalbec, Executive Director, Los Angeles County Medical Association, 17 October 1966, and Reuben Dalbec to Oliver Field, 25 October 1966, both in Box 341, Folder 0341–08, AMA.

23. Oliver Field to George Eddy, 24 July 1963, and Oliver Field to Dorothy Cooley, Chicago Tribune Co., 10 July 1963, both in Box 338, Folder 0338–01, AMA.

24. Trager 1971; "What's So Great about Health Foods?," *Life* 73, no. 13 (September 29, 1972): 45–47; Lyons 1973.

25. "The Facts About Those So-Called Health Foods," *Good Housekeeping* 174 (March 1972): 175–77.

26. See, e.g., Tobey 1939; advertisement, Washburn-Crosby Company, *Hygeia* 7, no. 4 (April 1929): 327.

27. E. H. Hays, M.D., to Arthur Cramp, 7 January 1933, and Arthur Cramp to E. H. Hays, 9 January 1933, both in Box 336, Folder 0336–01, AMA.

28. See Ladimer 1965 for an account of AMA–Better Business Bureau cooperation.

29. Better Business Bureau of Spokane to AMA, 19 August 1947, Box 338, Folder 0338–08, AMA.

30. *Health Frauds and Quackery, Part 3*, 277–78.

31. See Apple 1996 for the history of debates over whether vitamins should be classified as drugs or dietary supplements.

32. For a report on one such incident involving an undercover investigation, see "Naturopath Had Impressive Signs," *New York Times*, April 20, 1912, 10. In this case, Lust and his associate, Isidore Hertz, were fined one hundred dollars.

33. "'Prof.' Bragg Again," *Journal of the American Medical Association* 106, no. 16 (1936): 1408.

34. "Expert Urges Silencing of Radio Nutritionists," *Broadcasting* 61 (October 16, 1961):48; "Guide for Discussion with the Federal Communications Commission," June 20, 1961, both in Box 338, Folder 0338–06, AMA.

35. *Health Frauds and Quackery, Part 3*, 289–90.

36. On twentieth-century battles over book censorship, see Boyer 1968; de Grazia 1992.

37. *Health Frauds and Quackery, Part 3*, 294–95; see also Saegert and Saegert 1976, 167.

38. "Charges Drug Head with Fake Arthritis Cure," *Chicago Daily Tribune*, July 14, 1945, 10; United States v. Kordel, 66 F. Supp. 538 (N.D. Ill. 1946); *Kordel*, 164 F.2d 913; Kordel v. United States, 335 U.S. 345 (1948).

39. "U.S. Seizes Hauser's 'Live Longer' Molasses," *New York Herald Tribune*, March 10, 1951, 3; "Live Longer, Lasses," *Newsweek* 37, no. 13 (March 26 1951): 58–59.

40. "Farrar, Straus & Young," *Publishers' Weekly* 160, no. 11 (September 15, 1951): 1157–58.

41. See, e.g., "Warning!," *Bulletin of the National Health Federation* 3, nos. 9–10 (September–October 1957): 6.

42. Press Release, Food and Drug Administration, November 25, 1961, Box 338, Folder 0338–06, AMA; "Diet Book Seized," *Los Angeles Times*, January 24, 1962,

10; "Health Book Blasted as Pill Pusher," *Los Angeles Times*, July 7, 1962, 9; Hunter 1962; "FDA Attacks Taller Book: S&S Rebuts," *Publishers' Weekly* 182, no. 3 (July 16, 1962): 28–29; "'Calories Don't Count' Used as Tie-In, Seized," *Publishers' Weekly* 181, no. 5, (January 29, 1962): 191.

43. United States of America v. An Article of Drug Consisting of 250 Jars, etc., of U.S. Fancy Pure Honey, etc., 218 F. Supp. 208 (E.D. Mich. 1963); United States of America v. Articles of Drug in the Following Locations and Consisting of: Detroit, 1454 Broadway—250 Jars and/or Tins Variously Labeled in Part: "Cal's Tupelo Blossom U.S. Fancy Pure Honey" . . . Cal T. Albritton, Tallahassee, Fla. Net Wt. 1 Lb. . . . etc., and Detroit Vital Foods, Inc., 344 F.2d 288 (6th Cir. 1965).

44. "Detroit Vital Foods Sentenced on Five Misbranding Charges," *FDA Report on Enforcement and Compliance*, January 1966, 12; United States of America v. Detroit Vital Foods, Inc., Lelord Kordel and Alfred Feldten, 407 F.2d 570 (6th Cir. 1969); Herbert and Barrett 1981, 90.

45. Complaint No. 6843, Box 337, Folder 0337–03, AMA.

46. "FTC Says Book Made False Dieting Claims," *Wall Street Journal*, September 16, 1963, 8.

47. "FTC Hits Claims for Gayelord Hauser Book," *Publishers' Weekly* 184, no. 10 (September 2, 1963): 48; "FTC Charges Denied on Gayelord Hauser Book," *Publishers' Weekly* 184, no. 15 (October 7, 1963): 34–35.

48. United States of America v. An Undetermined Number of Cases, Each Case Containing 24 Bottles of an Article Labeled in Part: (Bottle) "Sterling Vinegar and Honey Aged in Wood Cider Blended with Finest Honey Contents 1 Pint Product of Sterling Cider Co., Inc., Sterling Mass." and an Undetermined Number of Copies of the Books Entitled "Folk Medicine" and "Arthritis and Folk Medicine," Both by Dr. C. Jarvis, Balanced Foods, Inc., 338 F.2d 157 (2d Cir. 1964).

49. "FDA Proposes Major Overhaul of Dietary Food Regulations," *FDA Report on Enforcement and Compliance*, July 1966, 3–5; Dietary Supplements and Vitamin and Mineral-Fortified Foods, No. 118, 31 Fed. Reg. 8525–27 (June 18, 1966).

50. "Parley in Capital Fights Quackery," *New York Times*, October 26, 1963, 30.

51. Advertisement, National Dietary Foods Association, *Washington Post*, August 30, 1966, A21; emphasis in the original.

52. *Health Frauds and Quackery, Day 1, Hearings Before the Senate Subcommittee on Frauds and Misrepresentations Affecting the Elderly of the Special Committee on Aging*, 88th Cong. 128 (1964) (testimony given on January 13); Schmeck 1973. See Apple 1996, 144–48 for a description and examples of such letters.

53. Health Research and Health Services Amendments of 1976, Pub. L. No. 94–278 90 Stat. 401 (1976). Health food companies still needed to be careful not to cross the line separating food from drug. To this day, advertisements for health food products in trade magazines typically include the disclaimer: "These statements have not been evaluated by the Food and Drug Administration. This product is not intended to diagnose, treat, cure, or prevent any disease."

54. *Vitamin, Mineral, and Diet Supplements, Hearings Before the House Sub-committee on Public Health and Environment of the Committee on Interstate and Foreign Commerce*, 93d Cong. 687 (1973) (testimony given on October 29, 30, and 31).

55. "NHF Leaders Feuding over Financial Crisis," *Natural Foods Merchandiser*, July 1980, 73, 104.

56. For example, "American Capsule News," *Bulletin of the National Health Federation* 4, nos. 7–8 (July–August 1958): 13. On the opposition of health food followers to fluoridation, see Ackerman 2004, 62.

57. "Communists Try Propaganda through Health Foods," *Howard Inches Report* 4, no. 9 (1959): 1, Box 5, Folder M759/5/14, Stanford; G. Allen 1973.

Chapter Six

1. See Ewen 1999 for a longer historical view of the place of style in commerce and politics.

2. All unattributed quotations come from interviews I conducted. In this and the following chapter, I rely heavily on interview data for my accounts of the events and issues discussed here.

3. However, see B. Henderson 1989 for an argument that the vegetarianism of Thoreau and Emerson was influenced by Buddhism.

4. Admirers included, for example, Fred Hirsch and Otto Carqué. See Hirsch 1928b; Yogananda 1930, 10–11.

5. On the incorporation of Zen Buddhism into the counterculture, see Tipton 1982.

6. On the history of Erewhon and Chico-San, see Shurtleff and Aoyagi 2011; Milbuty 2011.

7. For example, "The Kosher of the Counterculture," *Time* 96 (November 16, 1970): 59–60, 63; Lansing 1970.

8. *Natural Life Styles* 1, no. 1, 1971, 1.

9. Ibid.; see also *Natural Life Styles* 2, no. 1 (1972).

10. See Belasco 1989 for an extended discussion of how the counterculture's "countercuisine" was represented by the press.

11. "Writing the President," episode 102 of *All in the Family*, aired January 19, 1971; episode 13 of *Fernwood 2 Night*, aired July 20, 1977.

12. Wright 1972; Enterprise Investments, Inc., *A Brief Overview of Kahan & Lessin, Inc. as an Acquisition Opportunity* (St. Paul, 1983), 4, Miller.

13. See, e.g., Horvath 1957; "Selling Outside the Industry," *Health Foods Business* 25, no. 5 (May 1979): 50.

14. "Standards and Practices," Mrs. Gooch's, ca. 1985, Miller.

15. "Mrs. Gooch's Invites You To Have Fun Cooking Naturally" (circular), Mrs. Gooch's Natural Foods Ranch Markets, 1985, Miller; "Come to Mrs. Gooch's

Natural Cookery Cooking School" (circular), Mrs. Gooch's Natural Foods Ranch Markets, 1985, Miller.

16. "New Unit Lifts Gooch's Sales to $28.6 Million," *Natural Foods Merchandiser*, July 1984, 110.

17. On the importance of hip for contemporary commerce, see Frank 1997. See also Binkley 2007.

18. "FDA Clamps Lid on Bulk Food Sales," *Natural Foods Merchandiser*, July 1984, 1, 24.

Chapter Seven

1. This figure includes natural foods, beverages, supplements, and personal care products.

2. Ada J. Alberty, "Newfangled Ideas," 1939, Miller.

3. See, e.g., advertisement, Natural Foods Institute, *Eat to Live: Journal of Health* 4, no. 1 (April 1942): 13; advertisement, Schiff Vitamins, *Better Nutrition*, November 1953, 2.

4. "More Food or More Pills?" *Health-Wise and Healthways* 3, no. 4 (Winter 1945): 2 (published by Loma Linda Foods, Arlington, CA).

5. "Government Launches Crackdown on Andro Products," *Whole Foods* 2, no. 5 (May 2004): 8–9; Luke 2005; "DEA Classifies Three Compounds as Anabolic Steroids," *Whole Foods* 33, no. 2 (February 2010): 8.

6. "Rethinking the Pill," *Natural Foods Merchandiser* 36, no. 4 (April 2015): 27.

7. This figure does not include sales by online-only retailers.

8. "General Nutrition Centers Expand," *Los Angeles Times*, January 23, 1972, I12; Minsky 1979; "General Nutrition Starts Big Board Trading Today," *Wall Street Journal*, December 22, 1980, 10.

9. "Two New Shops to Open Soon," *Los Angeles Times*, February 14, 1971, WS9; Minsky 1979; General Nutrition Incorporated, *Annual Report for the Year Ended February 2 1985*, 10, Miller; Beazley1985b, 1985a. General Nutrition ended up acquiring Nature Food Centres in 1994.

10. General Nutrition Incorporated, *Annual Report for 1985*, 10; Richman 1988.

11. These eight wholesalers were Balanced Foods and Sherman Foods of the New York metropolitan area, Health Food Distributors of Detroit, Health Food Jobbers (later, Health Food Inc.) of Chicago, Pavo Co. of Minneapolis, Akin's of Tulsa, Kahan & Lessin of Los Angeles, and Landstrom of San Francisco.

12. Enterprise Investments, Inc., A Brief Overview of Kahan & Lessin, Inc. as an Acquisition Opportunity (St. Paul, 1983), 1, Miller.

13. "West Wins Presidency, But It's a Photo Finish," *Health Foods Business* 27, no. 9 (September 1981): 61.

14. "18 Seminars Highlight First Expo Program," *Health Foods Business* 27, no. 5 (May 1981): 84.

15. "Expo West 2015: Biggest Show to Date," *Whole Foods* 38, no. 5 (May 2015): 12.

16. In the food sector, discussions of industrialization have generally focused on agriculture.

17. Pacey 1971; "Organic Shops Move into the Big Stores," *Business Week*, no. 2184 (July 10, 1971): 76–77.

18. "Selling Outside the Industry," *Health Foods Business* 25, no. 5 (May 1979): 49–50.

19. Flyer, Independent Natural Food Retailers Association, Vic Boff Papers, Stark.

20. "Kahan & Lessin Company," May 15, 1979, Miller.

21. "Naturally," *Newsweek* 83, no. 16 (April 22, 1974): 92; Klein 1978.

22. "Iroquois Industries Purchase," *Wall Street Journal*, May 2, 1968, 29; "Iroquois Industries Purchase Bid," *Wall Street Journal*, January 22, 1968, 9.

23. "Miles Labs Set to Buy Fabricated-Food Maker," *Wall Street Journal*, December 22, 1969, 10; Hammer 1969; "Miles Labs Acquires Food Firm," *Wall Street Journal*, March 12, 1970, 32.

24. For an overview of this activity, see Howard 2009. Howard creates useful infographics, periodically updated, of natural food companies' corporate ties. See https://msu.edu/~howardp.

25. "IC to Buy Subsidiary of Ogden," *Chicago Tribune*, October 21 1986, B3; Sloane 1994; "Hain Food to Buy Celestial Seasonings," *New York Times*, March 7, 2000, C2; Hain Celestial Group 2014. On Hain's earlier acquisition by Archon Pure Products, see "A Conversation with . . . Dan Ritchie," *Health Food Age* 2, no. 3 (March 1972): 4–7; Wright 1972.

26. For profiles of Earthbound and Horizon, see Fromartz 2006.

27. Whole Foods has been written about extensively. For scholarly works, see, e.g., Johnston 2008; Johnston and Szabo 2011; Serazio 2011.

28. Martin 2007; "Whole Foods Settles F.T.C. Challenge," *New York Times*, March 7, 2009, B8.

29. "The Stuff of Life," *Newsweek* 75, no. 21 (May 25, 1970): 100; "The Perils of Eating, American Style," *Time* 100, no. 25 (December 18, 1972): 68–76; F. Allen 1972.

30. On the development of California Certified Organic Farmers, the National Organic Program, and organic standards, see Guthman 2004; Fromartz 2006; Farmer 2010; Goodman and Goodman 2001.

31. As of 2016, the answers to these questions were:

1. A period of three years from the last application of prohibited material is required before land can produce certified organic crops.

2. Some chemical substances, including chlorine, are allowed as a disinfectant, sanitizer, or algicide in postharvest handling of raw organic agricultural products, though when wash water is chemically treated, agricultural products must immediately be rinsed with clean water.

3. Approximately forty synthetic ingredients are allowed in the processing of foods labeled *organic*, including some used as thickening or stabilizing agents.

4. One hundred percent of the feed of both dairy and meat cows must be organic.

5. Livestock must have access to organic pasture, and at least 30 percent of their food intake must come from organic pasture, for at least 120 days a year. The exact number of days depends on the geographic region.

6. Wild-caught fish cannot be certified as organic.

7. Genetic engineering is a prohibited method for certified organic food. Engineered nanomaterial is evaluated on a case-by-case basis in the same manner as other synthetic and nonsynthetic substances.

32. For an account of the elaborate process of converting a conventional to certified organic farm, see Besonen 2010.

33. The cases were *Harvey v. Veneman*, 297 F.Supp.2d. 334 (D.Me.2004); *Harvey v. Johanns*, 462 F.Supp.2d 69 (2006). The courts eventually gave Harvey a partial victory, and changes were made to the regulations.

Chapter Eight

1. On the relationship between new markets and oppositional identities, see King and Pearce 2010.

2. For similar poll results from the beginning of the mainstreaming era, see Chou 1979, 167.

3. "Primer Pinpoints Foodie Trends," *Montreal Gazette*, August 29, 1998, W7; Kessler 1998.

4. See also Hirshberg 2008; Hollender and Breen 2010; Newman and Hotchner 2003.

5. See P. Allen 2004 for a discussion of the development of many such organizations in the 1990s, when the proliferation of advocacy groups began. For an account of numerous contemporary issues and advocacy groups, see Katz 2006.

6. One exception is the Center for Science in the Public Interest, which has sometimes been allied with and other times opposed to the natural foods industry.

7. For an extended account of the controversy over raw milk, see Gumpert 2009. For a history of pasteurization, see DuPuis 2002; Smith-Howard 2014.

References

Abramson, Ernst (1970). "Trade in Food Faddism and the Law." In *Food Cultism and Nutrition Quackery*, edited by Gunnar Blix, 93–103. Uppsala: Almqvist & Wiksells.

Ackerman, Michael (2004). "Science and the Shadow of Ideology in the American Health Foods Movement, 1930s–1960s." In *The Politics of Healing: Histories of Alternative Medicine in Twentieth-Century North America*, edited by Robert D. Johnson, 55–67. New York: Routledge.

Adams, Mark (2009). *Mr. America: How Muscular Millionaire Bernarr Macfadden Transformed the Nation Through Sex, Salad, and the Ultimate Starvation Diet*. New York: Harper.

Addison, Heather (2003). *Hollywood and the Rise of Physical Culture*. New York: Routledge.

Agin, Katie (2010). "Lean Manufacturing, 2.0." *Whole Foods* 33 (1): 28–34.

Albanese, Catherine L. (1990). *Nature Religion in America: From the Algonkian Indians to the New Age*. Chicago: University of Chicago Press.

Albright, Nancy (1982). *The Rodale Cookbook*. New York: Ballantine. First published in 1973.

Alcott, A. Bronson (1842). "Days from a Diary." *Dial* 2 (4): 409–37.

——— (1843). "Sayings." *Present* 1 (5–6): 170–72.

Alcott, Louisa May (1975). *Transcendental Wild Oats*. Harvard, MA: Harvard Common Press. First published in 1873.

[Alcott, William A.] (1835). "Objections to Animal Food," *Moral Reformer and Teacher on the Human Condition* 1:276–84.

Alcott, William A. (1859). *Vegetable Diet: As Sanctioned by Medical Men, and by Experience in All Ages, Including a System of Vegetable Cookery*. 2nd, rev., and expanded ed. New York: Fowler and Wells. First published in 1849.

Alkon, Alison Hope, and Julian Agyeman (2011). "Introduction: The Food Movement as Polyculture." In *Cultivating Food Justice: Race, Class, and Sustainability*, edited by Alison Hope Alkon and Julian Agyeman, 1–20. Cambridge, MA: MIT Press.

Allen, Floyd (1972). "The 1972 Organic Certification Program." *Organic Gardening and Farming*, February, 94–100.

Allen, Gary (1973). *Vitamins: Federal Bureaucrats Want to Take Yours!* Belmont, MA: American Opinion.

Allen, Patricia (2004). *Together at the Table: Sustainability and Sustenance in the American Agrifood System*. University Park: Pennsylvania State University Press.

Allen, Steve (1965). Introduction to *Bare Feet and Good Things to Eat*, by Gypsy Boots, i–iii. Los Angeles: Virg Nover Printer.

American Medical Association (1847). *Proceedings of the National Medical Conventions Held in New York, May, 1846, and in Philadelphia, May, 1847*. Philadelphia: T. K. & P. G. Collins.

Ansberry, Clare (1988). "General Nutrition to Offer Franchises, Open Outlets in Mass-Merchandise Stores." *Wall Street Journal*, March 10, 30.

Apple, Rima D. (1996). *Vitamania: Vitamins in American Culture*. New Brunswick, NJ: Rutgers University Press.

Archibald, Matthew E. (2010). "Sources of Self-Help Movement Legitimation." In *Social Movements and the Transformation of American Health Care*, edited by Jane C. Banaszak-Holl, Sandra R. Levitsky, and Mayer N. Zald, 227–45. New York: Oxford University Press.

Armstrong, Elizabeth A., and Mary Bernstein (2008). "Culture, Power, and Institutions: A Multi-Institutional Politics Approach to Social Movements." *Sociological Theory* 26 (1): 74–99.

Aronson, Naomi (1982). "Social Definitions of Entitlement: Food Needs 1885–1920." *Media, Culture and Society* 4 (1): 51–61.

Barlett, Peggy F. (1993). *American Dreams, Rural Realities: Family Farms in Crisis*. Chapel Hill: University of North Carolina Press.

Bauman, Zygmunt (1990). *Thinking Sociologically*. Oxford: Basil Blackwell.

Baur, John E. (1959). *The Health Seekers of Southern California, 1870–1900*. San Marino, CA: Huntington Library.

Beazley, J. Ernest (1985a). "General Nutrition Will Pay $14 Million to Settle Seven-Year-Old Antitrust Suit." *Wall Street Journal*, October 4, 9.

——— (1985b). "Under Attack: General Nutrition Inc. Is Besieged with Suits over Bold Sales Tactics," *Wall Street Journal*, June 28, 1.

Beeuwkes, Adelia M. (1956). "Characteristics of the Self-Styled Scientist." *Journal of the American Dietetic Association* 32 (7): 627–30.

———. (1960). "Food Faddism—A Growing Threat." *Postgraduate Medicine* 28: 75–81.

Belasco, Warren J. (1989). *Appetite for Change: How the Counterculture Took on the Food Industry, 1966–1988*. New York: Pantheon.

Bellah, Robert N., Richard Madsen, William M. Sullivan, Ann Swidler, and Steven M. Tipton (1986). *Habits of the Heart: Individualism and Commitment in American Life*. New York: Perennial Library.

Bentsen, Cheryl (1973). "Furore Over FDA Curb on Vitamin Sales." *Los Angeles Times*, October 18, F1, F16, F17.

Berger, Bennett M. (1981). *The Survival of a Counterculture: Ideological Work and Everyday Life among Rural Communards*. Berkeley: University of California Press.

Berman, Marshall (1988). *All That Is Solid Melts into Air: The Experience of Modernity*. New York: Penguin.

Bernardini, James G. (1976). " 'Health Foods Retailing' 40 Years of Service." *Health Foods Retailing* 40 (12): 58–69, 182–220.

Besonen, Julie (2010). "Going from Conventional to Organic." *Specialty Food* 40 (6): 72–82.

Bevir, Mark, and Frank Trentmann, eds. (2007). *Governance, Consumers and Citizens*. Houndmills, UK: Palgrave Macmillan.

Biddle, Frederic M. (1992). "Texas Food Retailer Buys Bread & Circus for $26M." *Boston Globe*, October 14, 1.

Biltekoff, Charlotte (2013). *Eating Right in America: The Cultural Politics of Food and Health*. Durham, NC: Duke University Press.

Binkley, Sam (2007). *Getting Loose: Lifestyle Consumption in the 1970s*. Durham, NC: Duke University Press.

Bobrow-Strain, Aaron (2012). *White Bread: A Social History of the Store-Bought Loaf*. Boston: Beacon Press.

Bonacich, Edna (1973). "A Theory of Middlemen Minorities." *American Sociological Review* 38 (5): 583–94.

Bond, Pamela (2011). "Should You Sell HCG Supplements?" *Natural Foods Merchandiser* 33 (12): 20–21.

Boots, Gypsy (1965). *Bare Feet and Good Things to Eat*. Los Angeles: Virg Nover Printer.

Borsodi, Ralph (1933). *Flight from the City: The Story of a New Way to Family Security*. New York: Harper & Brothers.

——— (1947–48). "The Case against Farming as a Big Business." *Land* 6 (4): 446–51.

Bourdieu, Pierre (1984). *Distinction: A Social Critique of the Judgement of Taste*. Translated by Richard Nice. Cambridge, MA: Harvard University Press. First published 1979.

Boyer, Paul S. (1968). *Purity in Print: The Vice-Society Movement and Book Censorship in America*. New York: Charles Scribner's Sons.

Boyle, T. Coraghessan (1993). *The Road to Wellville*. New York: Viking.

Bragg, Paul C. (1928). "Health Hints." *Los Angeles Times*, January 22, K29.

——— (1935). *Paul C. Bragg's Personal Health Food Cook Book and Menus*. 2nd ed. Burbank, CA: Paul C. Bragg. First published in 1930.

——— (1941). *The Four Generation Health Food Cook Book and Menus*. 2nd ed. Burbank, CA: Paul C. Bragg.

——— (1946). "How Hollywood Keeps Healthy." *Nature's Path* 50 (3): 138, 172.

Bragg, Paul C., with Patricia Bragg (1985). *The Miracle of Fasting: Proven Throughout History for Physical, Mental and Spiritual Rejuvenation.* Santa Barbara, CA: Health Science.

Brand, Stewart, ed. (1974). *The Updated Last Whole Earth Catalog: Access to Tools.* Menlo Park, CA: [Portola Institute].

Braun, W. H. Jr. (1964). "Report from Hollywood." *Better Nutrition*, February, 9, 16–17, 19.

Brennan, Bernard F. (1991). "Remarks on Marketing Ethics." *Journal of Business Ethics* 10 (4): 255–58.

Brooks, Jack, Harold J. Burelson, Mrs. Temple D. Corey, Leo Eber, Jim Sofer, Terry M. Staten, Wilma Voge, and John Weidner. (1970). "Special Orders . . . Books . . . Uniforms for Employees." *Health Foods Retailing* 34 (2): 24–26, 38–44.

Brown, Keith R. (2013). *Buying into Fair Trade: Culture, Morality, and Consumption.* New York: New York University Press.

Bruch, Hilde (1970). "The Allure of Food Cults and Nutrition Quackery." *Journal of the American Dietetic Association* 57 (4): 316–20.

Buchwald, Art (1959). "The Hollywood Health Faddists." *Los Angeles Times*, December 25, B5.

Bull, Malcolm, and Keith Lockhart (2007). *Seeking a Sanctuary: Seventh-day Adventism and the American Dream.* 2nd ed. Bloomington: Indiana University Press. First published in 1989.

Bunnell, A.O., ed. ([1902?]). *Dansville: Historical Biographical Descriptive 1789–1902.* Dansville, NY: Instructor Publishing.

Busch, Noel F. (1951). "You Can Live to Be a Hundred, He Says." *Saturday Evening Post* 224 (6): 30, 107–10.

Calhoun, Craig (1993). "'New Social Movements' of the Early Nineteenth Century." *Social Science History* 17 (3): 385–427.

——— (2012). *The Roots of Radicalism: Tradition, the Public Sphere, and Early Nineteenth-Century Social Movements.* Chicago: University of Chicago Press.

Calvert, Gene Paul, and Susan W. Calvert (1975). "Intellectual Convictions of 'Health' Food Consumers." *Journal of Nutrition Education* 7 (3): 95–98.

Canadian Patent Office (1895). *Canadian Patent Office Record.* Vol. 22. Ottawa: Government Printing Bureau.

Carpenter, Peg, and Lorraine Moffett (1967). "'Quackery' in Our Schools." *National Health Federation Bulletin* 13 (1): 4–7.

Carqué, Otto (1923). *Rational Diet: An Advanced Treatise on the Food Question.* Los Angeles: Times-Mirror Press.

——— (1925). *Natural Foods: The Safe Way to Health.* Los Angeles: Carqué Pure Food.

Carson, Gerald (1957). *Cornflake Crusade.* New York: Rinehart.

Carson, Rachel (1962). *Silent Spring.* Boston: Houghton Mifflin.

Cawley, Sherry Arent (2000). *Berrien County in Vintage Postcards.* Chicago: Arcadia Publishing.

Chaney, David C. (1996). *Lifestyles*. London: Routledge.

Chappell, Tom (1993). *The Soul of a Business: Managing for Profit and the Common Good*. New York: Bantam.

Chasin, Alexandra (2000). *Selling Out: The Gay and Lesbian Movement Goes to Market*. New York: Palgrave.

Chou, Marilyn (1979). "Changing Attitudes and Lifestyles Shaping Food Technology in the 1980s." In *Critical Food Issues of the Eighties*, edited by Marilyn Chou and David P. Harmon Jr., 149–90. New York: Pergamon Press.

Clouder, Scott, and Rob Harrison (2005). "The Effectiveness of Ethical Consumer Behaviour." In *The Ethical Consumer*, edited by Rob Harrison, Terry Newholm, and Deirdre Shaw, 89–104. London: Sage.

Cody, George (1996). "History of Naturopathic Medicine." In *A Textbook of Natural Medicine.*, vol. 1, edited by Joseph E. Pizzorno Jr. and Michael T. Murray, I:HistNM-1–I:HistNM-23. Bothell, WA: Bastyr University Publications.

Collins, Harry (2014). *Are We All Scientific Experts Now?* Cambridge: Polity Press.

Colman, F. H. (1933). "A California Utopia Passes." *Los Angeles Times*, August 6, G4, G14.

Conklin, William D. (1971). "The Jackson Health Resort, Pioneer in Its Field, As Seen by Those Who Knew It Well; Being an Account of the Institution's Fiftieth Anniversary . . . With Records of the Seventieth and the One Hundredth . . . And a Supplement." Unpublished manuscript, typescript.

Cooper, Lenna Frances (1917). *How to Cut Food Costs*. Battle Creek, MI: Good Health Publishing.

Council for Responsible Nutrition (2014). "The CRN Consumer Survey on Dietary Supplements: 2014." October. http://www.crnusa.org/CRNconsumersurvey/2014/.

Council on Foods of the American Medical Association (1939). *Accepted Foods and Their Nutritional Significance: Containing Descriptions of the Products Which Stand Accepted by the Council on Foods of the American Medical Association on September 1, 1939* Chicago: American Medical Assocation.

Cowen, Tyler (2002). *Creative Destruction: How Globalization Is Changing the World's Cultures*. Princeton, NJ: Princeton University Press.

Cox, Craig (1994). *Storefront Revolution: Food Co-ops and the Counterculture*. New Brunswick, NJ: Rutgers University Press.

Crawford, Charles W. (1951). "Beware the 'Health Food' Peddlers!" *American Magazine*, December, 24–25, 114–15.

Crecelius, Charles I. (1972). "The Annual Report of the President," *National Health Federation Bulletin* 18 (2): 1–4.

Curtis, Russell L. Jr., and Louis A. Zurcher Jr. (1973). "Stable Resources of Protest Movements: The Multi-Organizational Field." *Social Forces* 52 (1): 53–61.

Davis, Adelle (1947). *Let's Cook It Right: Good Health Comes from Good Cooking*. New York: Harcourt, Brace.

——— (1954). *Let's Eat Right to Keep Fit*. New York: Harcourt, Brace.

de Acosta, Mercedes (1960). *Here Lies the Heart*. New York: Reynal.

de Grazia, Edward (1992). *Girls Lean Back Everywhere: The Law of Obscenity and the Assault on Genius*. New York: Random House.

Delugach, Al (1984)."LaLanne Expands Line." *Los Angeles Times*, October 21, F4.

Deutsch, Ronald M. (1961). *The Nuts among the Berries*. New York: Ballantine.

DiMaggio, Paul J., and Walter W. Powell (1991). "The Iron Cage Revisited: Institutional Isomorphism and Collective Rationality in Organization Fields." In *The New Institutionalism in Organizational Analysis*, edited by Walter W. Powell and Paul J. DiMaggio, 63–82. Chicago: University of Chicago Press.

Dodds, Susanna W. (1886). *Health in the Household; or, Hygienic Cookery*. 2nd ed. New York: Fowler & Wells.

Dougherty, Philip H. (1986)."Prevention Magazine's New Focus." *New York Times*, August 4, D10.

Douglas, Karen Manges, and Regelio Saenz (2008). "Middleman Minorities." In *International Encyclopedia of the Social Sciences*, 2nd ed., edited by William A. Darity Jr., 147–48. Detroit: Macmillan Reference.

Dunne, Robert J. (2005). "Marginality: A Conceptual Extension." *Research in Race and Ethnic Relations* 12:11–27.

Dunning, Mary (1965). "It's Been an Uphill Battle." *Health Foods Retailing* 24 (2): 36–38.

DuPuis, E. Melanie (2002). *Nature's Perfect Food: How Milk Became America's Drink*. New York: New York University Press.

——— (2015). *Dangerous Digestion: The Politics of American Dietary Advice*. Oakland: University of California Press.

Dwyer, Johanna T., Randy F. Kandel, Laura D. V. H. Mayer, and Jean Mayer (1974a). "The 'New' Vegetarians." *Journal of the American Dietetic Association* 64:376–82.

Dwyer, Johanna T., Laura D. V. H. Mayer, Kathryn Dowd, Randy Frances Kandel, and Jean Mayer (1974b). "The New Vegetarians: The Natural High?" *Journal of the American Dietetic Association* 65:529–36.

Eder, Klaus (1996). *The Social Construction of Nature: A Sociology of Ecological Enlightenment*. Translated by Mark Ritter. London: Sage. First published in 1988.

Edgington, Ryan H. (2008). " "Be Receptive to the Good Earth": Health, Nature, and Labor in Countercultural Back-to-the-Land Settlements." *Agricultural History* 82 (3): 279–308.

Edwards, Nicola (2013). "Values and the Institutionalization of Indonesia's Organic Agriculture Movement." In *Social Activism in Southeast Asia*, edited by Michele Ford, 72–88. London: Routledge.

Ehret, Arnold (1924). *A Scientific Method of Eating Your Way to Health: Ehret's Mucusless-Diet Healing System*. Los Angeles: Ehret Literature.

——— (1926). *Rational Fasting for Physical, Mental and Spiritual Rejuvenation*. Los Angeles: Ehret Literature.

Enticott, Gareth (2003). "Risking the Rural: Nature, Morality and the Consumption of Unpasteurized Milk." *Journal of Rural Studies* 19 (4): 411–24.

Epstein, Steven (1996). *Impure Science: AIDS, Activism, and the Politics of Knowledge*. Berkeley: University of California Press.

Erhard, Darla (1973). "The New Vegetarians." *Nutrition Today* 8 (6): 4–12.

Ernst, Robert (1991). *Weakness Is a Crime: The Life of Bernarr Macfadden*. Syracuse, NY: Syracuse University Press.

Ewen, Stuart (1999). *All Consuming Images: The Politics of Style in Contemporary Culture*. Rev. ed. New York: Basic Books. First published in 1988.

Fair, John D. (1999). *Muscletown USA: Bob Hoffman and the Manly Culture of York Barbell*. University Park, PA: Pennsylvania State University Press.

Farmer, Ellen (2010). *Barney Bricmont, Founder, California Certified Organic Farmers*. Santa Cruz, CA: Regional History Project, University Library, UC Santa Cruz.

Featherstone, Mike (2007). *Consumer Culture and Postmodernism*. 2nd ed. London: Sage. First published in 1991.

Ferruzza, Charles (2012). "A Century of Meatless Eating in Kansas City." *Pitch* (blog). May 11. http://www.pitch.com/FastPitch/archives/2012/05/11/a-century-of-meatless-eating-in-kansas-city.

Field, Oliver F. (1982). "History of the U.S. Food and Drug Administration." Interview by Robert G. Porter. *Oral History Program*. Chicago, U.S. Food and Drug Administration.

Filer, George (1850). Letter to the editor, August 25, *American Vegetarian and Health Journal* 1 (1): 11.

Fishbein, Morris (1932). *Fads and Quackery in Healing: An Analysis of the Foibles of the Healing Cults, with Essays on Various Other Peculiar Notions in the Health Field*. New York: Blue Ribbon Books.

Fitzgerald, Deborah (2003). *Every Farm a Factory: The Industrial Ideal in American Agriculture*. New Haven, CT: Yale University Press.

Fligstein, Neil, and Doug McAdam (2012). *A Theory of Fields*. New York: Oxford University Press.

Foucault, Michel (1990). *The History of Sexuality: Volume I: An Introduction*. Translated by Robert Hurley. New York: Vintage. First published in 1976.

Fowler, Bertram B. (1936). *Consumer Cooperation in America: Democracy's Way Out*. New York: Vanguard Press.

Francis, Richard (1997). *Transcendental Utopias: Individual and Community at Brook Farm, Fruitlands, and Walden*. Ithaca, NY: Cornell University Press.

———— (2010). *Fruitlands: The Alcott Family and the Search for Utopia*. New Haven, CT: Yale University Press.

Frank, Thomas (1997). *The Conquest of Cool: Business Culture, Counterculture, and the Rise of Hip Consumerism*. Chicago: University of Chicago Press.

Fred, Emanuel (1961). "Pelll Needs Your Help," *Health Foods Retailing* 25 (2 [March–April]): 16–19.

Fromartz, Samuel (2006). *Organic, Inc.: Natural Foods and How They Grew*. Orlando: Harcourt.

Frost, Bob (1990). "The Pope of Soap." *California* 15 (11): 96–101.

Fulton, E. G. (1904). *Vegetarian Cook Book: Substitutes for Flesh Foods*. Mountain View, CA: Pacific Press.

Gaventa, John (1993). "The Powerful, the Powerless, and the Experts: Knowledge Struggles in an Information Age." In *Voices of Change: Participatory Research in the United States and Canada*, edited by Peter Park, Mary Brydon-Miller, Budd Hall, and Ted Jackson, 21–40. Toronto: Ontario Institute for Studies in Education Press.

Giddens, Anthony (1991). *Modernity and Self-Identity: Self and Society in the Late Modern Age*. Stanford, CT: Stanford University Press.

Gifford, Nellie (1973). "Eat It, It's Good for You." *Chicago Guide*, August, 81–89.

Gittelson, Natalie (1972). "The $2 Billion Health Food . . . Fraud?" *Harpers Bazaar* 106 (November): 32.

Goldstein, Richard (2011). "Jack LaLanne, 96, Fitness's Father, Dies." *New York Times*, January 24, A25.

Goodman, David, and Michael Goodman (2001). "Sustaining Foods: Organic Consumption and the Socio-Ecological Imaginary." In *Exploring Sustainable Consumption: Environmental Policy and the Social Sciences*, edited by Maurie J. Cohen and Joseph Murphy, 97–119. Oxford: Pergamon.

Goodwin, Jeff, and James M. Jasper (2004). "Caught in a Winding, Snarling Vine: The Structural Bias of Political Process Theory." In *Rethinking Social Movements: Structure, Meaning, and Emotion*, edited by Jeff Goodwin and James M. Jasper, 3–30. Lanham, MD: Rowman & Littlefield.

Goodwin, Lorine Swainston (1999). *The Pure Food, Drink, and Drug Crusaders, 1879–1914*. Jefferson, NC: McFarland.

Gottlieb, Robert (1993). *Forcing the Spring: The Transformation of the American Environmental Movement*. Washington, DC: Island Press.

Graham, Sylvester (1837). *Treatise on Bread, and Bread-Making*. Boston: Light & Stearns.

——— (1877). *Lectures on the Science of Human Life*. New York: S. R. Wells. First published in 1839.

Green, Harvey (1986). *Fit for America: Health, Fitness, Sport and American Society*. New York: Pantheon.

Green, Martin (1986). *Mountain of Truth: The Counterculture Begins: Ascona, 1900–1920*. Hanover, NH: University Press of New England.

Griggs, Barbara (1986). *The Food Factor*. Harmondsworth, UK: Viking.

Gumpert, David E. (2009). *The Raw Milk Revolution: Behind America's Emerging Battle Over Food Rights*. White River Junction, VT: Chelsea Green.

Gura, Philip F. (2007). *American Transcendentalism: A History*. New York: Hill and Wang.

Gusfield, Joseph R. (1980). "The Modernity of Social Movements: Public Roles and Private Parts." In *Societal Growth*, edited by Amos Hawle, 290–307. New York: Free Press.

—— (1981). "Social Movements and Social Change: Perspectives of Linearity and Fluidity." *Research in Social Movements, Conflict and Change* 4:317–39.

—— (1992). "Nature's Body and the Metaphors of Food." In *Cultivating Differences: Symbolic Boundaries and the Making of Inequality*, edited by Michèle Lamont and Marcel Fournier, 75–103. Chicago: University of Chicago Press.

Guthman, Julie (2004). *Agrarian Dreams: The Paradox of Organic Farming in California*. Berkeley: University of California Press.

Habermas, Jürgen (1975). *Legitimation Crisis*. Translated by Thomas McCarthy. Boston: Beacon Press. First published in 1973.

Hackett, Alice Payne, and James Henry Burke (1977). *80 Years of Best Sellers: 1895–1975*. New York: R. R. Bowker.

Haedicke, Michael A. (2014). "Small Food Co-ops in a Whole Foods® World." *Contexts* 13 (3): 32–37.

Hafner, Arthur W., James G. Carson, and John F. Zwicky (1992). *Guide to the American Medical Association Historical Health Fraud and Alternative Medicine Collection*. Chicago: American Medical Association.

Hain Celestial Group, Inc. (2014). *Committed to Sustainable Growth: 2014 Annual Report*. http://phx.corporate-ir.net/External.File?item=UGFyZW50SUQ9NTU 2OTQ0fENoaWxkSUQ9MjU0NTg5fFR5cGU9MQ==&t=1.

Hall, Daniel T., and John D. Fair (2004). "The Pioneers of Protein." *Iron Game History* 8 (3): 23–34.

Halling, Bliss O. (1947). "Bureau of Investigation." In *History of the American Medical Association*, edited by Morris Fishbein, 1034–38. Philadelphia: W. B. Saunders.

Hamilton, Malcolm, Peter A. J. Waddington, Susan Gregory, and Ann Walker (1995). "Eat, Drink and Be Saved: The Spiritual Significance of Alternative Diets." *Social Compass* 42 (4): 497–511.

Hammer, Alexander R. (1969). "Miles to Acquire a Food Concern." *New York Times*, December 20, 45.

Harrison, Rob, Terry Newholm, and Deirdre Shaw, eds. (2005). *The Ethical Consumer*. London: Sage.

Hartman, Harvey, and David Wright (1999). *Marketing to the New Natural Consumer: Understanding Trends in Wellness*. Bellevue, WA: Hartman Group.

Hau, Michael (2003). *The Cult of Health and Beauty in Germany: A Social History 1890–1930*. Chicago: University of Chicago Press.

Hauser, Bengamin Gayelord (1930). *Harmonized Food Selection: Including the Famous Hauser Body Building System*. New York: Tempo Books.

—— (1944). *Diet Does It*. New York: Coward-McCann.

—— (1950). *Look Younger, Live Longer*. New York: Farrar, Straus.

Haveman, Heather A., and Hayagreeva Rao (1997). "Structuring a Theory of Moral Sentiments: Institutional and Organizational Coevolution in the Early Thrift Industry." *American Journal of Sociology* 102 (6): 1606–51.

Hay, William Howard. (1934). Introduction to *The Official Cook Book of the Hay System*, rev. ed., by Esther L. Smith, xiii–xvii. Mount Pocono, PA: Pocono Haven.

Haynes, Harmony (1940). "The Man Garbo Would Diet For." *Photoplay*, February, 16, 76.

Hebdige, Dick (1979). *Subculture: The Meaning of Style*. London: Methuen.

Henderson, Bruce (1989). "Thoreau and Emerson: Vegetarianism, Bhuddism and Organic Form." In *Cooking by the Book: Food in Literature and Culture*, edited by Mary Anne Schofield, 170–78. Bowling Green, OH: Bowling Green State University Popular Press.

Henderson, Harold (1987). "These Are Vegetarian Times," *Chicago Reader*, December 10.

Henderson, Mary F. (1885). *Diet for the Sick: A Treatise on the Values of Foods, Their Application to Special Conditions of Health and Disease, and on the Best Methods of Their Preparation*. New York: Harper & Bros.

Herbert, Victor, and Stephen Barrett (1981). *Vitamins and "Health" Foods: The Great American Hustle*. Philadelphia: George F. Stickley.

Hewitt, Jean (1971). *The New York Times Natural Foods Cookbook*. New York: Quadrangle Books.

Hiatt, Shon R., Wesley D. Sine, and Pamela S. Tolbert (2009). "From Pabst to Pepsi: The Deinstitutionalization of Social Practices and the Creation of Entrepreneurial Opportunities." *Administrative Science Quarterly* 54 (4): 635–67.

Hilton, Matthew (2007). "Social Activism in an Age of Consumption: The Organized Consumer Movement." *Social History* 32 (2): 121–43.

Hine, Robert V. (1953). *California's Utopian Colonies*. San Marino, CA: Huntington Library.

Hirsch, Fred S. (1928a). "Health Center Newslets." *Los Angeles Times*, January 22, K27.

———— (1928b)."Health Center Newslets." *Los Angeles Times*, January 29, I27.

Hirshberg, Gary (2008). *Stirring It Up: How to Make Money and Save the World*. New York: Hyperion.

Hoblyn, Richard D. (1865). *A Dictionary of Terms Used in Medicine and the Collateral Sciences*. A New American from the Last London ed. Philadelphia: Henry C. Lea.

Hoff, Hebbel E., and John F. Fulton (1937). "The Centenary of the First American Physiological Society Founded at Boston by William A. Alcott and Sylvester Graham." *Bulletin of the Institute of the History of Medicine* 5 (8): 687–734.

Hoffman, Bob (1962). *Functional Isometric Constraction System of Static Contraction: Advance Course*. York, PA: Bob Hoffman Foundation.

Hollender, Jeffrey, and Bill Breen (2010). *The Responsibility Revolution: How the Next Generation of Businesses Will Win*. San Francisco: Jossey-Bass.

Holt, Douglas B. (2000). "Does Cultural Capital Structure American Consumption?" In *The Consumer Society Reader*, edited by Juliet B. Schor and Douglas B. Holt, 212–52. New York: New Press.

Horrocks, Thomas A (2008). *Popular Print and Popular Medicine: Almanacs and Health Advice in Early America*. Amherst: University of Massachusetts Press.

Horvath, Roland E. (1957). "How to Plan Your Store Lighting for More Sales." *Health Foods Retailing* 21 (2): 24–25, 54–56.

Howard, Philip H. (2009). "Consolidation in the North American Organic Food Processing Sector, 1997 to 2007." *International Journal of Sociology of Agriculture and Food* 16 (1): 13–30.

Hunt, Ridgely (1975). "Health Food Industry Is Commercially Hale and Hearty." *Chicago Tribune*, April 7, E7, E8.

Hunt, William R. (1989). *Body Love: The Amazing Career of Bernarr Macfadden*. Bowling Green, OH: Bowling Green State University Press.

Hunter, Marjorie (1962). "US Official Says Calorie Book Was a Promotion for Capsules." *New York Times*, July 7, 1, 15.

Huth, Andy (2016)."Crafting a New Future." *Natural Foods Merchandiser* 37 (4): 25–31.

Iacobbo, Karen, and Michael Iacobbo (2004). *Vegetarian America: A History*. Westport, CT: Praeger.

International Medical Missionary and Benevolent Association (1897). *Year Book of the International Medical Missionary and Benevolent Association*. Battle Creek, MI: International Medical Missionary and Benevolent Association.

Irvine, Clarke (1935). *"Health!" With Recipes and Remedies*. 5th ed. Hollywood, CA: Clarke Irvine. First published in 1927.

Jablow, Valerie, and Bill Horne (1999). "Farmers' Markets." *Smithsonian* 30 (3): 120–30.

Jenkins, J. Craig (1977). "Radical Transformation of Organizational Goals." *Administrative Science Quarterly* 22 (4): 568–86.

Jochnowitz, Eve (1997). "Health, Revolution, and a *Yidishe Tam*: Reading Yiddish Vegetarian Cookbooks as Women's Literature." In *Conference Proceedings: Di Froyen: Women and Yiddish: Tribute to the Past Directions for the Future*, pp. 52–56. New York: National Council of Jewish Women New York Section, Jewish Women's Resource Center.

Johnston, Josée (2008). "The Citizen-Consumer Hybrid: Ideological Tensions and the Case of Whole Foods Market." *Theory & Society* 37 (3): 229–70.

Johnston, Josée, and Shyon Baumann (2007). "Democracy versus Distinction: A Study of Omnivorousness in Gourmet Food Writing." *American Journal of Sociology* 113 (1): 165–204.

——— (2010). *Foodies: Democracy and Distinction in the Gourmet Foodscape*. New York: Routledge.

Johnston, Josée, and Michelle Szabo (2011). "Reflexivity and the Whole Foods Market Consumer: The Lived Experience of Shopping for Change." *Agricultural and Human Values* 28 (3): 303–19.

Just, Adolf (1903). *Return to Nature! The True Natural Method of Healing and Living and the True Salvation of the Soul: Paradise Regained.* Translated by Benedict Lust. New York: Benedict Lust. First published in 1896.

Kalus, Louis (1948). "Choice of Two Worlds" *American Vegetarian* 7 (2): 5, 8.

Katz, Sandor Ellix (2006). *The Revolution Will Not Be Microwaved: Inside America's Underground Food Movements.* White River Junction, VT: Chelsea Green Publishing.

Kellogg, E. E. (1897). *Every-Day Dishes and Every-Day Work.* Battle Creek, MI: Modern Medicine Publishing.

——— (1898). *Science in the Kitchen. A Scientific Treatise on Food Substances and Their Dietetic Properties, Together with a Practical Explanation of the Principles of Healthful Cookery, and a Large Number of Original, Palatable, and Wholesome Recipes.* Rev. ed. Battle Creek: Health Publishing. First published in 1892.

Kellogg, John Harvey (1903). *The Living Temple.* Battle Creek, MI: Good Health Publishing.

——— (1921). *The New Dietetics: What to Eat and How; A Guide to Scientific Feeding in Health and Disease.* Battle Creek, MI: Modern Medicine Publishing.

[Kellogg, John Harvey] (1918). "The Soy Bean." *Good Health* 53 (February): 111.

Kennedy, Gordon (1998). *Children of the Sun: A Pictorial Anthology: From Germany to California 1883–1949.* Ojai, CA: Nivaria Press.

Kerouac, Jack (1991). *On the Road.* New York: Penguin. First published in 1957.

Kerr, Peter (1984). "Gaylord Hauser, 89, Author; Proponent of Natural Foods." *New York Times*, December 29, 26.

Kessler, John (1998). "Dinner Conversation: Plenty to Munch on in Goofy Little Book about Food." *Atlanta Journal and Constitution*, July 31, 3Q.

Kilpatrick, James J. (1965). "A Lonesome Battle to Air Ideas." *Los Angeles Times*, August 24, A5.

——— (1967). "The Book and the Bureaucrat." *Los Angeles Times*, July 18, A5.

King, Brayden G. (2008). "A Political Mediation Model of Corporate Response to Social Movement Activism." *Administrative Science Quarterly* 53 (3): 395–421.

King, Brayden G., and Nicholas A. Pearce (2010). "The Contentiousness of Markets: Politics, Social Movements, and Institutional Change in Markets." *Annual Review of Sociology* 36:249–67.

Kirchfeld, Friedhelm, and Wade Boyle (1994). *Nature Doctors: Pioneers in Naturopathic Medicine.* Portland, OR: Medicina Biologica.

Klandermans, Bert (1992). "The Social Construction of Protest and Multiorganizational Fields." In *Frontiers in Social Movement Theory*, edited by Aldon D. Morris and Carol McClurg Mueller, 77–103. New Haven, CT: Yale University Press.

Klein, Joe (1978). "A Social History of Granola." *Rolling Stone*, February 23, 40–44.

Kneipp, Sebastian ([1901]). *The Kneipp Cure: An Absolutely Verbal and Literal Translation of "Meine Wasserkur" (My Water Cure)*. Complete American ed. New York: B. Lust.

Knupfer, Anne Meis (2013). *Food Co-Ops in America: Communities, Consumption, and Economic Democracy*. Ithaca, NY: Cornell University Press.

Kobrin, Rebecca, ed. (2012). *Chosen Capital: The Jewish Encounter with American Capitalism*. New Brunswick, NJ: Rutgers University Press.

Kotulak, Jean (1963). "Stands on Stomach at Interview." *Chicago Tribune*, June 30, S3.

Kotulak, Ronald (1974). "Organic Food Fad Big Fraud: Experts." *Chicago Tribune*, March 3, 18.

Kurzman, Charles (2008). "Meaning-Making in Social Movements." *Anthopological Quarterly* 81 (1): 5–15.

Kvidahl, Melissa (2016). "Supplements Spotlight 2015." *Natural Foods Merchandiser* 37 (4): 35–36.

Ladimer, Irving (1965). "The Health Advertising Program of the National Better Business Bureau." *American Journal of Public Health Nation's Health* 55 (8): 1217–27.

Lager, Mildred, and Dorothea Van Gundy Jones (1963). *The Soybean Cookbook*. New York: Devan-Adair.

Lane, Charles (1843). "The Consociate Family Life," *New Age, Concordium Gazette, & Temperance Advocate* 11 (1): 116–20.

Lansing, Elizabeth (1970). "The Move to Eat Natural." *Life* 69 (24): 44–52.

Latson, W. R. C. (1902). "On Dietary Reform." *Los Angeles Times*, December 23, A4.

Laufer, William S. (2003). "Social Accountability and Corporate Greenwashing." *Journal of Business Ethics* 43 (3): 253–61.

Layna, Anna (1958). "Beauty After Forty." *Health Culture* 65 (12): 28–29, 36.

Lee, Louise (1996). "Whole Foods Swallows Up Nearest Rival." *Wall Street Journal*, June 19, B1.

Lee, Paul (1972). Preface to *Whole Earth Cook Book*, by Sharon Cadwallader and Judi Ohr, vii–viii. Boston: Houghton Mifflin.

Lehman, Ernest (1951). "The Fantastic Story of Gayelord Hauser." *Cosmopolitan* 130 (3): 33–35, 114–19.

Levenstein, Harvey (1988). *Revolution at the Table: The Transformation of the American Diet*. New York: Oxford University Press.

Levitsky, Sandra R., and Jane C. Banaszak-Holl (2010). "Social Movements and the Transformation of American Health Care: Introduction." In *Social Movements and the Transformation of American Health Care*, edited by Jane C. Banaszak-Holl, Sandra R. Levitsky, and Mayer N. Zald, 3–18. New York: Oxford University Press.

Licata, Paul J. (1981). *National Nutritional Foods Association Report on the Natural Foods and Vitamin Market*. Westminster, CA: California Nutritional Products.

Linton, April, Cindy Chiayuan Liou, and Kelly Ann Shaw (2004). "A Taste of Trade Justice: Marketing Global Social Responsibility via Fair Trade Coffee." *Globalizations* 1 (2): 223–46.

Lockie, Stewart, and Darren Halpin (2005). "The 'Conventionalisation Thesis' Reconsidered: Structural and Ideological Transformation of Australian Organic Agriculture." *Sociologia Ruralis* 45 (4): 284–307.

Lounsbury, Michael, Marc Ventresca, and Paul M. Hirsch (2003). "Social Movements, Field Frames and Industry Emergence: A Cultural-Political Perspective on US Recycling." *Socio-Economic Review* 1 (1): 71–104.

Luders, Joseph (2006). "The Economics of Movement Success: Business Responses to Civil Rights Mobilization." *American Journal of Sociology* 111 (4): 963–98.

Luke, Emily (2005). "The Roar about Hormones." *Whole Foods* 28 (2): 38–40.

Lyons, Richard D. (1973). "Disputed Health Lobby Is Pressing for a Bill to Overturn Any Limits on Sales of Vitamins." *New York Times*, May 14, 17.

Mabrie, Sanford (1956). "Gaylord [*sic*] Hauser: America's No. 1 Huckster of Health." *Inside Story* 2 (6): 20–22, 62–64.

Macfadden, Bernarr (1901). *Strength from Eating: How and What to Eat and Drink . . . to . . . Develop . . . the Highest Degree of Health and Strength*. New York: Physical Culture.

Maintenance Company (1922). *History of the Philadelphia Bible-Christian Church for the First Century of Its Existence from 1817 to 1917*. Philadelphia: J. B. Lippincott.

Major, Nettie Leitch (1963). *C. W. Post: The Hour and the Man*. Washington, DC: Press of Judd & Detweiler.

Marshall, Lisa (2012). "Adding Up Supplement Costs." *Natural Foods Merchandiser* 33 (7): 24–25.

——— (2015). "Risk & Reward." *Natural Foods Merchandiser* 36 (6): 17–22.

Martin, Andrew (2007). "Whole Foods Makes Offer for a Smaller Rival." *New York Times*, February 22, C1, C12.

Marx, Karl, and Friedrich Engels (1978). "Manifesto of the Communist Party." In *The Marx-Engels Reader*, 2nd ed., edited by Robert C. Tucker, 469–500. New York: W. W. Norton. First published in 1848.

Maurer, Donna (2002). *Vegetarianism: Movement or Moment?* Philadelphia: Temple University Press.

May, Earl Chapin (1937). *The Canning Clan: A Pageant of Pioneering Americans*. New York: Macmillan.

McAdam, Doug, Sidney Tarrow, and Charles Tilly (2001). *Dynamics of Contention*. New York: Cambridge University Press.

McBean, Lois D., and Elwood W. Speckermann (1974). "Food Faddism: A Challenge to Nutritionists and Dietitians." *American Journal of Clinical Nutrition* 27:1071–78.

McCarthy, John D., and Mayer N. Zald (1977). "Resource Mobilization and So-
    cial Movements: A Partial Theory." *American Journal of Sociology* 82 (6):
    1212–41.

McKie, James W. (1974). "Changing Views." In *Social Responsibility and the Business
    Predicament*, edited by McKie, 17–40. Washington, DC: Brookings Institution.

Melucci, Alberto (1989). *Nomads of the Present: Social Movements and Individual
    Needs in Contemporary Society*. Philadelphia: Temple University Press.

Merrill, Arch (1958). "Dansville—Birthplace of First 'Flakes.'" *Rochester Demo-
    crat and Chronicle*, October 5, 1958, 4H.

Merrill, Harwood F., ed. (1948). *The Responsibilities of Business Leadership*. Cam-
    bridge, MA: Harvard University Press.

Metcalfe, William (1872). *Out of the Clouds: Into the Light. Seventeen Discourses
    on the Leading Doctrines of the Day, in the Light of Bible Christianity. Together
    with a Memoir of the Author, By His Son, Rev. Joseph Metcalfe*. Philadelphia:
    J. B. Lippincott.

Meyer, David S., and Sidney Tarrow (1998). "A Movement Society: Contentious
    Politics for a New Century." In *The Social Movement Society: Contentious Poli-
    tics for a New Century*, edited by Meyer and Tarrow, 1–28. Lanham, MD: Row-
    man & Littlefield.

Meyer, Donald (1988). *The Positive Thinkers: Popular Religious Psychology from
    Mary Baker Eddy to Norman Vincent Peale and Ronald Reagan*, rev. ed., with a
    new introduction. Middletown, CT: Wesleyan University Press. First published
    in 1965.

Meyer-Renschhausen, Elisabeth, and Albert Wirz (1999). "Dietetics, Health Re-
    form and Social Order: Vegetarianism as a Moral Physiology. The Exam-
    ple of Maximilian Bircher-Benner (1867–1939)." *Medical History* 43 (3): 323–
    41.

Micheletti, Michele (2003). *Political Virtue and Shopping: Individuals, Consumer-
    ism, and Collective Action*. New York: Palgrave Macmillan.

Milbuty, Peter (2011). "Chico-San and Organic Brown Rice: A Personal History."
    Macrobiotics Today 51 (1): 14–19.

Millar, Robin (1972). "Viewpoint on Nutrition Spreads on Radio-TV." *Los Ange-
    les Times*, June 25, AB7, AB11.

Miller, Laura J. (2006). *Reluctant Capitalists: Bookselling and the Culture of Con-
    sumption*. Chicago: University of Chicago Press.

Miller, Laura J., and Emilie Hardman (2015). "By the Pinch and the Pound: Less and
    More Protest in American Vegetarian Cookbooks from the Nineteenth Century
    to the Present." In *Protest on the Page: Essays on Print and the Culture of Dissent
    Since 1865*, edited by James L. Baughman, Jennifer Ratner-Rosenhagen, and
    James P. Danky, 111–36. Madison: University of Wisconsin Press.

Miller, Timothy (1998). *The Quest for Utopia in Twentieth-Century America, Vol-
    ume I: 1900–1960*. Syracuse: Syracuse University Press.

——— (1999). *The 60s Communes: Hippies and Beyond.* Syracuse: Syracuse University Press.

Minsky, Terri (1979). "Health-Food Chains, in a Rapid Expansion, Cause Some Heartburn." *Wall Street Journal,* September 28, 1, 35.

Mintel International Group (2008). *Organic Food—US.* Chicago: Mintel International Group.

Mitchell, Ruth Comfort. 1904. "To a Health-Food Girl." *Sunset* 13 (5): 489.

Moeller, Susan D. (1996). "Pictures of the Enemy: Fifty Years of Images of Japan in the American Press, 1941–1992." *Journal of American Culture* 19 (1): 29–42.

Muller, Jerry Z. (2010). *Capitalism and the Jews.* Princeton, NJ: Princeton University Press.

Murphy, Priscilla Coit (2005). *What a Book Can Do: The Publication and Reception of Silent Spring.* Amherst: University of Massachusetts Press.

Murray, Erastus H. (1873). Improvement in Food from Wheat and Processes of Preparing the Same. US Patent 139,600, filed June 3.

Murray, Frank (1985). "Gayelord Hauser—A Remembrance," *Health Foods Retailing* 49 (3): 30–31, 40.

Murray, Frank, with Jon Tarr (1984). *More Than One Slingshot: How the Health Food Industry Is Changing America.* Richmond, VA: Marlborough House.

"'Natural' Tops Product Claims in 2008" (2009). *Whole Foods* 32 (3): 9.

Nearing, Helen (1980). *Simple Food for the Good Life: An Alternative Cookbook.* New York: Delacorte Press.

Nearing, Helen, and Scott Nearing (1954). *Living the Good Life: Being a Plain Practical Account of a Twenty Year Project in a Self-Subsistent Homestead in Vermont together with Remarks on How to Live Sanely and Simply in a Troubled World.* Harborside, ME: Social Science Institute.

Nelson, Harry (1974). "Organic Food Report Supported." *Los Angeles Times,* February 26, 19.

Neltner, Thomas G., Heather M. Alger, Jack E. Leonard, and Maricel V. Maffini (2013). "Data Gaps in Toxicity Testing of Chemicals Allowed in Food in the United States." *Reproductive Toxicology* 42:85–94.

New, Peter Kong-Ming, and Rhea Pendergrass Priest (1967). "Food and Thought: A Sociologic Study of Foods Cultists." *Journal of the American Dietetic Association* 51 (1): 13–18.

Newman, Paul, and A. E. Hotchner (2003). *Shameless Exploitation: In Pursuit of the Common Good.* New York: Nan E. Talese.

Nicholson, Asenath (1835). *Nature's Own Book.* 2nd ed. New York: Wilbur & Whipple.

Nissenbaum, Stephen (1980). *Sex, Diet, and Debility in Jacksonian America: Sylvester Graham and Health Reform.* Westport, CT: Greenwood Press.

Numbers, Ronald L. (1976). *Prophetess of Health: A Study of Ellen G. White.* New York: Harper & Row.

———— (2003). "Sex, Science, and Salvation: The Sexual Advice of Ellen G. White and John Harvey Kellogg." In *Right Living: An Anglo-American Tradition of Self-Help Medicine and Hygiene*, edited by Charles E. Rosenberg, 206–26. Baltimore: Johns Hopkins University Press.

O'Connor, Anahad (2013). "Pills That Aren't What They Seem." *New York Times*, November 5, D1, D5.

Offe, Claus (1985). "New Social Movements: Challenging the Boundaries of Institutional Politics." *Social Research* 52 (4): 817–68.

Olsen, M. Ellsworth (1972). *A History of the Origin and Progress of Seventh-Day Adventists*. New York: AMS Press. First published in 1925.

Olson, Robert E. (1955). "Research, Fads, and Practical Dietetics." *Journal of the American Dietetic Association* 31 (8): 777–82.

———— (1958). "Food Faddism—Why?" *Nutrition Reviews* 16 (1): 97–99.

Pacey, Margaret D. (1971). "Nature's Bounty." *Barron's* 51 (19): 5, 15, 16.

———— (1972). "Not All Milk and Honey." *Barron's* 52 (37): 11, 24, 26, 27.

Paumgarten, Nick (2010). "Does Whole Foods' C.E.O. Know What's Best for You?" *New Yorker* 85 (43): 36–47.

Pellow, David Naguib (2007). *Resisting Global Toxics: Transnational Movements for Environmental Justice*. Cambridge, MA: MIT Press.

Perry, Nathaniel, and David Cambell (1837). "To Agriculturists," *Graham Journal of Health and Longevity* 1 (7): 56.

Petrina, Stephen (2008). "Medical Liberty: Drugless Healers Confront Allopathic Doctors, 1910–1931." *Journal of Medical Humanities* 29 (4): 205–30.

Phillipps, Stanley (1976). "The HF Industry Has Come of Age." *Health Foods Retailing* 40 (12): 71–78, 238–58.

Piacentini, Maria, Lynn MacFadyen, and Douglas Eadie (2000). "Corporate Social Responsibility in Food Retailing." *International Journal of Retail & Distribution Management* 28 (11): 459–69.

Polletta, Francesca (2008). "Culture and Movements." *Annals of the American Academy of Political and Social Science* 619:78–96.

Powell, Horace B. (1956). *The Original Has This Signature—W. K. Kellogg*. Englewood Cliffs, NJ: Prentice-Hall.

Powell, Rachel, and John Clarke (1976). "A Note on Marginality." In *Resistance through Rituals: Youth Subcultures in Post-War Britain*, edited by Stuart Hall and Tony Jefferson, 223–29. London: HarperCollins Academic.

Pratt, Charles Orlando (1966). "NHF Lawyer Charges AMA with Oppression of Health Freedom." *National Health Federation Bulletin* 12 (10): 3–7.

Pratt, E. L. (1949a). "Gould Falsehood." *American Vegetarian* 7 (11): 1.

———— (1949b). "The Veracity of the Jews." *American Vegetarian* 7 (10): 1, 8.

Quarter, Jack (2000). *Beyond the Bottom Line: Socially Innovative Business Owners*. Westport, CT: Quorum Books.

Ransome, Paul (2005). *Work, Consumption and Culture: Affluence and Social Change in the Twenty-First Century*. London: Sage.

Rao, Hayagreeva (2009). *Market Rebels: How Activists Make or Break Radical Innovations*. Princeton, NJ: Princeton University Press.

Rao, Hayagreeva, Calvin Morrill, and Mayer N. Zald (2000). "Power Plays: How Social Movements and Collective Action Create New Organizational Forms." *Research in Organizational Behaviour* 22:237–81.

Research Department of Prevention (1981). *Health Food Store Shoppers: A Lifestyle and Product Usage Profile*. Emmaus, PA: Prevention.

Richman, Alan (1988). "1987: A Perplexing Year." *Health Foods Business*, March, 36–46.

Ridgeway, James (1963). "The AMA, the FDA and Quacks," *New Republic* 149 (19): 31–33.

Roach, Randy (2004). "Splendid Specimens: The History of Nutrition in Bodybuilding." *Wise Traditions in Food, Farming and the Healing Arts* 5 (3): 25–38.

Robinson, Dores Eugene (1965). *The Story of Our Health Message*. 3rd ed. Nashville: Southern Publishing Association. First published in 1943.

Robinson, Jennifer Meta, and J. A. Hartenfeld (2007). *The Farmers' Market Book: Growing Food, Cultivating Community*. Bloomington, IN: Quarry Books.

Rodale, J. I. (1965). *Autobiography*. Emmaus, PA: Rodale Press.

Rodale, J. I., and Ruth Adams, eds. (1954). *The Health Finder: An Encyclopedia of Health Information from the Preventive Point-of-View*. Emmaus, PA: Rodale Books.

Rodale, Robert (1961). "Every Man a Homesteader." *Organic Gardening and Farming* 8 (5): 16–19.

Ronco, William (1974). *Food Co-ops: An Alternative to Shopping in Supermarkets*. Boston: Beacon Press.

Root, Waverly, and Richard de Rochemont (1976). *Eating in America: A History*. New York: William Morrow.

Roszak, Theodore (1995). *The Making of a Counter Culture: Reflections on the Technocratic Society and Its Youthful Opposition*. Berkeley: University of California Press. First published in 1969.

Roth, Julius A. (1977). *Health Purifiers and Their Enemies*. New York: Prodist.

Saegert, Joel, and Merry Mayne Saegert (1976). "Consumer Attitudes and Food Faddism: The Case of Vitamin E." *Journal of Consumer Affairs* 10 (2): 156–69.

Saegert, Joel, Eleanor Young, and Merry Mayne Saegert (1978). "Fad Food Use among Anglo- and Mexican-Americans: An Example of Research in Consumer Behavior and Home Economics." *Advances in Consumer Research* 5 (1): 730–33.

Sandomit, Richard (2004). "Jack LaLanne Is Back (Sort Of), Helping Viewers Feel Guilty Again." *New York Times*, March 12, D3.

Sarnoff, Rachel Lincoln (2015). "The New DIY." *Natural Foods Merchandiser* 36 (7): 21–22.

Schiff, Eugene (1957). "The Pelll Committee Reports," *Health Foods Retailing* 21 (4 [July–August]):19.

Schmeck, Harold M. Jr. (1973). "Vitamin Sales and Labeling Face Tighter Regulations by the F.D.A." *New York Times*, August 2, 1, 23.

Schurman, Rachel, and William A. Munro (2010). *Fighting for the Future of Food: Activists versus Agribusiness in the Struggle Over Biotechnology*. Minneapolis: University of Minnesota Press.

Schwartz, Hillel (1986). *Never Satisfied: A Cultural History of Diets, Fantasies and Fat*. New York: Anchor Books.

Schwarz, Richard W. (1970). *John Harvey Kellogg, M.D.* Nashville: Southern Publishing Association.

———— (1972). "The Kellogg Schism: The Hidden Issues." *Spectrum: Journal of the Association of Adventist Forums* 4 (4): 23–39.

Scott, Donald M. (1980). "The Popular Lecture and the Creation of a Public in Mid-Nineteenth-Century America." *Journal of American History* 66 (4): 791–809.

Sears, Clara Endicott (1915). *Bronson Alcott's Fruitlands*. Boston: Houghton Mifflin.

Seidman, Gay W. (2003). "Monitoring Multinationals: Lessons from the Anti-Apartheid Era." *Politics & Society* 31 (3): 381–406.

Serazio, Michael (2011). "Ethos Groceries and Countercultural Appetites: Consuming Memory in Whole Foods' Brand Utopia." *Journal of Popular Culture* 44 (1): 158–77.

Shephard, Sue (2000). *Pickled, Potted, and Canned: How the Art and Science of Food Preserving Changed the World*. New York: Simon & Schuster.

Shi, David E. (1985). *The Simple Life: Plain Living and High Thinking in American Culture*. New York: Oxford University Press.

Shils, Edward (1975). "Center and Periphery." In *Center and Periphery: Essays in Macrosociology*, 3–16. Chicago: University of Chicago Press.

Shprintzen, Adam D. (2013). *The Vegetarian Crusade: The Rise of an American Reform Movement, 1817–1921*. Chapel Hill: University of North Carolina Press.

Shurtleff, William, and Akiko Aoyagi (2011). *History of Erewhon—Natural Foods Pioneer in the United States (1966–2011): Extensively Annotated Bibliography and Sourcebook*. Lafayette, CA, Soyinfo Center. http://www.soyinfocenter.com/pdf/142/Erewhon2.pdf.

Shyrock, Richard H. (1931). "Sylvester Graham and the Popular Health Movement, 1830–1870." *Mississippi Valley Historical Review* 18 (2): 172–83.

Simmel, Georg (1904). "Fashion." *International Quarterly* 10 (1): 130–55.

Simmons Market Research Bureau (1981). *Health Food Store Shoppers: A Lifestyle and Product Usage Report*. Emmaus, PA: Prevention.

Sine, Wesley D., and Brandon H. Lee (2009). "Tilting at Windmills? The Environmental Movement and the Emergence of the U.S. Wind Energy Sector." *Administrative Science Quarterly* 54 (1): 123–55.

Singer, Natasha (2013). "Supplements Called Risky Are Destroyed." *New York Times*, July 17, B2.

Singer, Natasha, and Peter Lattman (2013a). "F.D.A. Issues Warning on Workout Supplement." *New York Times*, April 13, B1, B2.

—— (2013b). "Is the Seller to Blame?" *New York Times*, March 17, BU1, BU6–7.

—— (2013c). "US Moves to Seize Dietary Supplement from GNC Warehouses." *New York Times*, June 22, B2.

Slater, Don (1997). *Consumer Culture and Modernity*. Cambridge: Polity Press.

Sloane, Leonard (1994). "A Small Specialty Foods Company Moves to Revitalize Some Longtime Brands." *New York Times*, December 28, D6.

Slocum, Rachel (2007). "Whiteness, Space and Alternative Food Practice." *Geoforum* 38 (3): 520–33.

Smith, Andrew F. (1996). *Pure Ketchup: A History of America's National Condiment with Recipes*. Columbia, SC: University of South Carolina Press.

Smith, Ralph Lee (1960). *The Health Hucksters*. New York: Thomas Y. Crowell.

Smith-Howard, Kendra (2014). *Pure and Modern Milk: An Environmental History since 1900*. New York: Oxford University Press.

Snow, David A. (2004). "Social Movements as Challenges to Authority: Resistance to an Emerging Conceptual Hegemony." In *Authority in Contention*, edited by Daniel J. Myers and Daniel M. Cress, 3–25. Amsterdam: Elsevier.

Snow, David A., and Robert D. Benford (1992). "Master Frames and Cycles of Protest." In *Frontiers in Social Movement Theory*, edited by Aldon D. Morris and Carol McClurg Mueller, 133–55. New Haven, CT: Yale University Press.

Soper, Kate, Martin Ryle, and Lyn Thomas, eds. (2009). *The Politics and Pleasures of Consuming Differently*. Houndmills, UK: Palgrave Macmillan.

Soule, Sarah A. (2009). *Contention and Corporate Social Responsibility*. New York: Cambridge University Press.

Spielman, Michael (1979). "The Annual Survey of Health Food Stores in America." *Health Foods Business* 25 (3): 45–56.

Stare, Fredrick J. (1970). "Current Nutrition Nonsense in the United States." In *Food Cultism and Nutrition Quackery*, edited by Gunnar Blix, 51–58. Uppsala: Almqvist & Wiksells.

—— (1992). "Combatting Misinformation—A Continuing Challenge for Nutrition Professionals." *Nutrition Today* 27 (3): 43–46.

—— (1996). "Nutrition Professor for 5 Decades Plus." *Nutrition Today* 31 (4): 148–54.

Starr, Amory (2000). *Naming the Enemy: Anti-Corporate Movements Confront Globalization*. London: Zed Books.

Starr, Paul (1982). *The Social Transformation of American Medicine*. New York: Basic Books.

Stein, Jeannine (1988). "Jack LaLanne Presses On." *Los Angeles Times*, May 24, F1, F2, F6.

Stewart, Kimberly Lord (2003). "Meat-Label Madness." *Natural Foods Mercahndiser* 24 (3): 72–74.

Stewart, Mrs. P. P. (1854). "Correspondence," *American Vegetarian and Health Journal* 4 (8): 161–62.

Strasser, Susan (1989). *Satisfaction Guaranteed: The Making of the American Mass Market*. Washington, DC: Smithsonian Institution Press.

Stryker, Robin (1994). "Rules, Resources, and Legitimacy Processes: Some Implications for Social Conflict, Order, and Change." *American Journal of Sociology* 99 (4): 847–910.

Suddaby, Roy, and Royston Greenwood (2005). "Rhetorical Strategies of Legitimacy." *Administrative Science Quarterly* 50:35–67.

Swift, Lindsay (1973). *Brook Farm: Its Members, Scholars, and Visitors*. Secaucus, NJ: Citadel Press. First published in 1900.

Szasz, Andrew (2007). *Shopping Our Way to Safety: How We Changed from Protecting the Environment to Protecting Ourselves*. Minneapolis: University of Minnesota Press.

Tardosky, Cathy C. (1990). "A Store Grows in Manhattan: NYC's Brownie's Looks Forward to Next 50 Years." *Whole Foods*, March, 74–78.

Thomas, Anna (1978). *The Vegetarian Epicure Book Two*. New York: Knopf.

Thompson, Craig J., and Gokcen Coskuner-Balli (2007). "Countervailing Market Responses to Corporate Co-Optation and the Ideological Recruitment of Consumption Communities." *Journal of Consumer Research* 34:135–52.

Tipton, Steven M. (1982). *Getting Saved from the Sixties: Moral Meaning in Conversion and Cultural Change*. Berkeley: University of California Press.

Tobey, James A. (1939). "Baking Technology and National Nutrition." *Scientific Monthly* 49 (5): 464–68.

Tompkins, Kyla Wazana (2012). *Racial Indigestion: Eating Bodies in the 19th Century*. New York: New York University Press.

Tonell, Tess (1970). "News Around the Corner." *Health Foods Retailing* 34 (6): 102–3, 114.

Tovey, Hilary (1999). "'Messers, Visionaries and Organobureaucrats': Dilemmas of Institutionalisation in the Irish Organic Farming Movement." *Irish Journal of Sociology* 9:31–59.

Trager, James (1971). "Health Food: Why and Why Not." *Vogue* 157 (January 1): 122–23, 134, 136.

Turner, Ralph H., and Lewis M. Killian (1987). *Collective Behavior*. 3rd ed. Englewood Cliffs, NJ: Prentice-Hall.

United States Department of Agriculture (1910). "Notice of Judgment No. 470, Food and Drugs Act." In *Food and Drugs Act, Notices of Judgment Nos. 251–500*. Washington, DC: US Government Printing Office.

United States Department of Agriculture, Food Safety and Inspection Service (2015). "Meat and Poultry Labeling Terms." Last modified August 10. http:// www.fsis.usda.gov/wps/portal/fsis/topics/food-safety-education/get-answers /food-safety-fact-sheets/food-labeling/meat-and-poultry-labeling-terms/meat -and-poultry-labeling-terms.

Unity School of Christianity (1923). *The Unity Inn Vegetarian Cook Book: A Collection of Practical Suggestions and Receipts for the Preparation of Non-Flesh Foods in Palatable and Attractive Ways*. Kansas City, MO: Unity School of Christianity.

Van Dyke, Nella, Sarah A. Soule, and Verta Taylor (2004). "The Targets of Social Movements: Beyond a Focus on the State." In *Authority in Contention*, edited by Daniel J. Myers and Daniel M. Cress, 27–51. Amsterdam: Elsevier.

Vasi, Ion Bogdan (2011). *Winds of Change: The Environmental Movement and the Global Development of the Wind Energy Industry*. New York: Oxford University Press.

Veblen, Thorstein (1953). *The Theory of the Leisure Class: An Economic Study of Institutions*. New York: Mentor. First published in 1899.

Veit, Helen Zoe (2013). *Modern Food, Moral Food: Self-Control, Science, and the Rise of Modern American Eating in the Early Twentieth Century*. Chapel Hill: University of North Carolina Press.

Vogel, David (2005). *The Market for Virtue: The Potential and Limits of Corporate Social Responsibility*. Washington, DC: Brookings Institution Press.

Warde, Alan (1997). *Consumption, Food, and Taste: Culinary Antinomies and Commodity Culture*. London: Sage.

Waters, Alice (1990). "The Farm-Restaurant Connection." In *Our Sustainable Table*, edited by Robert Clark, 113–22. San Francisco: North Point.

Weber, Klaus, Kathryn L. Heinze, and Michaela DeSoucey (2008). "Forage for Thought: Mobilizing Codes in the Movement for Grass-Fed Meat and Dairy Products." *Administrative Science Quarterly* 53 (3): 529–67.

Weber, Max (1976). *The Protestant Ethic and the Spirit of Capitalism*. Translated by Talcott Parsons. New York: Charles Scribner's Sons. First published in 1904–1905.

——— (1978). "The Distribution of Power within the Political Community: Class, Status, Party." In *Economy and Society: An Outline of Interpretive Sociology*, vol. 2, translated by Guenther Roth and Claus Wittich, 926–40. Berkeley: University of California Press. First published in 1922.

Wedemeyer, Bernd (1994). "Body-building or Man in the Making: Aspects of the German Bodybuilding Movement in the Kaiserreich and Weimar Republic." *International Journal of the History of Sport* 11 (3): 472–84.

Weindling, Paul (1989). *Health, Race and German Politics between National Unification and Nazism, 1870–1945*. Cambridge: Cambridge University Press.

Weiss, Harry B., and Howard R. Kemble (1967). *The Great American Water-Cure Craze: A History of Hydropathy in the United States*. Trenton, NJ: Past Times Press.

West, Eric D. (1972). "The Psychological Health of Vegans Compared with Two Other Groups." *Plant Foods for Human Nutrition* 2:147–49.

Whelan, Elizabeth M., and Fredrick J. Stare (1975). *Panic in the Pantry: Food Facts, Fads and Fallacies*. New York: Atheneum.

White, Ellen G. (1903). "The Role of Christ's Object Lessons; Concern Over Health Food Companies and Restaurants; Soul Winning to be Emphasized" (letter to Lucinda Hall). May 11. *Manuscript Releases* 17 (1285): 294. Ellen G. White Estate. https://egwwritings.org/?ref=en_17MR.294&para=63.1580

—— (1905). "Restaurant Work" (speech). September 23. *Manuscript Releases* 8 (577): 173. Ellen G. White Estate. https://egwwritings.org/?ref=en_8MR.171&para=52.865.

—— (1942). *The Ministry of Healing.* Mountain View, CA: Pacific Press. First published in 1905.

—— (1970). "No Monopoly on the Health Food Work," in *The Health Food Ministry: As Presented in the Writings of Ellen G. White, Testimonies,Vol. 7, Section III: "Health Foods," Mimeograph Collection, "The Health Food Work," Miscellaneous Items.* Washington, DC: Prepared for the World Food Service of the General Conference by Ellen G. White Publications. First published June 18, 1900.

White, Philip L. (1958). "The Program of the Council on Foods and Nutrition of the American Medical Association." *Nutrition Reviews* 16 (3): 65–66.

Whorton, James C. (1982). *Crusaders for Fitness: The History of American Health Reformers.* Princeton, NJ: Princeton University Press.

—— (2002). *Nature Cures: The History of Alternative Medicine in America.* New York: Oxford University Press.

Wickstrom, Lois (1974). *The Food Conspiracy Cookbook: How to Start a Neighborhood Buying Club and Eat Cheaply.* San Francisco: 101 Productions.

Wild, Peter (2008). *William Pester: The Hermit of Palm Springs.* Johannesburg, CA: Shady Myrick Research Project.

Wilder, Russell M. (1956). "A Brief History of the Enrichment of Flour and Bread." *Journal of the American Medical Association* 162 (17): 1539–41.

Wilson, Brian C. (2014). *Dr. John Harvey and the Religion of Biologic Living.* Bloomington: Indiana University Press.

Worthington, Eustis (1837). "More Facts." *Graham Journal of Health and Longevity* 1 (9): 65.

Wright, Robert A. (1972). "Health Foods—Only a Fad?" *New York Times*, October 15, F1, F5.

Wynne, Brian (1996). "May the Sheep Safely Graze? A Reflexive View of the Expert-Lay Knowledge Divide." In *Risk, Environment and Modernity: Towards a New Ecology*, edited by Scott Lash, Bronislaw Szerszynski, and Brian Wynne, 44–83. London: Sage.

Yergin, Daniel (1973). "Supernutritionist." *New York Times Magazine*, May 20, 32–33, 58–66, 71.

Yogananda, Paramahansa (1930). *Descriptive Outline, General Principles and Merits of Yogoda; or, a System for Harmonious and Full Development of Body, Mind and Soul.* Los Angeles: Yogoda Sat-Sanga Art of Super-Living Society of America.

Young, James Harvey (1967). *The Medical Messiahs: A Social History of Health Quackery in Twentieth-Century America*. Princeton, NJ: Princeton University Press.

Zablocki, Benjamin D., and Rosabeth Moss Kanter (1976). "The Differentiation of Life-Styles." *Annual Review of Sociology* 2:269–98.

Zietsma, Charlene, and Thomas B. Lawrence (2010). "Institutional Work in the Transformation of an Organizational Field: The Interplay of Boundary Work and Practice Work." *Administrative Science Quarterly* 55 (2): 189–221.

Zinkin, Harold, and Bonnie Hearn (1999). *Remembering Muscle Beach: Where Hard Bodies Began: Photographs and Memories*. Santa Monica: Angel City Press.

Zwiebach, Elliot (2001). "Whole Foods Buys Harry's as Base to Go Southern." *Supermarket News*, August 20, 1.

Index